PRESENTED TO:

..................................................................................

FROM:

..................................................................................

DATE:

..................................................................................

# TOUCHED
## *by the*
# TRUTH

 DEVOTIONAL

COUNTRYMAN®
An Imprint of Thomas Nelson Publishers

THOMAS NELSON
*Since 1798*

*Touched by the Truth*
© 2018 Thomas Nelson

Published in Nashville, Tennessee, by Thomas Nelson. Thomas Nelson is a registered trademark of HarperCollins Christian Publishing, Inc.

Unless otherwise noted, Scripture quotations are taken from the New King James Version®. © 1982 by Thomas Nelson. Used by permission. All rights reserved.

Scripture quotations marked KJV are from Scripture quotations marked KJV are from the King James Version. Public domain.

Scripture quotations marked NASB are from the New American Standard Bible®, Copyright © 1960, 1962, 1963, 1968, 1971, 1972, 1973, 1975, 1977, 1995 by The Lockman Foundation. Used by permission. (www.Lockman.org).

ISBN 978-1-4002-1583-6

Original package design © 2018 Thomas Nelson
Cover design by Halie Cotton
Images © Shutterstock

*Printed in China*

19 20 21 22 23 GRI 9 8 7 6 5 4 3 2 1

# INTRODUCTION

Fifty devoted men of God helped to create the devotions in *Touched by the Truth*. We pray the truths you discover bring to light God's eternal hope, salvation, and saving grace. Psalm 25:5 says, "Lead me in Your truth and teach me, for You are the God of my salvation; On You I wait all the day." As you read each devotion through the coming year, allow God's truth to draw you ever closer to the heavenly Father.

It is our prayer that God will touch your heart with His truth as you spend time with Him and meditate on His Word every day.

Dr. Johnny M. Hunt
Senior Pastor
First Baptist Church Woodstock
Woodstock, Georgia

# TOUCHED
## *by the*
# TRUTH

*MyDaily* DEVOTIONAL

# CONTENTS

# WEEK 1—MONDAY

*Turning Bad Situations into Good Situations*

*Joseph said to them, "Do not be afraid, for am I in the place of God? But as for you, you meant evil against me; but God meant it for good, in order to bring it about as it is this day, to save many people alive. Now therefore, do not be afraid; I will provide for you and your little ones." And he comforted them and spoke kindly to them.*

GENESIS 50:19–21

T he story of Joseph is a beautiful and glorious picture of God's providence. Joseph had every right to be angry and to be a "debt settler." However, he realized that God had orchestrated his life and destination. Joseph was very keen to trust God's sovereignty and His overarching providence.

One major takeaway from Joseph's story is the calming truth that God is ultimately and always in charge of the affairs of humans.

Only God can take a bad situation and turn it into a good one. This Old Testament story is once again magnified in Romans 8:28: "All things work together for good." Not only did Joseph's situation work together for his good, but it affected so many lives in the future.

God is preparing us for what He already has planned. Joseph's faith in the different situations built incredible character inside of him. We can't control what comes into our lives, but we can determine how we respond.

What a picture this story paints of how God can take an ugly situation and, with the stroke of His brush, paint *beauty*.

........................................................................................................

*Lord, grant that I may see the "big picture" of Your painting of my life so I might respond as I ought. In Jesus' name, amen.*

Dr. Johnny Hunt, First Baptist Church Woodstock, Woodstock, GA

# WEEK 1—TUESDAY

*Covetousness Is Idolatry*

*"You shall not covet your neighbor's house; you shall not covet your neighbor's wife, nor his male servant, nor his female servant, nor his ox, nor his donkey, nor anything that is your neighbor's."*

EXODUS 20:17

There always seems to be a "bottom line." The bottom line in the Ten Commandments is the truth that the external acts we commit are always driven by our internal thoughts.

To covet is to want. Covetousness results in a never-satisfied life that knows little contentment. The apostle Paul included the sin of covetousness in his "sin lists" (Romans 1:28–30; Colossians 3:5–10). He even went so far as to define covetousness as idolatry in Colossians 3:5.

Making idols out of people, places, and things is easy at times, sometimes without meaning to. Idols have the potential to occupy the place reserved for our Lord. An idol is anything that comes between us and our love for Christ. May the Lord reveal the things in our lives we hold too tightly. Only He is worthy of this place of honor.

May we avoid covetousness and instead be thankful for what the Lord gives us.

········································································

*Lord, my heart is so prone to wander and turn away from You. Grant that my passion would be always for You, amen.*

# Week 1—Wednesday

*God Is So Good*

*Now the Lord descended in the cloud and stood with him there, and proclaimed the name of the Lord. And the Lord passed before him and proclaimed, "The Lord, the Lord God, merciful and gracious, longsuffering, and abounding in goodness and truth."*

Exodus 34:5–6

The Lord promised Moses that He would answer his request to see God's glory (Exodus 33:18). Moses thought that in order to know God intimately, he needed to commune with Him face-to-face. In Exodus 34 the Lord told Moses that He would pass before him, but He would hide him in the cleft of the rock and allow Moses to see only His back, not His face.

What God proclaimed about Himself in Exodus 34:6 is a revelation of His glory. God is merciful in that He does not give us what we deserve. If He did, none would ever be able to stand before Him.

The Lord is gracious in that not only does He not give us what we deserve, but He gives us what we don't deserve. The Lord's undeserved and unmerited gifts include His gracious forgiveness.

The Lord is long-suffering and patient with us. We can be grateful that God does not deal with our rebellion immediately, or not one of us would have ever been saved.

The Lord is a good, good Father. His goodness leads us to repentance and redemption

......................................................................................................

*Lord, we have so many reasons to praise You. Today I praise You for Your goodness, amen.*

Dr. Johnny Hunt, First Baptist Church Woodstock, Woodstock, GA

# WEEK 1—THURSDAY
## Consecrate Yourselves

*"For I am the LORD your God. You shall therefore consecrate yourselves, and you shall be holy; for I am holy. Neither shall you defile yourselves with any creeping thing that creeps on the earth. For I am the LORD who brings you up out of the land of Egypt, to be your God. You shall therefore be holy, for I am holy."*

LEVITICUS 11:44–45

L eviticus reminds us of who we were before we met God and what He made us to be. He is holy, and He makes us holy. Holiness is often defined as "Christ in us." It is not something we can achieve on our own. Rather Christ is the way to holiness.

Leviticus 11:45 reminds us that it was God who brought us out of bondage in order to move us into a life that would display Christ in us.

In the New Testament Paul referred to the Corinthians as "saints" (1 Corinthians 1:2). This name is a reminder that God saved us and then set us aside as His own personal possessions. We are sanctified (or "consecrated") to the Lord. We are no longer our own, but we are His. Because of this new and glorious relationship, we are to be separated from all else and dedicated to Him alone.

God's sovereign sanctification is the process of God's working in and through us from when we come to know Him until the day we see Him. This work will never totally perfected until we see Him. This gives us confidence that He is alive and at work in His children.

............................................................................................................

*Lord, thank You for what You started in me at salvation, and thank You for continuing it until I see You, amen.*

# WEEK 1—FRIDAY

## A Prayer of Blessing

*"The LORD bless you and keep you; the LORD make His face shine upon you, and be gracious to you; the LORD lift up His countenance upon you, and give you peace."*

NUMBERS 6:24–26

In Philippians 2:13, "It is God who works in you both to will and to do for His good pleasure," the apostle Paul gives clarity to the fact that as God moves within our lives, we can bring Him pleasure. All of us have people in our lives whom we desire to please. Yet we are aware that we are dependent upon "God's working in us." His grace at work in us inclines us to do that which brings Him pleasure.

The prayer of blessing listed in today's passage was used by the priests to bless the people. This is also a prayer of blessing that we often wish to say over those we love. God's blessing brings His favor. We need God's favor, and we also welcome God's protection. This prayer speaks of God's guarding our hearts and minds through Christ Jesus our Lord (Philippians 4:7).

The shining of God's face upon us reminds me of the old saying, "He's his dad's favorite." The Father's face enlightens, renews, and comforts His own.

Numbers 6:25–26 teaches the New Testament principle that grace always precedes peace. It is through God's gracious display on the cross and the forgiveness offered that we experience the peace of God, which is indeed Christ Himself (Ephesians 2:14).

........................................................................................................

*Lord Jesus, Your favor is given even though it is not deserved. Your graciousness is so wonderfully seen and felt day by day, amen.*

Dr. Johnny Hunt, First Baptist Church Woodstock, Woodstock, GA

# Week 1—Weekend
## It Will Go Well with Us

*"Therefore you shall be careful to do as the Lord your God has commanded you; you shall not turn aside to the right hand or to the left. You shall walk in all the ways which the Lord your God has commanded you, that you may live and that it may be well with you, and that you may prolong your days in the land which you shall possess."*

DEUTERONOMY 5:32–33

We are often hard-pressed to find any of God's promises that are not conditional. His praises are predicated on our obedient responses. What father would bless a child in response to disobedience?

Moses had been given God's truths to teach to his children. There are truths that promise great rewards in life. The *therefore* in verse thirty-two takes us back to what the Lord had taught His servant Moses. Moses in turn would teach his own household as well as the families of Israel, encouraging the teachings in their homes. In like manner we are to obey what we have been taught. It's not the truth we know but the truth we obey that makes the difference in our lives and our families.

The command to walk in His ways speaks of what we do and what we say. As we choose to live His way, He promises us life even as Jesus did. He cares that we have and abundant life. Too many are making a living without really living the life He intended.

We cannot only live, but our living will go well with us. The Lord was indeed speaking of His promise of inheritance. We have the same promise of a future with God here on earth as well as in heaven.

........................................................................................

*O Mighty God, You alone are worthy of my life of obedience. Help me to do what is right in Your sight, amen.*

# Week 2—Monday

*Teaching Your Children How to Love God*

*And these words which I command you today shall be in your heart. You shall teach them diligently to your children, and shall talk of them when you sit in your house, when you walk by the way, when you lie down, and when you rise up.*

Deuteronomy 6:6–7

Parents teach their children all kinds of things. They teach them how to spell words, throw a football, and even how to cross the street. These things and many more like them need to be taught to children by their parents or guardians.

Yet the greatest thing we can teach our children is how to love God.

If our children are going to be raised to love the Lord their God with all their hearts, with all their souls, and with all their minds, then parents must consistently teach their children the truth of God's Word. Parents accomplish this when they teach their children how to love God all throughout the day and every day.

Sharing a daily devotional time with children can be effective, but the most diligent and consistent way to teach children how to love God is to lead by example. We can take them to a local church so others can help teach and show them how to love God. The church's role is not to take the place of a parent, but being a part of the church community allows our children to worship God with others and to grow as a family of God.

................................................................................

*Father, remind me daily to teach the children the value and priority of loving God. In Jesus' name, amen.*

Dr. Ronnie Floyd, Cross Church, Springdale, AR

# WEEK 2—TUESDAY

*Proclaiming the Name of the Lord*

*For I proclaim the name of the LORD: ascribe greatness to our God. He is the Rock,*
*His work is perfect; for all His ways are justice, a God of truth and without injustice;*
*righteous and upright is He.*

DEUTERONOMY 32:3–4

Every day we talk about many topics with others. Our conversations might be stories about our children, the sale in the store we just left, job challenges, or even last night's ball game. We're not shy to talk about what matters to us.

If our relationship with God really matters to us, we need to be unashamed in proclaiming the name of the Lord to others. We can touch people with the truth of God's Word when we are faithful to share His great name with others. Why wouldn't we want to do that?

God is great, and no one is greater!

God is our Rock, and no one is stronger!

God is perfect in all His ways, and no one is purer!

God is just in all things, and no one is fairer!

God is true at all times, and no one is truer!

God is upright in all things, and no one is straighter!

At all times and in all things, proclaim the name of the Lord!

.......................................................................................

*Father, no one is greater than You! Empower me to proclaim Your name today!*
*Amen.*

# Week 2—Wednesday
## Standing Up to Serve the Lord!

*Now therefore, fear the Lord, serve Him in sincerity and in truth, and put away the gods which your fathers served on the other side of the River and in Egypt. Serve the Lord! And if it seems evil to you to serve the Lord, choose for yourselves this day whom you will serve, whether the gods which your fathers served that were on the other side of the River, or the gods of the Amorites, in whose land you dwell. But as for me and my house, we will serve the Lord.*

Joshua 24:14–15

We've now been on earth long enough to witness a shift in our culture. We've gone from standing erect with our hand over our heart to proudly salute our nation's flag as the national anthem is sung, to seeing some people disrespect our flag and nation by kneeling. They believe that by kneeling, they're standing up for their rights.

Standing up for your nation is great. But standing up to serve the Lord is the greatest stand you can take in your life.

As you live each day, stand up to serve the Lord. While others may be unashamed in proclaiming their own allegiances to culture, flags, and earthly things, take your stand boldly and serve the Lord unashamedly.

The temptation to go after other pursuits will be in front of you daily, and it will pull on you and your family. Yet take your stand courageously. Stand up and serve the Lord. Let the world know that as for you and your family, you will serve the Lord.

........................................................................................

*Father, empower my family to be bold in our witness as we stand up to serve the Lord. Amen.*

Dr. Ronnie Floyd, Cross Church, Springdale, AR

# Week 2—Thursday

*Following in the Footsteps of Greatness*

*And Solomon said: "You have shown great mercy to Your servant David my father, because he walked before You in truth, in righteousness, and in uprightness of heart with You; You have continued this great kindness for him, and You have given him a son to sit on his throne, as it is this day."*

1 Kings 3:6

The Bible proclaims that King David was a man after God's own heart. This statement about him takes into account his entire life and leaves no question about his greatness.

Can you imagine what it must have been like to be David's son? While I imagine Solomon felt pressure from time to time to as great a man as his father, he didn't discuss his worries in today's verse. Rather, Solomon applauded the kindness God gave to him for being able to follow his father as the king.

When Solomon became king, this was not a pronouncement of his greatness, but a declaration of God's greatness.

This passage of Scripture demonstrates both Solomon's humility before God and his respect for King David, his father. Regardless of your parental heritage, you can always walk in humility when you follow your heavenly Father, for none is greater than He. Follow God and walk in the footsteps of His greatness.

........................................................................................................

*God, I choose to follow You all the days of my life, amen.*

# WEEK 2—FRIDAY

## *Calling Out to God When You Get Sick*

*Then he turned his face toward the wall, and prayed to the LORD, saying, "Remember now, O LORD, I pray, how I have walked before You in truth and with a loyal heart, and have done what was good in Your sight." And Hezekiah wept bitterly.*

2 KINGS 20:2–3

The prophet Isaiah told King Hezekiah that the king would die soon. When Isaiah shared this grim news, he also told King Hezekiah it was the time to get his affairs in order. How did the king respond?

The first thing King Hezekiah did when he received the news was to call out to God. As he prayed to the Lord, he reminded God how he had walked, with a faithful heart, before Him and others in God's truth. When Hezekiah became sick, prayer was not his last choice, but his first choice.

Calling out to God when you get sick should always be your first choice. When Hezekiah called out to God first, the Lord responded and told the prophet Isaiah to go back to King Hezekiah and inform him that God would give him an additional fifteen years to live. God heard King Hezekiah's prayer and rewarded him with this extension of grace.

God can do what others cannot do. Even though you can go to the best medical doctors and hospitals that you can possibly afford, still call out to God for His help. God can heal us physically in many ways and by using different methods. God also offers us eternal healing by taking His children to heaven where there is no more sickness.

....................................................................................................

*God, You are my healer. Heal me today, amen.*

Dr. Ronnie Floyd, Cross Church, Springdale, AR

# WEEK 2—WEEKEND
## *Walking in Godliness This Weekend*

*Blessed is the man who walks not in the counsel of the ungodly, nor stands in the path of sinners, nor sits in the seat of the scornful; but his delight is in law of the Lord, and in His law he meditates day and night.*

PSALM 1:1–2

E very day presents innumerable challenges to walking with the Lord. As the pressures of our jobs and the schedules of families occur daily, walking each day isn't easy. Yet when we do, the blessings are so many.

Sometimes when the weekends come and the pressure is relieved a bit, we can might feel entitled, thinking that the weekends are ours. We choose to do as we please. Walking in godliness throughout the weekend is often our greatest challenge spiritually. We may become lax in reading the Bible and praying to the Lord.

God's call to walk in godliness is not just a call during the week, but it is a call even during the weekends. We must be intentional in walking with the Lord every day.

During this weekend, choose to relax, but not spiritually. Choose this weekend to begin each day with God, even if you sleep in. Read your Bible and meditate on it this weekend. Talk to God on Saturday about your past week, and on Sunday talk to Him about the week ahead.

........................................................................................................................

*Father, I choose godliness this weekend, amen.*

# Week 3—Monday

*The Choice to Rejoice*

*But let all those rejoice who put their trust in You; let them ever shout for joy, because You defend them; let those also who love Your name be joyful in You. For You, O Lord, will bless the righteous; with favor You will surround him as with a shield.*

PSALM 5:11–12

As believers in the Lord Jesus, we are to be joyful and glad as we walk with the King. Most of us can do it—when everything is going well. But how do we shout for joy when life has kicked us to the curb? How can we rejoice if everything is going wrong?

Rejoicing is a choice, and it is not based on circumstances. Rejoicing is based on the Lord and His goodness and grace. Paul, writing from his incarceration in Rome, wrote in Philippians 4:4, "Rejoice in the Lord always; again I will say, rejoice!" (NASB). Make no mistake: Paul didn't rejoice about imprisonment (that was not his heart's desire); he rejoiced in the Lord . . . and that is the key.

Circumstances change with the wind, but the Lord never changes. As we focus on Him, we can rejoice and shout praises to His name. We can know that His blessings come even in the hard times. He is faithful to us every step of the way, and He uses our difficulties to teach us to trust Him.

So what do you say? Will you make the choice to rejoice in the Lord?

.......................................................................................................................

*God, help me set my eyes on You. Help me remember that You are my Rock and my Fortress. Thank You for loving me and surrounding me with Your favor. I am so blessed. Jesus, how can I fail to rejoice? Amen.*

Dr. Jeff Schreve, First Baptist Church, Texarkana, TX

# WEEK 3—TUESDAY

*The Truth Sets You Free*

LORD, *who may abide in Your tabernacle? Who may dwell in Your holy hill? He who walks uprightly, and works righteousness, and speaks the truth in his heart.*

PSALM 15:1–2

What thoughts play in your mind as you go through your day? Are they thoughts that build you up in the Lord? Are they thoughts that encourage your faith, or are they thoughts that tear you down and fill your heart with fear and woe?

David wrote Psalm 15. He experienced lots of trouble in his life. Although he was anointed the future king of Israel as a youth, David lived for years on the run from King Saul and his army. Potential death seemed to accompany his every move. David could have easily succumbed to the fear and the lies of the devil, but he refused to do so. Instead, he walked in God's ways and spoke God's truth in his heart, over and over again.

It is critical to know the truth and speak the truth in our hearts, moment by moment. The destructive lies of the devil constantly come at us. His lies are so easy for us to believe because they so often coincide with our fears.

The devil says, "God doesn't love you. God has left you. You can't be forgiven. You will surely fail." The way to defeat his lies is with God's truth. God does love you. He is with you. He forgives the worst of sins and will provide for you as you trust Him.

.............................................................................................

*Lord, I confess my tendency to believe the devil's lies. Today I choose to believe Your truth and speak it continually in my heart. Thank You, Jesus, amen.*

# Week 3—Wednesday

*In God We Trust*

*O house of Aaron, trust in the Lord; He is their help and their shield. You who fear the Lord, trust in the Lord; He is their help and their shield.*

Psalm 115:10–11

Many years ago, my godly father-in-law was in the hospital, fighting for his life. A stroke had put him in a coma for many weeks. When he finally awoke, I asked him what the Lord had said to him during this trial. I have never forgotten his reply: "Trust Me." But what exactly does that mean to trust the Lord, and how do we do it?

Trusting the Lord means you rely upon Him, put your confidence and hope in Him, and firmly believe He will meet your needs. It means you look to Him—the God who spoke the world into existence—and refuse to fret over problems.

My sister, Valerie, faced financial problems at the end of the year. She did not have the money to pay her property taxes. Instead of worrying about this big problem, she chose to trust her heavenly Father, and she thanked Him in advance for meeting her need. Do you know how God responded to her unwavering faith? He blessed her by providing a high-paying, short-term job assignment that came out of nowhere. That temporary gig paid her taxes almost to the penny!

......................................................................................................

*Father God, I am facing big trials, but I choose to trust You to meet my needs, no matter how bleak my circumstances may seem. I know You are good and in control of all. I know that You will see me through. In Jesus' name, amen.*

Dr. Jeff Schreve, First Baptist Church, Texarkana, TX

# WEEK 3—THURSDAY

## *The Divine Counselor*

*I will bless the LORD who has given me counsel; my heart also instructs me in the night seasons. I have set the LORD always before me; because He is at my right hand I shall not be moved.*

PSALM 16:7–8

Have you ever received help from a godly counselor? I certainly have. A godly counselor is a wonderful blessing from the Lord. This wise person can provide you with direction and insight as you work through difficult problems.

David had many counselors in his life. His chief counselor, however, was the Lord. As David spent unhurried time with God—pouring out his heart, his hurts, and his fears—he received much-needed counsel from the King of kings. God showed David what to do, and David did it. David wasn't perfect, but he was genuine, and he kept his eyes on the Lord. That was the secret of his success.

Are you heavy-hearted today? Are you facing big decisions and you don't know what to do? The Counselor is ready, willing, and able to help you. If you will seek His face, rest in His glorious presence, and set His will before your eyes, the wonderful results will amaze you.

*Lord, I need You. I need to spend time in Your presence and have You show me what to do. When you show me, Lord, I promise to follow Your will. Give me the strength and grace to do what You say. I praise You for You are good, and Your will is perfect, amen.*

# WEEK 3—FRIDAY

*Praying from a Pure Heart*

*You have tested my heart; You have visited me in the night; You have tried me and have found nothing; I have purposed that my mouth shall not transgress. Concerning the works of men, by the word of Your lips, I have kept away from the paths of the destroyer. Uphold my steps in Your paths, that my footsteps may not slip.*

PSALM 17:3–5

David was very familiar with troubles and trials. He spent many days on the run from people who wanted to kill him. Most people do not like the trials, but deep down David knew trials were necessary to keep him humble and close to God.

In today's psalm, David cried out for protection from his enemies, from those who were trying to kill him—and you think you have problems! David desperately needed the Lord to show up on his behalf. As David prayed, he reminded God that his heart was pure. Because of this, he prayed with confidence. God tested his heart and found no unconfessed sin. David had repented of his sin and he was forgiven.

What does God see when He judges your heart? Are you hiding any sinful action or attitude? Is there anyone you need to forgive? Is there anything you need to confess and get right with Him? You hinder your prayers when you hide sin in your heart. But when you confess sin and forsake it, the Lord works mightily on your behalf.

........................................................................................

*Lord, I don't want to let sin have a place in my heart. Please show me if something is not right within me, and I will get it out of the shadows and into Your light. In Jesus' name, amen.*

Dr. Jeff Schreve, First Baptist Church, Texarkana, TX

# Week 3—Weekend
## Through the Dark Valley

*Yea, though I walk through the valley of the shadow of death, I will fear no evil; for You are with me; Your rod and Your staff, they comfort me. You prepare a table before me in the presence of my enemies; You anoint my head with oil; my cup runs over. Surely goodness and mercy shall follow me all the days of my life; and I will dwell in the house of the LORD forever.*

PSALM 23:4–6

The father of modern missions is William Carey. He served forty-one consecutive years in India, never taking a furlough. While his ministry was foundational and paved the way for many others to follow, his journey was not without heartache and pain. After a short time in India, he ran out of money, contracted malaria, and had to bury his five-year-old son. His wife had a nervous breakdown from which she never recovered. Carey experienced the valley of the shadow of death. Can you relate?

When you walk through the valley of the shadow of death, remember: you walk through it! God never intends for you to dwell there permanently. Everyone experiences loss and deals with tremendous storms and dark nights of the soul. Yet you need not fear. The Lord will not leave you. He will lead you through!

*God, I thank You that I do not have to live in despair. I can trust You as You lead me through the darkest night with Your nail-scarred hands. Help me, Lord, to keep moving forward with You. In Jesus' name, amen.*

# Week 4—Monday
*Show Me—Teach Me—Lead Me!*

*Show me Your ways, O Lord; teach me Your paths. Lead me in Your truth and teach me, for You are the God of my salvation; on You I wait all the day.*

Psalm 25:4–5

The Lord said David was a "man after My own heart, who will do all My will" (Acts 13:22). Indeed he was. David served, followed, and loved the Lord. Because of his faithfulness, God chose his family to be the one through whom the Messiah would come.

As we move through the Psalms, we find truths that show us why David was a man after God's heart. Notice how David prays here: "Show me Your ways, O Lord; teach me Your paths" (v. 4). This implies a forsaking of his own ways and a readiness to cast aside his own ways to follow God's ways. There are the ways of men and the ways of God, the paths of sin and the paths of righteousness, the ways of truth and the ways of error. There is the right way, and there is the wrong way, and far too many believers want all of God's blessings their own way as well.

However, David says, "Lead me in Your truth and teach me." God can't lead someone who won't follow! To be a follower of God, you must yield to Him. A longing in your hearts for Him to guide you into truth must exist. The secret to receiving more truth is being obedient to the truth you already have. Become a true follower of God, and He will teach you more.

......................................................................................

*Lord, I want to follow You. I surrender my heart and will to You. Show me Your ways, teach me, and lead me. And I will follow You. In Jesus' name, amen.*

Dr. Rob Zinn, Immanuel Baptist Church, Highland, CA

# Week 4—Tuesday

*How to Walk with the Lord*

*The humble He guides in justice, and the humble He teaches His way. All the paths of the LORD are mercy and truth, to such as keep His covenant and His testimonies.*

PSALM 25:9–10

D r. Andrew Murray referred to the Psalms as the prayer book of God's saints. In the book of Psalms, the spirit of prayer and the spirit of praise are twin spirits; they are indivisible. In Psalm 25:4–5 we glimpse David's heart. He had surrendered to God's will, teachings, and ways. Thus David's prayer was for God to show His way, teach His paths, and lead him into truth.

Now, as we look at our text, we see the attitude required to pray that kind of prayer. Humility. Jesus says in Matthew 5:5, "Blessed are the meek." James 4:6 says, "God resists the proud, but gives grace to the humble." Meekness is not weakness; rather it is power under control. Meekness is the realization that who we are is the result of what God and others have done for us.

God teaches justice and gives guidance to those who come before Him with humble hearts. A person's age, color, ethnicity, wealth, or education is unimportant. Our attitudes make a huge difference! The proud will not prosper until they humble themselves before the Lord. Then they will find mercy and truth—mercy to forgive and to cleanse and truth to guide, strengthen, and satisfy. To step off Lord's path is to get out of the channel of supply.

......................................................................................

*Lord, teach me how to walk in humility. In Jesus' name, amen.*

# WEEK 4—WEDNESDAY

*A Heart for God*

*Examine me, O LORD, and prove me; try my mind and my heart. For Your lovingkindness is before my eyes, and I have walked in Your truth.*

PSALM 26:2–3

I n today's passage, you can see three characteristics of one who has a heart for God. First, he has faith in God. In Psalm 26:1 David said, "I have also trusted in the LORD; I shall not slip." David put his faith in God; his confidence was in the Lord. God had proven Himself to David time and time again, and David knew he could count on the Lord. It is amazing how many talk about faith but don't live by faith. Have we noticed how the Lord puts us in situations so we can learn to trust Him? The more we serve Him, the more we learn we need Him, and the stronger our faith becomes.

Second, David desired to be tested by God: "Examine me, O LORD, and prove me; try my mind and heart" (v. 2). When we seek to be examined by God, it matters very little how we are judged by others. In Psalm 139:23, David wrote, "Search me, O God, and know my heart; try me, and know my anxieties."

Third, David was obedient to God: "And I have walked in Your truth" (v. 3). To walk in God's truth is to walk in His way and walk in the light. Jesus said in John 14:15, "If you love Me, keep My commandments." To obey God is to follow His law. How are you being obedient to God? God blesses your obedience.

......................................................................................

*Lord, help me to be faithful and follow You. In Jesus' name, amen.*

Dr. Rob Zinn, Immanuel Baptist Church, Highland, CA

# WEEK 4—THURSDAY
## *Wait on the Lord*

*Wait on the LORD; be of good courage, and He shall strengthen your heart; wait, I say, on the Lord!*

PSALM 27:14

Waiting is one of the most difficult things to do. We like to see things happen on our schedules. I once heard three phrases that spoke to my heart: "sit still" (Ruth 3:18), "stand still" (Exodus 14:13), and "be still" (Psalm 46:10).

"Sit still" was Naomi's counsel to Ruth, who would have accomplished nothing if she hadn't trusted and waited for Boaz to keep his promises. We often feel anxious and want to help God out. When we take matters into our own hands, we only make matters worse.

"Stand still" was the command of Moses to the people of Israel as the Egyptian army pursued them. God had the situation under control, and He led His people safely through the sea. There is a time to stand and a time to march; we must remain alert to know which one God wants us to do.

"Be still, and know that I am God" (Psalm 46:10) is a wonderful antidote for a restless spirit. It's easy for us to feel impatient with the Lord. God's hands can accomplish the impossible. For example, Paul wrote he was "confident of this very thing, that He who has begun a good work in you will complete it until the day of Jesus Christ" (Philippians 1:6).

Put yourself at the feet of the Lord. Listen to His command to "sit still," "stand still," or "be still." Always trust Him.

.............................................................................................................

*Lord, help me to trust You. In Jesus' name, amen.*

# Week 4—Friday

## *Attitude or Altitude*

*Sing praise to the LORD, you saints of His, and give thanks at the remembrance of His holy name. For His anger is but for a moment, His favor is for life; weeping may endure for a night, but joy comes in the morning.*

PSALM 30:4–5

David exemplified an attitude of gratitude. His heart overflowed with praise to God—so much that He invited all of God's saints to sing and give thanks at the remembrance of His holy name. With this declaration David remembered all that God had given him: strength, safety from his enemies, and healing.

Stop right now and think of what God has done for you. Many times we take for granted the blessings of God. We should be thankful and give praise to God. We sometimes say that no one knows what we're going through. Remember all that David went through and be encouraged.

"For His anger is for a moment, His favor is for life." God disciplines us because He loves us and is growing us in His grace. We all face trials and failures. When we turn to the Lord, He is always there to forgive, to restore, and continue His work.

The last phrase of David in this verse reminds us that we're all human. We all suffer sorrow, but such sorrow is only temporary. God promises eternal life where we will always be with Him. The troubles of this life are only for a short time. We are children of God, and He loves us. Let us rejoice!

---

*Father, thank You for Your faithfulness. Help me to see through the circumstances and know You're working for my good. In Jesus' name, amen.*

Dr. Rob Zinn, Immanuel Baptist Church, Highland, CA

# WEEK 4—WEEKEND
## *The Reality of Life*

*In You, O LORD, I put my trust; let me never be ashamed; deliver me in Your righteousness. Bow down Your ear to me, deliver me speedily; be my rock of refuge, a fortress of defense to save me. For You are my rock and my fortress; therefore, for Your name's sake, lead me and guide me.*

PSALM 31:1–3

As we come to this verse, we see the reality of what we saw yesterday. In Psalm 30 David talks about what we face for a moment compared to what we look forward to for eternity. First, we see his confidence in God, followed by his submission to God. Later we see his supplication to God. He is in distress, grief, and sorrow. His strength has failed, his body wasted away. He feels forgotten and broken. He is going through the trials of life. So where does he turn?

"In you, O LORD, I have put my trust" (v. 1). He knows the Lord, loves the Lord, and his trust and confidence are in the Lord. He serves a God who hears his prayers, serves as his Rock, and guides him. And we also trust the Lord our God is God. Jesus said, "I will never leave you nor forsake you" (Hebrews 13:5). If we will follow His Word, God will never abandon us. He will remain right by our sides as we go through our lives.

Let us never forget that God is a rock and fortress. We can always trust Him to keep us safe.

........................................................................................

*Thank you, Lord, for being my rock and my salvation. I submit myself to You. In Jesus' name, amen.*

# WEEK 5—MONDAY

*I Didn't See It Coming*

*Pull me out of the net which they have secretly laid for me, for You are my strength.*
*Into Your hand I commit my spirit; You have redeemed me, O LORD God of truth.*

PSALM 31:4–5

With these few words the psalmist tells us he has problems. There are many who don't like him. They hatched a secret scheme to trap him. And since he didn't see it coming, he's fallen into the trap.

It's not fun to talk about it, but we often face the same thing. No matter how hard we try to be kind to everyone, some people, for one reason or another, don't like us. Some won't be content merely to dislike us; they will try to do harm. And like David's enemies, they will rarely come with a frontal attack. They may smile and pretend to care, but the whole time, they're building a trap and we fall in.

When this happens, Christians must remember they don't have to sink to the level of their enemies. You can't let their behavior change who you are. Though toxic people may make trouble, you have something far more powerful. You have the knowledge that God is on your side! You can afford to love. You can afford to be generous. You are a child of the King, and no trap can hold you. If you fall in, He will pull you out.

.........................................................................................................................

*Dear Father, I want to love everyone, even my enemies, as Jesus taught me to do. Help me to spot traps before I step into them. You see and know everything, so I trust You. When I fall in, though, please rescue me. In Jesus' name, amen.*

Mark Hoover, NewSpring Church, Wichita, KS

# WEEK 5—TUESDAY
### Your Will Be Done

*For the word of the Lord is right, and all His work is done in truth. He loves*
*righteousness and justice; the earth is full of the goodness of the LORD.*

PSALM 33:4–5

W ow! Look at those four words: *right*, *truth*, *justice*, and *goodness*. In
all honesty do you feel that's the world you're about to face today?
Frankly it can seem like the opposite. A world filled with wrong, lies, injustice, and meanness. At first glance it can be challenging to believe "the earth
is full of the goodness of the LORD" (v. 5). Yet it's true.

When you become God's child, your destiny becomes forever determined
only by His grace. Your life and future are in His hands. Although the world
you'll face today is dysfunctional, it's only temporary and not your home.
Your day and your life are under His control. And just as today's verse says,
God will forever be right, He'll tell you only the truth, He's completely fair,
and He's always good.

The challenge is to keep your focus on God and on what He's doing. After
all He's the One in charge.

................................................................................

*Dear Father, whatever I face today, I believe Your Word. My life is in Your hands.*
*You are always right, You always tell the truth, and You are always good. Help*
*me to keep my eyes on You. Please keep me from being discouraged by the ugli-*
*ness I encounter, and let me see Your mighty hand at work in my life. In Jesus'*
*name, amen.*

# Week 5—Wednesday

*Waiting Room*

*Our soul waits for the LORD; He is our help and our shield. For our heart shall rejoice in Him, because we have trusted in His holy name. Let Your mercy, O LORD, be upon us, just as we hope in You.*

PSALM 33:20–22

Waiting is hard work. And the psalmist isn't just talking about the annoyance of waiting in line at the grocery store. It's the kind of waiting that starts with a pressing need and threatens danger, loss, and despair if help doesn't come in time. Worrying when this happens is natural. What if we run out of time? Why are we sitting still when the situation is desperate? Waiting is painful, unless we are waiting for the Lord.

Two words in our verse stand out today. The first word is *for*. Our waiting isn't just wasted time. We are waiting "for the LORD." That changes everything. The God we are waiting for has a history of rescuing His people. He's delivered His people from fiery furnaces, lions' dens, and advancing armies. He knows the trouble we are in, and He cares.

The other word is *trusted*. We wait confidently because our God can be counted on to arrive. He has promised never to leave nor forsake us. Time can never run out on His plan for our lives. Our God is always on time.

........................................................................................

*Heavenly Father, I have needs and problems in my life that are time sensitive. Keep me from rushing ahead in desperation and making things worse. Help me to remember that You are on Your way. In Jesus' name, amen.*

Mark Hoover, NewSpring Church, Wichita, KS

# WEEK 5—THURSDAY
## *Conundrum*

*Rest in the LORD, and wait patiently for Him; do not fret because of him who prospers in his way, because of the man who brings wicked schemes to pass. Cease from anger, and forsake wrath; do not fret—it only causes harm. For evildoers shall be cut off; but those who wait on the LORD, they shall inherit the earth.*

PSALM 37:7–9

O ne of life's toughest questions is: Why do bad things happen to good people? Scripture suggests another question is even more perplexing. Why do good things happen to bad people? Reading through the Psalms, you'll notice this especially seems to get under the psalmist's skin. Watching people prosper while doing horrible deeds makes him question nearly everything he's ever believed. And it makes him mad.

The word *fret* means to be in a slow burn. Not the kind of anger that blazes up and burns out quickly, but the kind that lingers and then turns into bitterness. Do we ever feel like this when we watch someone succeed who's caused us great trouble?

If so, God's Word today has three thoughts. First, in our upside-down world, this happens. Second, when we feel angry about it, "it only causes harm"—to ourselves and others. Third, and most importantly, the long-term prosperity of the wicked is only an illusion. This is God's world. And those who wait on Him will be blessed.

............................................................................................................

*Dear Father, watching toxic people get ahead while I'm struggling is hard for me to understand. Help me to remember that I am Your child, this world is not my home, and I will be with You forever. In Jesus' name, amen.*

# Week 5—Friday

*One Step at a Time*

*The steps of a good man are ordered by the Lord, and He delights in his way. Though he fall, he shall not be utterly cast down; for the Lord upholds him with His hand. I have been young, and now am old; yet I have not seen the righteous forsaken, nor his descendants begging bread. He is ever merciful, and lends; and his descendants are blessed.*

Psalm 37:23–26

Look at the words *steps* and *way* in the first sentence because they explain so much about our relationship with God. "Steps" refers to our individual moments. And that's how we live: one step, one moment at a time. But time passes so quickly, and all those steps add up to a whole life.

As we live each moment, God is there, directing our steps. But He sees so much more. He sees our whole lives. He knows how each step will ultimately fit into the way. How many times do we go through experiences that in the moment seem to make no sense? But looking back, we smile and say, "God was all over that!"

The psalmist reminds us that we have an issue, though. We are imperfect people trying to follow a perfect God. Sometimes while taking those steps, we stumble and fall. But He never abandons us. He lovingly picks us up, and the journey continues . . . until we arrive home.

*Dear heavenly Father, today's journey will have many steps. Since You have seen each one already, help me to keep my mind on You, looking constantly for Your guidance. Thank You for being with me throughout my whole journey until I am home in heaven with You. In Jesus' name, amen.*

Mark Hoover, NewSpring Church, Wichita, KS

# WEEK 5—WEEKEND

*Out of the Pit*

*I waited patiently for the LORD; and He inclined to me, and heard my cry. He also brought me up out of a horrible pit, out of the miry clay, and set my feet upon a rock, and established my steps. He has put a new song in my mouth—praise to our God; many will see it and fear, and will trust in the LORD.*

PSALM 40:1–3

Yesterday we learned even though God directs our steps, sometimes we stumble and fall. But today's passage says occasionally situations are far worse. We may fall into a horrible pit, a situation with no way out. Or we may get stuck in miry clay, a problem that threatens to swallow us whole.

We're sometimes inclined to allow despair to overwhelm us. When we look at our circumstances, we see nothing but hopelessness. Bystanders, staring at our plight, can make things worse. The curious ask us for an explanation. Some blame us for falling in. Even the well-intentioned offer us little more than sympathy.

But if you're in the pit or the clay today, help is on the way. You have a God who sees your tears. He hears your desperate cry for help, and He has the power to rescue.

The psalmist finishes with this thought: others will see what God does for us, and they will be drawn to Him. If today finds you in the pit or miry clay, look up. Help is coming!

........................................................................

*Dear heavenly Father, I am so thankful that You are my God. With You in control my situation may be desperate but never hopeless. In Jesus' name, amen.*

# WEEK 6—MONDAY

*I Choose to Proclaim the Goodness of God*

*I have proclaimed the good news of righteousness in the great assembly; indeed, I do not restrain my lips, O LORD, You Yourself know. I have not hidden Your righteousness within my heart; I have declared Your faithfulness and Your salvation; I have not concealed Your lovingkindness and Your truth from the great assembly.*

PSALM 40:9–10

Have you ever had an experience so wonderful in your life that you couldn't keep the good news to yourself? Perhaps there was a time when a significant gift you received or a goal you achieved was so overwhelming that you felt compelled to tell everyone.

For the psalmist, the deeply moving experience of God's favor and faithfulness toward him resulted in an open, unashamed declaration of the goodness of God. The faithfulness of God so overwhelmed David that he could not keep silent concerning the good news of God's work in and around him.

Similarly those who have come to know Jesus Christ and the freedom of forgiveness found in Him, find it most difficult to remain silent about His work of grace in their lives. Because of all the good blessings God has provided us through His Son, we too should be those who faithfully declare the good news of God in Christ Jesus to others. The good news of Jesus Christ crucified, risen, and coming again is the message we must be faithful to proclaim from grateful hearts overwhelmed by the love and goodness of God.

........................................................................

*Father, I ask for strength and courage today to declare the good news of Jesus Christ faithfully to any and all who will hear me. Compel my lips to speak openly of Your faithfulness. In Jesus' name I pray, amen.*

Steven Blanton, Ebenezer Baptist Church, Hendersonville, NC

# WEEK 6—TUESDAY
## I Choose to Pursue the Presence of God

*Oh, send out Your light and Your truth! Let them lead me; let them bring me to
Your holy hill and to Your tabernacle. Then I will go to the altar of God, to God my
exceeding joy; and on the harp I will praise You, O God, my God.*

PSALM 43:3–4

W e are never more tempted to forget essential biblical truth than in
times of trouble and distress. In the fog and confusion of troubling
times, we must cling to the truths of God's Word as the anchor that faithfully
holds us throughout the storms of life. When the psalmist was being misrepresented and overwhelmed by the unwarranted treatment of "deceitful and
unjust" men (Psalm 43:1), he was wise to call to the Lord in his distress.

When many would be tempted to allow difficult circumstances to drive
them far from the Lord, the psalmist's difficulties drove him desperately to
the source of his joy and strength—the presence of God. The psalmist asked
the Lord for light and truth so they might bring him to the "holy hill" and
"tabernacle" of the Lord.

When distress and discouragement come our way, we should follow the
psalmist's example. In the darkness of despair, the light of faith guides wearied hearts to the throne of grace. Amidst the deep wounds produced from
the loose lips of deceitful people, the truth of God's Word provides embattled
souls the unshakable resolve to carry on in the day of adversity.

..............................................................................................

*Father, when I face difficult circumstances, I ask You to give me the wisdom and
strength necessary to run to You alone as the limitless source of joy and encouragement my soul so desperately needs. In Jesus' name I pray, amen.*

# WEEK 6—WEDNESDAY

*I Choose to Acknowledge the Sin in My Life*

*For I acknowledge my transgressions, and my sin is always before me. Against You, You only, have I sinned, and done this evil in Your sight—that You may be found just when You speak, and blameless when You judge.*

PSALM 51:3–4

L iar. *Adulterer. Murderer.* Three words that aptly describe the life of David at the time he penned Psalm 51. However, David willingly confessed his sin and asked the Lord to forgive him. Had the psalmist ultimately decided to hide and deny his sin, he would have never come to know God's forgiveness and restoration.

Even today, when believers break God's commands, the Spirit of God lovingly and faithfully works within to reveal the truth about their sin, urgently providing awareness and courage to confess and repent. Just as an earthly father disciplines his child, our heavenly Father convicts and disciplines His children so they might avoid being destroyed by the consequences of their sin.

Sin unconfessed and uninhibited will always result in destruction and death. However, if we acknowledge, confess, and repent of our sin, the Lord promises to forgive our sins and to cleanse us from all unrighteousness (1 John 1:9). The key to experiencing healing and restoration in Christ Jesus is first to acknowledge one's sin, repent of the sin, and believe that God forgives.

........................................................................................

*Father, how grateful I am that You are faithful to forgive my sin when I confess my transgressions to You. I ask You to reveal sin in my life so I might be forgiven and know the joy of being redeemed. In Jesus' name I pray, amen.*

Steven Blanton, Ebenezer Baptist Church, Hendersonville, NC

# WEEK 6—THURSDAY

## I Choose to Recognize My Need for Truth

*Behold, I was brought forth in iniquity, and in sin my mother conceived me. Behold, You desire truth in the inward parts, and in the hidden part You will make me to know wisdom. . . . Create in me a clean heart, O God, and renew a steadfast spirit within me.*

PSALM 51:5–6, 10

The psalmist understood that sin had deeply affected his heart, and he was capable of any decision or action, given the right time and circumstances. Before his sin with Bathsheba, before his plot to cover his tracks, before his decision to have Uriah killed, the ability to carry out all manner of evil lay waiting for the right time and place deep within the heart of the shepherd-king.

However, in Psalm 51, at the height of his brokenness, David embraced his need for a supernatural restoration of the heart. In repentance David longed for God to create within him a "clean heart." The Lord awakened David to his need for renewal and increased his desire for the life-changing truths of God's Word.

It is no coincidence that a genuine desire for God always accompanies a genuine desire to know God's Word and keep His commands. God's Word, His truth and wisdom, transforms the "inward parts" of the soul.

...........................................................................................................

*Father, I ask You for a fresh encounter with the truth of Your Word. May I experience the truths of Your Word in such a way that I will abandon the desires of my sinful nature and embrace Your sanctifying truth. I ask this in Jesus' name, amen.*

# WEEK 6—FRIDAY
## *I Choose to Express My Need to God*

*I will cry out to God Most High, to God who performs all things for me. He shall send from heaven and save me; He reproaches the one who would swallow me up. God shall send forth His mercy and His truth.*

PSALM 57:2–3

T he Lord performs "all things" for those who call to Him in faith. The psalmist believed that if he called to God in desperation, the Lord would answer Him. Similarly the Lord Jesus answers those who cry out to Him for salvation.

Our Savior has reproached and conquered him who would swallow up the soul! Upon the cross, Jesus Christ conquered the forces of hell and broke the curse of sin. Because of Christ's work on the cross, believers now have direct access to the heavenly Father. Because of what Christ did for us, we can rejoice today, knowing that we can be partakers of the same hope and intimacy the psalmist had with the Father.

What a blessing to know that He who is "full of grace and truth" (John 1:14) now resides within us, providing a limitless source of guidance and direction for our lives. We have access to the mercy, grace, and truth needed for our lives through a humble plea to the Father for His help and assistance. If we ask, God will be faithful to hear and answer.

........................................................................................................................

*Father, help me not to grow so distracted that I forget I have direct access to You through Jesus Christ. I humbly ask You to provide clear direction from the truth of Your Word so I might know Your will and obey Your commands. I ask this in Jesus' name, amen.*

Steven Blanton, Ebenezer Baptist Church, Hendersonville, NC

# WEEK 6—WEEKEND
## *I Choose to Stand Beneath the Banner of Truth*

*You have given a banner to those who fear You, that it may be displayed because of the truth. That Your beloved may be delivered, save with Your right hand, and hear me.*

PSALM 60:4–5

I n the time of the psalmist, the banner could be likened to a flag raised atop a high pinnacle or hill. The banner was raised so that the people of a particular tribe or nation would know to rally and assemble for the sake of communication or in preparation for a battle against an incoming threat.

The passage reminds us that God has provided a banner of truth to those who fear Him and trust Him by faith. As the people of God we are those who must be faithful to recognize and rally beneath the banner of God's truth. Under His banner of truth, we find deliverance from the deceptive work of the enemy and shelter from the destructive ways of the world.

By God's grace let us be those who raise high the banner of truth in our hearts, our homes, and our churches. Our strength as the people of God depends upon our commitment to know the Word of God. As we build our lives on our "most holy faith" (Jude v. 20), may God help us to be empowered, equipped, and enabled by the truths of the Bible.

...........................................................................................

*Father, I pray to be faithful to calling my heart, my family, and my friends to rally beneath the banner of truth that is Your Word. In You alone can I find deliverance from sin and victory against the enemy. I trust You and ask all this in Jesus' name, amen.*

# Week 7—Monday

*Our Greatest Privilege*

*But as for me, my prayer is to You, O Lord, in the acceptable time; O God, in the multitude of Your mercy, hear me in the truth of Your salvation.*

Psalm 69:13

The Christian's greatest privilege is prayer. It is an amazing gift that we can communicate directly to the Father who loves us. We can talk to him at any time during the day, no matter what is going, and He will listen. But many times we use prayer as our last resort. Without thinking clearly, when difficult times come—and they will come—we will run to the phone instead of to the throne. We will turn to others before we turn to God.

God wants to be the source for everything we need in life. The Bible tells us God inclines His ear when we pray (Psalm 116:2). That means He leans in to hear us. The great God of heaven is listening for our prayers, and He leans in always ready to respond. Remember, nothing is too hard for God (Jeremiah 32:27), and when we are down to nothing, God is up to something—no matter what we may be facing.

Let us not neglect our greatest privilege—the privilege of prayer.

.............................................................................................

*God, thank You for the awesome privilege of prayer. May it be a priority each day and not just a possibility, amen.*

Dr. Benny Tate, Rock Springs Church, Milner, GA

# Week 7—Tuesday

## Significance Comes Through Serving

*For a day in Your courts is better than a thousand. I would rather be a doorkeeper in the house of my God than dwell in the tents of wickedness. For the Lord God is a sun and shield; the Lord will give grace and glory; no good thing will He withhold from those who walk uprightly. O Lord of hosts, blessed is the man who trusts in You!*

Psalm 84:10–12

The psalmist said to live in the court of the Lord, he would rather be a lowly doorkeeper and serve in the house of God than to experience all the world offers. He understood that significance in life is found through serving others.

The Bible teaches that God created everyone to serve (1 Peter 4:10–11). Four things happen when you serve. First, you use your gifts. Second, others benefit. Third, you glorify God. Fourth, you experience fulfillment in your heart.

The secret to life is not in receiving, but in giving. Jesus said, "He who is greatest among you shall be your servant" (Matthew 23:11). You can be great! Anyone can serve.

Start serving today. You can begin right where you are. Ask God to put people in your path to whom you can be a blessing. As you serve others, you will be the one who benefits the most!

........................................................................................................

*God, send people into my life today so I can serve them and they can see You. Amen.*

# WEEK 7—WEDNESDAY
## Smarter Than a Rock

*Teach me Your way, O LORD; I will walk in Your truth; unite my heart to fear Your name. I will praise You, O Lord my God, with all my heart, and I will glorify Your name forevermore. For great is Your mercy toward me, and You have delivered my soul from the depths of Sheol.*

PSALM 86:11–13

In 2007 the Fox television network launched a program called "Are You Smarter Than a Fifth Grader?" The adults could win one million dollars if they correctly answered questions based on a fifth-grade curriculum. Since watching that program, I have often wanted to ask some Christians, "Are you smarter than a box of rocks?"

Jesus said even the rocks would praise him if people do not (Luke 19:40). We should certainly hope the rocks will not have to do what God created us to do. Praise is what God seeks from us and is truly the purest thing we can give Him. We may give Him our lives, but He gave us life first. We may give Him our tithes, but He gave them to us first. The least we can give Him is our praise.

God gives us a mandate to praise Him, but we also have a reason to praise Him. He is loving, gracious, merciful, unchanging, and longsuffering. He is our joy, our peace, our healer, and the lifter of our heads. Let us never cease to praise Him. We are smarter than rocks!

........................................................................................

*God, I praise You for who You are and what You have done for me, amen.*

Dr. Benny Tate, Rock Springs Church, Milner, GA

# WEEK 7—THURSDAY
## *Something to Shout About*

*Righteousness and justice are the foundation of Your throne; mercy and truth go before Your face. Blessed are the people who know the joyful sound! They walk, O LORD, in the light of Your countenance.*

PSALM 89:14–15

The "joyful sound" in this verse is the shout of God's people when they saw the Lord lifted high. The Bible encourages us to shout to God. Psalm 47:1 says, "O, clap your hands, all ye people; shout unto God with the voice of triumph" (KJV). Many times we shout and make noise at sporting event or even at a county fair. We clap and cheer. But when we come to church, we act like we're at a funeral. This should not be the case, because we are meant to rejoice and shout about Jesus.

The psalmist also exhorts: "Make a joyful shout to the Lord, all you lands!" (Psalm 100:1). Rejoicing in the Lord is a recurring theme in the book of Psalms. Christians should be excited at all the blessings God has bestowed upon them. When the world looks at Christians, they should see people who rejoice daily in the Lord's blessings.

........................................................................................................................

*Lord, may I always have a shout in my heart for You! Let me never take Your blessings for granted, and may others see my rejoicing in You, amen.*

# Week 7—Friday

*Learning from Eagles*

*Surely He shall deliver you from the snare of the fowler and from the perilous pestilence. He shall cover you with His feathers, and under His wings you shall take refuge; His truth shall be your shield and buckler.*

Psalm 91:3–4

God uses symbolic illustrations and practical examples to teach us about His love and protection. In today's passage He says He will cover us with His feathers, and under His wings we will take refuge. The eagle can teach us a lot. The Bible mentions eagles dozens of times, and according to Revelation 4:7 John saw a creature like an eagle flying around the throne of God!

The eagle is an interesting animal. Eagles are carnivores their whole lives. Wouldn't we also benefit from feeding on the meat of the Word of God? Eagles also seek the direct light of the sun and have two sets of eyelids for this purpose. They *want* to look directly at the sun. In the same way we would be better if we always kept our eyes toward the Son. Eagles are not afraid of storms. They fly above storms and use the wind as an undercurrent to glide and soar. Likewise we have the wings of the Holy Spirit to sustain and carry us through the storms of life.

We can learn a lot from eagles.

........................................................................................................

*Lord, thank You for wrapping me up in Your feathers and protecting me, amen.*

Dr. Benny Tate, Rock Springs Church, Milner, GA

# WEEK 7—WEEKEND

## *Jesus Is Coming Soon*

*Let the field be joyful, and all that is in it. Then all the trees of the woods will rejoice before the LORD. For He is coming, for He is coming to judge the earth. He shall judge the world with righteousness, and the peoples with His truth.*

PSALM 96:12–13

J esus is coming soon! I often tell others if they are believers, they shouldn't be looking for a hole in the ground. They should be looking for a hole in the sky. They shouldn't be looking for the undertaker. They should be looking for the upper taker. Don't look for the antichrist; look for Jesus Christ. Jesus is coming soon!

Today's passage informs us to await the coming of the Lord with joy. All of creation will rejoice at the coming of the Lord, including us. As followers of God we must not fear this coming judgment. He will reward us for the work we have done on earth to build His kingdom, and those who chose not to follow God will receive their just punishment. We can rejoice in knowing that He will set up His throne on earth and rule in truth and righteousness. This will be a wonderful day!

Live as if you expect Jesus to come back today.

......................................................................................................

*God, help me to live as if Your return is imminent! Amen.*

# Week 8—Monday

*The Truth About Approaching God*

*Make a joyful shout to the Lord, all you lands! Serve the Lord with gladness; come before His presence with singing.*

Psalm 100:1–2

The way we approach God matters. In Psalm 100:1–2 the psalmist shares the truth about approaching God by addressing who should approach God, how to approach God, and when to approach God.

Who should approach God? "All you lands" should make a joyful shout to the Lord! For example, if a local business advertises a promotion with a sign that reads: "All Competitor Coupons Accepted. Some Restrictions Apply," which is it, all or some coupons accepted? *All* never means "some"—it always means all. One day every group in every land will be represented at the feet of King Jesus in worship, so all people should approach God.

How should God be approached? Believers should approach God with gladness, not madness or sadness. We gladly worship God through service, and we gladly serve God through worship.

When should God be approached? Jesus, through His death and resurrection, made approaching God anytime, anywhere a reality. We should approach God daily.

......................................................................................

*Father, thank You for allowing me the opportunity to approach You every day. Forgive me when I fail to approach You with gladness. In Jesus' name, amen.*

Dr. Sam Greer, Ph.D, Red Bank Baptist Church, Chattanooga, TN

# Week 8—Tuesday

## *The Truth About Authenticity Before God*

*Enter into His gates with thanksgiving, and into His courts with praise. Be thankful to Him, and bless His name. For the LORD is good; His mercy is everlasting, and His truth endures to all generations.*

PSALM 100:4–5

I n recent years the sales of athletic apparel have grown more than the actual participation in athletics. People in America wear more athletic apparel while working out less. The term describing this phenomenon is *athleisure*, and it was officially adopted into the *Merriam-Webster's Dictionary* in April 2016. Wearing athletic clothing just to wear it is inauthentic. Similarly, how often do we dress the part but fail to worship God authentically?

How can we avoid being inauthentic in worship? We must remember that we have an audience of One. The psalmist wrote that we should "enter into His gates with thanksgiving, and into His courts with praise. Be thankful to Him, and bless His name." Authentic worship begins by not performing for the masses. It doesn't matter what others do or think about our worship. We are not aiming to please others with our worship, only God. Authentic worship comes from approaching God with a thankful and sincere heart.

........................................................................................................

*Father, thank You for being authentic with me. Forgive me when I am inauthentic with You. May I worship You authentically each day. In Jesus' name, amen.*

# Week 8—Wednesday
*The Truth About the Amenities of God*

*Bless the LORD, O my soul, and forget not all His benefits: Who forgives all your iniquities, who heals all your diseases, who redeems your life from destruction, who crowns you with lovingkindness and tender mercies, who satisfies your mouth with good things, so that your youth is renewed like the eagle's.*

PSALM 103:2–5

Whenever our family can take a weekend trip or a vacation, my wife, Tonya, searches for a hotel with the best value and certain amenities. Often these amenities, or the lack thereof, are the deciding factors for our vacation lodging

However, even when the amenities of this world are no more, the amenities of the Lord remain. The psalmist wrote that we must "forget not all His benefits." What are these amenities described as "benefits"?

*God forgives.* Maybe you need to repent for not forgiving yourself when God has already forgiven you in Jesus.

*God heals.* Some diseases God heals on earth, but God heals all diseases in heaven.

*God redeems.* God delivers us from the power of sin on earth and the presence of sin in heaven.

*God crowns.* He doesn't just flippantly say, "You are not guilty." God crowns us with mercy.

*God satisfies.* Why do we look for satisfaction everywhere else when God alone satisfies?

......................................................................................................

*Father, thank You for all Your amenities, but thank You most of all for Yourself.
In Jesus' name, amen.*

Dr. Sam Greer, Ph.D, Red Bank Baptist Church, Chattanooga, TN

# WEEK 8—THURSDAY
## *The Truth About Gospel Appointments*

*I will praise You, O LORD, among the peoples, and I will sing praises to You among the nations. For Your mercy is great above the heavens, and Your truth reaches to the clouds.*

PSALM 108:3–4

Have you ever gone to a doctor's appointment, only to feel as though the appointment was pointless? Perhaps you had a reason for going, but once you left, you didn't feel as though it was especially helpful. Most appointments tend to be scheduled with a point in mind. Gospel appointments are no different.

What are gospel appointments? Gospel appointments, gospel conversations, life-on-life evangelism, relational evangelism, or whatever phrase you are familiar with, are those opportunities when you must communicate the good news of Jesus through personal interactions. Although these gospel appointments may not be on your calendar, God has them circled on His calendar.

David wrote today's passage in a time of crisis, and he made a couple of points about all gospel appointments. First, we are not the point of gospel appointments. Second, we are the pointers who point people to Jesus in gospel appointments.

...........................................................................................

*Father, please help me be mindful of each gospel appointment You bring my way. May I point people to the good news of Jesus Christ. In Jesus' name, amen!*

# WEEK 8—FRIDAY

*The Truth About Being in Awe of God*

*The works of His hands are verity and justice; all His precepts are sure. They stand fast forever and ever, and are done in truth and uprightness. He has sent redemption to His people; He has commanded His covenant forever: holy and awesome is His name.*

PSALM 111:7–9

According to scientists, less than five percent of the ocean has been explored. In 2016 astrophysicists and astronomers agreed that only five percent of the entire universe is visible. Despite all scientific advances, scientists are ninety-five percent in the dark when it comes to the exploration of the entire universe and the oceans' depths. So why are men and women in awe of themselves and what they have done?

Psalm 111:7–9 presents God as the only One worthy of your wonder and awe. Why should you be in wonder and awe of God? God is the Creator. God is the Creator who designed the world. Are you in awe of God as Creator?

God is the Sustainer. God's precepts are sure, as they are given in truth and last forever. God sustains all that He creates. Are you in awe of God as Sustainer? God is the Savior. God's greatest miracle is the redemption of all people by making them into new creatures in Christ. Are you in awe of God as Savior?

God is the Lord. He demands that His commandments be obeyed. As Savior, Jesus obeyed God the Father; as Lord, Jesus deserves your obedience. Are you in awe of God as Lord?

·····························································································

*Father, may I be in awe of you as Creator, Sustainer, Savior, and Lord. In Jesus' name, amen.*

Dr. Sam Greer, Ph.D, Red Bank Baptist Church, Chattanooga, TN

# WEEK 8—WEEKEND

## The Truth About Abiding in God

*You who fear the LORD, trust in the LORD; He is their help and their shield. The LORD has been mindful of us; He will bless us; He will bless the house of Israel; He will bless the house of Aaron. He will bless those who fear the Lord, both small and great.*

PSALM 115:11–13

D oes God play favorites? Does God pour out more of His favor on those who favor Him? Does God bless certain people more than others? Psalm 115:11–13 is a reminder that God will bless all of those who trust and fear Him, both small and great. The matter of abiding in God matters. But why?

God's blessings are unconditional. God's standard of blessing a person is never based upon what is on the outside; rather, God looks to the heart of a person. If you trust and fear the Lord, you will be blessed.

God's blessings are inclusive. God shows favoritism *to* those who trust and fear Him; however, God shows no favoritism *among* those who trust and fear Him. Those who fear the Lord, both small and great, will be blessed.

God's blessings are immeasurable. God will never forget those who fear Him, and He will never forget to bless those who fear Him. The psalmist emphatically said that God will bless those who trust Him. God's blessings are immeasurably multiplied on those who fear Him.

........................................................................................

*Father, You alone are to be feared and trusted. Thank You for all Your immeasurable blessings. May I continue to trust You. In Jesus' name, amen.*

# WEEK 9—MONDAY

*Let Everyone Praise the Lord*

*Praise the LORD, all you Gentiles! Laud Him, all you peoples! For His merciful kindness is great toward us, and the truth of the LORD endures forever. Praise the LORD!*

PSALM 117:1–2

Today's verses remind us that we are called to praise the Lord. The Scriptures make this command in many places, and as Christ followers, we should be quick to praise the Lord always. We praise the Lord for who He is, our Creator. He knew us before He formed us. On the cross, Jesus took our sins upon Himself, and we now have His forgiveness and redemption.

This passage also includes a special invitation to the Gentiles. Even though Gentiles are not Jewish, they have been invited to be part of God's family and have been given the opportunity for the redemption that was first offered to the Jewish people.

We also praise the Lord for where He leads us. We certainly have blessings upon this earth, but they pale in comparison to the blessings we will have with our Savior forever in eternity.

*Lord, forgive me when I withhold my praise from You. Sometimes my circumstances make me look inward instead of looking to You. Help me be quick to praise You in all things. And, Lord, I praise You most for who You are and for Your forgiveness and redemption, amen.*

Dr. Marty Jacumin, Bay Leaf Baptist Church, Raleigh, NC

# WEEK 9—TUESDAY
## *True Fulfillment*

*Blessed are the undefiled in the way, who walk in the law of the LORD! Blessed are those who keep His testimonies, who seek Him with the whole heart!*

PSALM 119:1–2

As human beings, we crave happiness. This can most clearly be seen on the magazine shelves of any bookstore.

Some magazines focus on our hobbies. We can learn how to improve our golf scores or how to catch bigger fish. Perhaps we find our happiness in motorcycles or automobiles. Others see money as the source of ultimate happiness in their lives. For them magazines will teach how to invest in the stock market, how to buy land, and even how to store up gold and silver. Others base their happiness on their earthly homes. They can learn how to fix up and decorate their homes or even expand the size of their homes.

God's Word reminds us of the true source of happiness. Today's text tells us we are happiest when we walk in the law of the Lord. This means we should walk in a way that honors Christ by keeping His Word and allowing it to be the guide for our lives. We are to seek Him with our whole hearts. Everything within us should desire to obey our Lord.

*Father, remind me that You know what will make me happy and that is walking with You. Help me seek You with my whole heart. In You I know I will find true happiness and true fulfillment in life, amen.*

# WEEK 9—WEDNESDAY

*Close and Clean*

*With my whole heart I have sought You; oh, let me not wander from Your commandments! Your word I have hidden in my heart, that I might not sin against You.*

PSALM 119:10–11

Years ago I asked my friend Johnny how I could pray for him. He responded with a simple request, asking me to pray that he would be close and clean. He wanted to be close to Jesus Christ.

Johnny also wanted to be clean before the Lord. He wanted to walk in the statutes of the Lord and obey His Word. We should all have this desire. Our text today reminds us that we need to stay rooted in the Word of God. We need to be reminded of its commands and its precepts. We need to read, study, memorize it, and let it guide our lives. We should not look to what's accepted in our culture or what's even accepted by people within the church. God's Word needs to guide our actions.

I have asked many people to pray for me in the same way that Johnny asked me to pray for him years ago. I now ask you to pray for one another in the same way. Pray that we would walk as God would have us walk so we can be people who are quick to obey the Lord.

................................................................................

*Father, help me not only to know Your work but also help me to obey Your Word. I desire to be close and clean before You. Give me strength when temptation comes, and let me seek to be obedient. Let people not only hear my testimony, but let them also see the testimony of a changed life because of what You have done within me, amen.*

Dr. Marty Jacumin, Bay Leaf Baptist Church, Raleigh, NC

# Week 9—Thursday

*What Do You Treasure?*

*I have rejoiced in the way of Your testimonies, as much as in all riches. I will meditate on Your precepts, and contemplate Your ways. I will delight myself in Your statutes; I will not forget Your word.*

PSALM 119:14–16

What do you treasure? I treasure time I spend with my grandson. If you are a grandparent, you understand. People love their children, but there's something extra special about a grandchild. I love to spend time with my grandson. I feel as if I'm investing in his life, and I want him to learn as much as he can. I also love to tell others about him

Today's text speaks of God's Word and the value we place on it. The psalmist values the Word of God above all riches. He places the highest value on it. Because he places this value on it, he spends time in the Word. He meditates and contemplates on it. The psalmist also says he delights in the Word of God. Just as a grandparent delights in spending time with a grandchild, the writer delights in the Truth.

A great question to ask yourself is if you value God's Word. The time you spend in it will reveal the answer.

*Father, forgive me when I don't value Your Word. Forgive me when I don't see it as more valuable than all riches. Help me to meditate on Your Word and to tell others about You. Help me to love You more, amen.*

# WEEK 9—FRIDAY
*Your Choice to Make*

*I have chosen the way of truth; Your judgments I have laid before me. I cling to
Your testimonies; O LORD, do not put me to shame! I will run the course of Your
commandments, for You shall enlarge my heart.*

PSALM 119:30–32

I occasionally meet people at our local coffee shop. I find it fascinating to
listen to people as they order their coffee. Very seldom will you hear someone order a black coffee. You are more likely to hear someone order a skinny
vanilla soy latte with an extra pump of espresso or a mocha Frappuccino with
extra whipped cream. Hearing these orders reminds me that we love choices.
Simply having a cup of coffee is wonderful, but we also love all the different
ways we can order our coffee.

Our text for today reminds us that obedience to God is a choice. The
writer says he has the statutes of the Lord before him and that he chooses to
walk as God would have him walk. When we trust Christ as Savior, He does
not take away our free will. We also must remember that our sinful natures
are still present within us. We must put on the armor of God daily and choose
to walk in obedience to Christ. In a world full of choices, this is the most
important decision we make each day.

*Dear Lord, help me to choose obedience each day. Forgive me for when I willing-
ly disobey Your Word. Help me each day to walk closer with You, amen.*

Dr. Marty Jacumin, Bay Leaf Baptist Church, Raleigh, NC

# Week 9—Weekend
## *The Help We Need*

*Teach me, O LORD, the way of Your statutes, and I shall keep it to the end. Give me understanding, and I shall keep Your law; indeed, I shall observe it with my whole heart. Make me walk in the path of Your commandments, for I delight in it.*

PSALM 119:33–35

As we studied yesterday, obedience to God is a choice. The good news is that God will help us as we seek to walk in obedience to Him. The psalmist cries out to God and asks to be taught the statutes of the Lord. How amazing to know that God will be our tutor if we will cry out to Him. He will teach us His statutes and equip us to walk with Him.

As we read our text today, we discover that the psalmist asks to go even deeper. He asks God for understanding. He wants to obey God, but he also wants to do it with a heart that is fully devoted to God. He wants to understand God's Word and why God wants him to walk in obedience.

The final section brings the verse to a thrilling end. Perhaps the psalmist fears he will not choose correctly, so he asks the Lord to make him walk in obedience. This connotes a special desire to cry out to God and not be willing to accept anything but obedience to Him. May that be the desire of our hearts every day as Christ followers.

........................................................................................

*Dear God, help me never to settle for half-hearted obedience to You. Teach me, give me understanding, and make me follow Your ways, amen.*

# Week 10—Monday

*Revive Me and Use Me*

*Consider how I love Your precepts; revive me, O Lord, according to Your lovingkindness. The entirety of Your word is truth, and every one of Your righteous judgments endures forever.*

Psalm 119:159–160

What a great prayer to begin a Monday morning: "Revive me, O Lord." The psalmist's cry for personal renewal and revival reminds me of the old spiritual song, "Not my brother or my sister, but it's me, O Lord, standing in the need of prayer." All of us need a fresh touch from God daily. In this text King David not only calls out for personal revival, but he also includes how that personal renewal from the Lord makes its way to us. Renewal comes as we spend time reading and meditating on the Word of God. He is for us. He is not against us. He wants to revive and replenish our barren souls. He can and He will as we meditate upon His precepts, Word of truth, and judgments.

Once you encounter the Lord and He revives you, go and be a blessing to someone else. S. Truett Cathy, founder of Chick-fil-A, was training his employees how to relate to customers. He asked his employees, "Do you know how you can tell someone needs encouragement?"

Some of the replies were, "They look sad." "They are crying." "They are yelling at the children!"

Cathy smiled and simply replied, "They walk in the door."

*O Lord God, You are awesome. I love You, and I love Your Word. Revive me, restore my downcast soul, and lift me up by the power of Your Word. And now help me encourage someone today, amen.*

Dr. Danny Forshee, Great Hills Baptist Church, Austin, TX

*If You, LORD, should mark iniquities, O Lord, who could stand? But there is forgiveness with You, that You may be feared. I wait for the LORD, my soul waits, and in His word I do hope.*

PSALM 130:3–5

The key to living an abundant and blessed life is to experience forgiveness, and then to forgive. The psalmist tells us that the Lord is a forgiving God. When we confess our sins to God, He forgives us because He is faithful and just (1 John 1:9). God longs to forgive us. We confess and He pardons. Proverbs 28:13 states, "He who covers his sins will not prosper, but whoever confesses and forsakes them will have mercy."

Because God forgives our sins, we can forgive those who sin against us. Our text gives us great insight into how we can forgive when someone hurts us. Fear God, wait on God, and trust Him. When we do this, He enables us to forgive those who mistreat us. Forgiveness is a beautiful thing to have and give away. When we choose not to forgive, it is like drinking poison and hoping that it kills the other person. Choosing not to forgive harms us in many ways, including causing physical, emotional, and mental anguish.

As you have freely received God's forgiveness for your sins, freely offer forgiveness to those who have harmed you. With God's help you can do it!

*Dear God, thank You for forgiving me of all my sins. I rejoice in Your salvation. Please empower me to choose to forgive those who wrong me. I cannot do this with my own strength, but by Your power, Lord, I can do all things, amen.*

# Week 10—Wednesday

*Trust and Obey*

*The LORD has sworn in truth to David; He will not turn from it: "I will set upon your throne the fruit of your body. If your sons will keep My covenant and My testimony which I shall teach them, their sons also shall sit upon your throne forevermore."*

PSALM 132:11–12

God made promises to King David, and whenever God makes a promise, we can rest assured that He will bring it to pass. The Bible abounds with examples of promises God makes to His children. The promises in our text today are very specific. God gave them to King David. The promises and subsequent blessings can be summed up this way—obey God, and your sons and posterity will reign as kings in Israel.

Unfortunately the sons of King David and the children of Israel did not obey God's commands, and as a result the kingdom was taken away from them. However, there is one notable exception. Jesus Christ, the King of kings, a descendant of King David, obeyed God the Father in all things. Now He sits upon not only the throne of the kingdom of God but also the throne of the heart of every person who confesses Jesus Christ as their Lord.

The promises made to King David and his descendants remind us of a promise God makes to all parents. Proverbs 20:7 states, "The righteous man walks in his integrity; his children are blessed after him." May God help us walk alongside Him so our children will be blessed.

.........................................................................................................................

*Dear God, thank You for always keeping Your promises. Help me to obey Your commandments. Thank You for the love You give me and the desire of Your heart to bless me. I love You! Amen.*

Dr. Danny Forshee, Great Hills Baptist Church, Austin, TX

# WEEK 10—THURSDAY
## *Praise, and Then Petition*

*I will worship toward Your holy temple, and praise Your name for Your lovingkindness and Your truth; for You have magnified Your word above all Your name. In the day when I cried out, You answered me, and made me bold with strength in my soul.*

PSALM 138:2–3

The psalmist lifts his hands in praise to God before he lifts his heart in making petitions to God. He bows his heart in heartfelt worship, and he also lifts his voice in praise to God. Why? He praises the Lord because of His lovingkindness, truth, and Word. After a season of worship and praise, he brings his petition to the Lord. He recalls how he had cried out to God for help. God had answered him, and then emboldened his inner soul.

Our primary objective in life is to know God. When we know Him, we will then worship Him and tell others about Him. Will hardship and pain come to the child of God on this earth? Absolutely! But in seasons of prosperity and drought, our responsibilities remain the same—worship first, and then make petitions. It is so easy to neglect the first part of this spiritual process. We often rush into God's presence demanding His help, but failing to ponder just how awesome is our God.

As you read today's devotion, you may be in a very difficult place. You might think this season of life will never pass. Let me encourage you to keep worshipping during waiting. God sees, He hears, and He acts! Be faithful.

. . . . . . . . . . . . . . . . . . . . . . . . . . . . . . . . . . . . . . . . . . . . . . . . . . . . . . . . . . . . . . . . . . . . . . . . . . . . . . . . . . . . . . . . .

*Lord, I believe. Help my unbelief in those dark nights of the soul when I fail to give You praise and trust in You. Deliver me, God, from these difficult hours in Your perfect timing. As I worship You I will wait on You, amen.*

# Week 10—Friday

*A Bowl of Ice Cream*

*The LORD is righteous in all His ways, gracious in all His works. The LORD is near to all who call upon Him, to all who call upon Him in truth. He will fulfill the desire of those who fear Him; He also will hear their cry and save them.*

PSALM 145:17–19

A little boy asked his mom if he could say the dinner blessing. The boy prayed, "God, thank You for this food we are about to receive and the ice cream my mom will give me. With liberty and justice for all, amen."

Some in the restaurant chuckled at this little boy's prayer, but not all laughed. One lady was offended, and she said, "Kids these days! Asking God for ice cream! He ought to be ashamed."

The little boy started to cry. A gentleman watching all of this transpire walked over to the boy and said, "I heard your prayer, and I happen to know God, and He loved your prayer. The mean lady could use some ice cream." When the waitress brought the boy a big bowl of ice cream, he took it to the mean woman and said, "Here you go, ma'am, a little ice cream is good for the soul, and my soul is good." [1]

God is for you, and He is not against you. Some will be against you and will hurt you. Let me encourage you to call upon the Lord in your time of trial. The text today proclaims that God will fulfill your desire, hear your cry, and save you.

........................................................................................................

*God, help me to not take to heart the insults and hurt that others direct toward me. Help me instead to cast my burden upon You, amen.*

Dr. Danny Forshee, Great Hills Baptist Church, Austin, TX

# WEEK 10—WEEKEND
## *True Happiness*

*Happy is he who has the God of Jacob for his help, whose hope is in the Lord his God, who made heaven and earth, the sea, and all that is in them; who keeps truth forever, who executes justice for the oppressed, who gives food to the hungry. The LORD gives freedom to the prisoners.*

PSALM 146:5–7

Quarterback Tom Brady has made many happy fans in New England. With all his accomplishments, many believe he is the best quarterback ever to play in the National Football League. Sorry to all the Joe Montana, Roger Staubach, and Terry Bradshaw fans. But as John Adams once said, "Facts are stubborn things." The Super Bowl appearances and wins make Brady the best, and, again, for New England Patriot fans, he has brought a lot of football happiness.

Now if a mere mortal can bring football fans joy and gladness, then how much more can the Creator bring true joy and happiness to His children? Our text teaches us that those who know God are truly happy. The one true God made heaven and earth, keeps truth forever, defends the oppressed, gives food to the needy, and freedom to the imprisoned. What a mighty God is He! All who hope in Him put their faith and trust in Him—they are truly happy.

........................................................................................

*Lord, thank You for being the source of true happiness. Forgive me when I doubt You and do not trust You as I should. I commit this day to walk by faith and lean on You for everything. I renew my hope and trust in You at this moment, amen.*

# Week 11—Monday

## The Shield

*For the LORD gives wisdom; from His mouth come knowledge and understanding; He stores up sound wisdom for the upright; He is a shield to those who walk uprightly.*

PROVERBS 2:6–7

I recently heard Pastor Bill Purvis say, "The voices you listen to determine the choices you make." We have the very words of God in the form of Scripture. We don't need to hear more from God about what we should do or where we should go; we just need to obey more of what He has already told us.

Proverbs 2:7 reminds us that when we follow His Word, He will be our protection. I serve as the chaplain for the police department in Byron, Georgia. In December 2016, I received a dreaded call from the police chief in the middle of the night. A suspect had shot two Byron officers during a drug raid. One had minor injuries, but Officer James Wynn had taken a shotgun blast to the arm and torso.

It has been more than a year, and Officer Wynn is just about to return to work after multiple surgeries and extensive rehabilitation. I saw the vest that he wore the night of the raid. My knees went limp when I saw three buckshot rounds embedded in the area of the heart. Officer Wynn had boldly faced the enemy and experienced pain and suffering, but his heart was protected.

That is what God promises to do for us when we live according to the wisdom that only He gives. We may go through trials, but God will protect our hearts. He will be our tactical vests.

*Lord, give me the strength today to live according to Your Word and not my desires, amen.*

Tim Sizemore, Lighthouse Baptist Church, Macon, GA

# Week 11—Tuesday
## *Stand Out*

*Let not mercy and truth forsake you; bind them around your neck, write them on the tablet of your heart, and so find favor and high esteem in the sight of God and man.*

PROVERBS 3:3–4

I am a huge Alabama football fan. I often wear shirts reflecting that fact. Whenever I walk through the grocery store and meet another Bama fan, do you know what he or she says? "Roll Tide!" My wife pokes fun at me, saying it reminds her of how people passed lepers and yelled, "Unclean! Unclean!"

People recognize I am a Bama fan because of what I wear. Solomon says in his own way that we should be so full of mercy and truth that it stands out like a big crimson A embroidered on our shirt!

I passed a guy in a parking lot on the day of the national championship game. He wore an Alabama shirt. I gave the normal "Roll Tide!" greeting. He looked at me funny and said, "Oh, no. This is my wife's shirt. I just borrowed it."

Anyone can wear a borrowed shirt or say he is a Christian, but what's inside will come out. Our hearts must be branded with mercy and truth. They must be the core of who we are. How do we build up that core? By putting it into practice.

........................................................................................................

*Lord, help me today to be faithful to Your Word and to the commitments that I make. Help me show mercy to others in the way that You have shown mercy to me, amen.*

# Week 11—Wednesday

*In Our Hearts*

*My son, give attention to my words; incline your ear to my sayings. Do not let them depart from your eyes; keep them in the midst of your heart; for they are life to those who find them, and health to all their flesh. Keep your heart with all diligence, for out of it spring the issues of life.*

PROVERBS 4:20–23

Have you ever heard the saying, "You are what you eat"? What you put into your body affects everything about you. Earlier in Proverbs 4, Solomon personified wisdom and talked of pursuing her as if she were a beautiful young woman who had caught the eye of a bachelor. The metaphor illustrates the importance of pursuing wisdom.

In verses 20–23, Solomon speaks of the two most useful and most dangerous organs of a man: his eyes and his ears. We use these organs to receive information. Solomon wants his son to take it all in. Solomon tells his son not only to hear his instructions but to store them "in the midst of your heart."

Where is the safest place for a child to ride in the car? To what part of the home do you run when a tornado is coming? The middle (the "midst") is the most protected and safe place. The author implies that we should not be content merely to possess wisdom. Rather we should store it deep within the center of our hearts where it will not be easily lost.

........................................................................................................

*Lord, keep my eyes focused on things that will bring Your wisdom to my heart. Tune my ears to hear what will guide me to You, amen.*

Tim Sizemore, Lighthouse Baptist Church, Macon, GA

# WEEK 11—THURSDAY
## *Treasured Obedience*

*My son, keep my words, and treasure my commands within you. Keep my commands and live, and my law as the apple of your eye. Bind them on your fingers; write them on the tablet of your heart.*

PROVERBS 7:1–3

T he Hebrew phrase translated "apple of your eye" literally means "as the little man in thine eye." The translation is the picture of the reflection you would see if you looked closely into the pupil of one's eye. In order for you to see this reflection, you would need to be close to someone's face. You wouldn't be able to focus on anything else.

Solomon is teaching his son about the dangers of sexual sin in Proverbs 7. Solomon wants his son to avoid sexual immorality by focusing on God's commands.

My father is the team chaplain for the Macon Mayhem, a minor league professional hockey team. Last year they won their league championship. Dad received a gargantuan championship ring. He wears it with pride. The ring is a reminder of a lot of right choices that resulted in extraordinary success and celebration.

Commands and laws are not always fun to follow at the time, but they ultimately pay off like all those practices and workouts did for the Mayhem. We should wear the teachings of God as Dad wears that ring. We should write them in stone, on the tablets of our hearts, so our desire to follow His laws won't be erased easily.

........................................................................................................

*Lord, keep me focused on You today, amen.*

# Week 11—Friday

*Sticks and Stones*

---

*There is one who speaks like the piercings of a sword, but the tongue of the wise promotes health. The truthful lip shall be established forever, but a lying tongue is but for a moment.*

Proverbs 12:18–19

S ticks and stones may break my bones, but words will never hurt me" is a lie! A hurtful word can be as crippling as any broken bone. The tongue can be a mighty weapon in several ways.

I once thought my calling was to keep people humble. However, I don't know if my blunt words made them humble as much as made them mad. What I do know is that I hurt them. I am ashamed of the person I was. I went around tearing people down when I could have just as easily been building them up. When I started looking at people as God does, I realized that what I was doing was hurtful.

Today I look for opportunities to be an encourager. The same tongue that causes pain and cuts people open can encourage healing and close wounds. How we utilize our eyes and ears will primarily affect our health; how we use our tongue will mainly impact the wellness of others.

Another danger the tongue harbors is the ability to lie. Solomon is clear that lies will eventually be uncovered and the truth will come out. Commit now always to be honest and seek opportunities to lift others up with encouraging words. You can be a healer with your words.

............................................................................................................

*Lord, use me today to lift someone up. Help me to be an encourager, amen.*

Tim Sizemore, Lighthouse Baptist Church, Macon, GA

# Week 11—Weekend

*I Meant to Do That . . .*

*The preparations of the heart belong to man, but the answer of the tongue is from the Lord. All the ways of a man are pure in his own eyes, but the Lord weighs the spirits. Commit your works to the Lord, and your thoughts will be established.*

PROVERBS 16:1–3

I am so thankful that the Lord often blocks my plans. I find incredible peace knowing that God searches my heart, knows my heart, and has the last say. One might say that He sometimes protects me from myself.

Every act of sin is evidence of a fallen humanity with a sinful nature. The Lord gives us free will, but as we find in the book of Revelation, He will have the last word. Man's heart will plot to do many evil things, some he will accomplish, but thankfully God will speak last.

Have you ever played pool with people who refused to call their shots? It is easy to say that you meant to make the 5-ball bank off two rails, travel the length of the table, and drop into the corner pocket . . . after it happens. Even though others in the room can't see the depths of your heart, they can see your other shots and be reasonably sure that was not your intention when you struck the cue ball.

We may fool others and even ourselves, but God sees our real motives. Solomon makes the point that if we set our hearts to do the work of God and not our own, then God will guide our thoughts.

*Father God, guide my thoughts today. Help me to incline my heart to advancing Your kingdom and looking for ways to serve You rather than myself, amen.*

# Week 12—Monday

*God's Lamp Examines Our Soul*

---

*The spirit of a man is the lamp of the LORD, searching all the inner depths of his heart. Mercy and truth preserve the king, and by lovingkindness he upholds his throne.*

PROVERBS 20:27–28

A s a small boy, long before becoming a Christian, I desperately wanted a toy that my friend had, but one my parents would not buy for me. One evening while playing with him, the darkness in me rose up and I slipped his toy into my pocket. When I got home that evening, I could not wait to enjoy my "new" toy. The experience, however, was not what I expected. Instead of happiness I found myself saddened by what I had done. I confessed to my father, who then walked me across the street to apologize as I sobbed uncontrollably. Something inside me had seriously disagreed with my actions. Many years passed before I came to understand what that "something" was.

God created life by breathing into man. In this passage God's lamp is a metaphor for the breath of God inside of people. When God breathes life into a person, that person receives a spirit that can evaluate his actions and motives. Some call it a conscience. God's infused Spirit is what makes man different from all the rest of creation. Man can understand right and wrong. He can understand moral, intellectual, and spiritual matters.

As God's lamp evaluates our deepest actions and thoughts, the darkness is exposed and God begins His work to make us more like Him. When this takes place we naturally become more loving and loyal.

---

*Father, I ask that You expose and cleanse any darkness in my life today and make me more like You, amen.*

Dr. Steve Folmar, First Baptist Church of Houma, Houma, LA

# WEEK 12—TUESDAY

## *Are Your Parents Your Best Friends?*

*Listen to your father who begot you, and do not despise your mother when she is old. Buy the truth, and do not sell it, also wisdom and instruction and understanding. The father of the righteous will greatly rejoice, and he who begets a wise child will delight in him.*

PROVERBS 23:22–24

I n ancient culture it was expected that a young man would listen to his father because his father literally gave him life. It was an action of respect. And it was understood that one received truth and gained wisdom from his parents.

A young man was expected to make his parents proud by being respectful and by growing in wisdom. Part of that growth also led to taking care of his parents in their old age.

Today we need a clarion call for young people to heed the instruction of their parents and to exhibit a true respect that honors them throughout life—especially in their old age.

I often tell young people that one of the best decisions they can make is to allow their parents to be their best friends. I try to get them to understand that their parents are their biggest fans. Naturally parents want their children to succeed. They want their children to have wonderful lives. Unfortunately all too often children reject their parents' wisdom and instruction instead of embracing the truths they share.

*Father, I ask that You give our children the wisdom to trust their parents: the ones who love them more than anyone other than You, amen.*

# WEEK 12—WEDNESDAY
## Celebrate Life!

*Live joyfully with the wife whom you love all the days of your vain life which He has given you under the sun, all your days of vanity; for that is your portion in life, and in the labor which you perform under the sun. Whatever your hand finds to do, do it with your might; for there is no work or device or knowledge or wisdom in the grave where you are going.*

ECCLESIASTES 9:9–10

E cclesiastes tells us that life here on earth is short and should be lived joyfully! Living joyfully encompasses every aspect of life, including marriage.

Solomon says that a man should make his wife his best friend. He encourages men to strive to enjoy her physically, emotionally, and spiritually. When Solomon says "enjoy your wife," he means it wholeheartedly.

God created Eve to complete Adam. God's design was for a man and woman to complete each other in every way. It's like two pieces of a puzzle coming together. He wants them to enjoy each other in their marriage relationship. In fact it should be a celebration of life!

Celebrating life means to enjoy your work and your hobbies as long as they line up with God's Word. However, many have been raised on a brand of Christianity that teaches anything enjoyable or fun must be bad. But nothing is wrong with celebrating the life God has graciously given to you. This is not only practical advice for life; it is also a command from the Word of God.

......................................................................................................................

*God, give me the ability to enjoy the wonderful blessings You provide for me, amen.*

Dr. Steve Folmar, First Baptist Church of Houma, Houma, LA

# Week 12—Thursday
## *God Gives Perfect Peace*

*Open the gates, that the righteous nation which keeps the truth may enter in. You will keep him in perfect peace, whose mind is stayed on You, because he trusts in You. Trust in the LORD forever, for in YAH, the LORD, is everlasting strength.*

ISAIAH 26:2–4

I saiah writes this word of confidence to God's people who were involved in the Dispersion. He reminds them that the ones who trust in Holy God, the ones who remain strong in their trust for Him, the ones who rely on Him, will come back one day to the city of God. They will be welcomed with open arms and find perfect peace. How reassuring is that?

Life is riddled with sin, and we live an imperfect existence. Just like our Christian ancestors, we too will find ourselves dispersed from God. We will have times in our lives when we will find ourselves feeling distant from God.

However, we must remember that when our life situations are not perfect, we must continue to trust Him. He is the God of eternal strength, peace, and promise. He promises perfect peace and protection—something only He can provide.

What must we do for this perfect peace and protection? Trust Him individually and trust Him as a nation. Keep His truths and our minds focused on Him. Be committed to Him. Doing so won't always be easy, but the reward will be worth it—perfect peace!

.................................................................................................

*Father, give me the strength to remain close and committed to You even when the circumstances of life cause me to feel distant from You, amen.*

# WEEK 12—FRIDAY

*God Promises a Better World*

*The work of righteousness will be peace, and the effect of righteousness, quietness and assurance forever. My people will dwell in a peaceful habitation, in secure dwellings, and in quiet resting places.*

ISAIAH 32:17–18

Israel's history has often been one of war. Throughout history hostile people and nations have attached Israel. Even today, enemies surround Israel and seek to destroy them.

The promise in Isaiah was for Israel and is still valid today. The good news is that the promise is for Christians too. Isaiah's promise involves the coming Messiah who will reign in righteousness. Once the Messiah comes, for the first time honest judgments will be made. Some people will be affirmed for their righteousness, and some will be exposed for their sins.

The Messiah will also bring an atmosphere of peace, secure dwellings, and quiet resting places. These concepts seem totally foreign and an improbable reality when we consider today's chaotic world. But all of God's children can look forward with anticipation to Jesus, the righteous judge, who will come and bring a true utopia to the lives of His people.

*Lord, may I be encouraged that the best is yet to come. I eagerly anticipate the coming of Jesus. I pray today and ask You to come quickly! Amen.*

Dr. Steve Folmar, First Baptist Church of Houma, Houma, LA

# WEEK 12—WEEKEND

*Keep Your Worship Pure*

*"To whom then will you liken Me, or to whom shall I be equal?" says the Holy One.*
*Lift up your eyes on high, and see who has created these things, who brings out their*
*host by number; He calls them all by name, by the greatness of His might and the*
*strength of His power; not one is missing.*

ISAIAH 40:25–26

Throughout their history, Israel often worshipped idols, which was a direct violation of God's law. If we are honest, we have too!

God created the heavens and the stars. He also created the materials that men use to build false idols. However, whenever our worship turns away from God and shifts to something He created, it is improper and dangerous.

God wants us to worship Him. He invites us to compare, "To whom then will you liken Me, or to whom shall I be equal?" He tells us to look up at the stars and realize that by His power, He created them, He named them, and He put them in the heavens. Being amazed by God's creation is not wrong, but we must be careful that we worship the Creator, not the creation.

*Today, Lord, I ask You to guide my worship and help me remain focused on You. I pray You keep my worship pure and help me refrain from worshipping anything other than You, amen.*

# WEEK 13—MONDAY

*Trusting God's Word*

*"Remember the former things of old, for I am God, and there is no other; I am God, and there is none like Me, declaring the end from the beginning, and from ancient times things that are not yet done, saying, 'My counsel shall stand, and I will do all My pleasure.'"*

ISAIAH 46:9–10

Everything we do as believers must be based upon the foundation of God's Word. I hear people say, "I believe the Bible is inerrant, infallible, and the inspired Word of God." I agree with this statement because this is a core conviction that guides my daily life.

We all must stand on something or else we are like the waves of the ocean being tossed about with no clear direction. The Word of God is the guiding light to our lives as believers, but we must trust what it says in order to experience the benefits God has in store for us. God told Abraham to go without telling Abraham where he was going. The best part of that story is that Abraham went anyway. Abraham knew something that we can all learn from: just trust Him, because He knows what is best for our lives. When we understand that we can take God at His Word, then we can begin to walk with Him as never before!

........................................................................................

*God, today I want to take my relationship with You further than yesterday. I want to trust You with my whole life. I give thanks for all Your counsel that comes from Your holy Word. I pray that I will be obedient to Your commands even if I don't understand them fully the moment You ask, amen.*

Dr. Kevin C. Williams, First Baptist Church, Villa Rica, GA

# WEEK 13—TUESDAY
## A Willing Substitute

*He was oppressed and He was afflicted, yet He opened not His mouth; He was led as a lamb to the slaughter, and as a sheep before its shearers is silent, so He opened not His mouth. He was taken from prison and from judgment, and who will declare His generation? For He was cut off from the land of the living; for the transgressions of My people He was stricken.*

ISAIAH 53:7–8

The Celts had an old tradition: if someone was sentenced to death for a crime, the only way he could be set free was for someone to take his place willingly. There was once a young teenage boy who had been caught in a crime punishable by death. His family was in agony and distraught over losing their only son. The day before the boy was to be executed, he was set free. He ran away as fast as he could but was overcome by the thought of knowing who took his place, so he sneaked to the back of the crowd as the execution was about to take place. He was shocked to see that his own father was beheaded in his place.

Jesus did the same for us the day He went to the cross as our willing substitute. He took our sins upon Himself, setting us free from sin, death, and hell. All we have to do is repent and believe to receive this free gift of salvation.

*Jesus, thank You for being my willing substitute. I was guilty and deserved death, but You took my place. Understanding this is hard, but I am thankful for Your free gift of salvation! Thank You for loving me, amen.*

# Week 13—Wednesday

*Living with Integrity*

"For I, the LORD, love justice; I hate robbery for burnt offering; I will direct their work in truth, and will make with them an everlasting covenant. Their descendants shall be known among the Gentiles, and their offspring among the people. All who see them shall acknowledge them, that they are the posterity whom the LORD has blessed."

ISAIAH 61:8–9

I am a former military police officer and currently a pastor, so a word that matters a lot to me is *integrity*. This word means "completeness, wholeness," or, simply put, it means "to do things right."

A living example of the word *integrity* can be seen in a fruit. You see, every time you peel a banana, you will always find a banana. If you cut open an orange, you will always find an orange. Every time you open a watermelon, you find a watermelon. Why? These fruits have integrity. They are on the inside what they appear to be on the outside.

God wants Christians to have integrity. This passage says He will "direct their work in truth." A believer should be the same inside and out. If you have integrity, you cannot act one way at church, and then be completely different outside the church. The Bible also says to let your yes be yes and your no be no (Matthew 5:37). In other words, mean what you say and say what you mean. If you do this, God says He will bless you and others will acknowledge God is at work in your life. This comes from living with integrity.

................................................................

*God, help me to live my life with integrity so I may bring glory and honor to Your name. May people see You living through me, amen.*

Dr. Kevin C. Williams, First Baptist Church, Villa Rica, GA

# WEEK 13—THURSDAY
## *Drifting*

*"If you will return, O Israel," says the LORD, "Return to Me; and if you will put away your abominations out of My sight, then you shall not be moved. And you shall swear, 'The LORD lives,' in truth, in judgment, and in righteousness; the nations shall bless themselves in Him, and in Him they shall glory."*

JEREMIAH 4:1–2

The nation of Israel often found itself in trouble with God because the people drifted into idolatry time and time again. The people were taken into captivity because they took their eyes off God's statutes and commands and followed false gods.

One of my professors at Fruitland Baptist Bible College told us a story about when he was a boy working with his father plowing a field. He always wanted to use the mule and plow as his father did, so one day his dad let him. My teacher wanted to make a straight line like his dad did, but when he got back to his dad, his line was a zigzag. His dad told him, "Son, pick out a fence post, keep your eyes on it, and walk straight at it." He followed his dad's instructions, and this time when he turned around to look, he had a straight line.

That is much like following Jesus in our lives. If we take our eyes off Jesus, we will drift into areas that get us into trouble and out of fellowship with God. As a result our lives will be big zigzags. However, if we keep our eyes on Jesus and follow Him, our lives can be straight. So if we are drifting from Him, let's put our eyes on Him and return to the straight path.

........................................................................................

*God, help me to keep my eyes on You and follow You in all that I do, amen.*

# WEEK 13—FRIDAY
## Hard-Hearted

*"Run to and fro through the streets of Jerusalem; see now and know; and seek in her open places if you can find a man, if there is anyone who executes judgment, who seeks the truth, and I will pardon her. Though they say, 'As the LORD lives,' surely they swear falsely." O LORD, are not Your eyes on the truth? You have stricken them, but they have not grieved; You have consumed them, but they have refused to receive correction. They have made their faces harder than rock; they have refused to return.*

JEREMIAH 5:1–3

Have you ever known someone who was hard-hearted? Today's passage talks about such people and the dangers of having hearts hardened against God. People who turn from God and avoid His correction can find themselves in serious spiritual trouble. In the New Testament Jesus tells a parable of the sower, and in this parable the seed falls on four different types of soil. The seed in the parable represents God's Word, and the soils refer to people's hearts. The second soil He mentions is "stony places" (Matthew 13:5), which represents people's hearts that are calloused to the gospel. Hebrews 3:13 also warns against allowing one's heart to be hardened by sin.

The question is how do you get past this? You must guard your heart and keep it soft toward the things of God. You must learn to love people. One area that leads to having a hard heart is being unforgiving. But, instead, it is only hurting you and turning your heart away from the things of God. Learn to love people and forgive them, and you will find your joy, but if you choose the other path it will be a hard one.

..............................................................................................................

*Lord Jesus, help me not to have a hard heart. Help me to keep my heart soft toward You, amen.*

Dr. Kevin C. Williams, First Baptist Church, Villa Rica, GA

# Week 13—Weekend

*Return*

*"Behold, I will bring it health and healing; I will heal them and reveal to them the abundance of peace and truth. And I will cause the captives of Judah and the captives of Israel to return, and will rebuild those places as at the first. I will cleanse them from all their iniquity by which they have sinned against Me, and I will pardon all their iniquities by which they have sinned and by which they have transgressed against Me. Then it shall be to Me a name of joy, a praise, and an honor before all nations of the earth, who shall hear all the good that I do to them; they shall fear and tremble for all the goodness and all the prosperity that I provide for it."*

JEREMIAH 33:6–9

Watching people fall is not fun. However, watching them return to the right place is always a fulfilling feeling. I have a friend who was hurt and blamed God for his demise. I watched him turn his back on his family, lose his job, go into depression, and leave his church. Talking to him was like talking to a brick wall. He didn't want to hear anything about God and was in rebellion. Much like the parable of the prodigal son, one day he came to his senses, repented, and returned to his family, job, and church. He thought he wouldn't be accepted, but he was surprised when he saw everyone loved him and accepted him back completely.

That is what God wants for our lives when we have strayed away from Him. Today's passage promises restoration to God's people, if they will turn from their sins and turn back to worshipping and loving Him. God wants us to repent and come back and be met with His forgiveness and love. That is a wonderful feeling!

........................................................................................................

*God, forgive me when I fail You, amen.*

# Week 14—Monday

*He's Got Your Back*

*Through the LORD's mercies we are not consumed, because His compassions fail not. They are new every morning; great is Your faithfulness. "The LORD is my portion," says my soul, "therefore I hope in Him!"*

LAMENTATIONS 3:22–24

God's got our backs! The stresses of this world consumed by sin can wear on us, leaving us feeling overwhelmed, helpless, empty, and alone. When going through difficult times we can feel like we wear out our welcome or lose closeness with our family, friends, and confidants.

People tire of others relying on them. How refreshing to know the Lord never tires of us! His love, mercy, and compassion are alive and well and new every day. How comforting to know that deep down in our inner beings, in the depths of our souls, we know He is our portion and our hope.

Darkness, depression, and struggles can cause people to lose hope. As believers we know the Lord never gives up on us. He is always there, day and night, to encourage, strengthen, guide, and comfort in our time of need. We never get on His nerves. He always has time for us. He never fails us. He is faithful. He always has our backs!

Jeremiah 29:11 tells us that the Lord does not have plans for disaster for us, but plans for a future and great hope. On this earth He walks with us through the valleys, leading us to the ultimate mountaintop in heaven one day.

........................................................................

*Lord Jesus, guide me through life's struggles, valleys, and pitfalls. Thank You for constantly being there. Thank You for always having my back, amen.*

Brian Fossett, Fossett Evangelistic Ministries, Dalton, GA

# Week 14—Tuesday

*Pitfall of Pride*

*At the same time my reason returned to me, and for the glory of my kingdom, my honor and splendor returned to me. My counselors and nobles resorted to me, I was restored to my kingdom, and excellent majesty was added to me. Now I, Nebuchadnezzar, praise and extol and honor the King of heaven, all of whose works are truth, and His ways justice. And those who walk in pride He is able to put down.*

DANIEL 4:36–37

According to Proverbs 16:18, pride comes before a fall. The Lord cannot stand pride. Pride blinds us from seeing His hand at work all around us. Pride is a lie that tells us we are in control, not God. Pride says we have accomplished everything on our own. Many prideful men and women have lost it all—family, friends, wealth, and stature—due to pride.

Do not let pride become the foundation on which you build your kingdom. Thank goodness God gives second chances. He is a God of restoration and reconciliation. No matter how far you have fallen, or what all you have lost, He can restore you.

The Lord's Word is truth. He desires to work His truth in us, so we will walk in truth and integrity. However, we are freewill agents. We must acknowledge our need for Him and His guidance and direction in our lives. Pride is a sin that will continually obstruct our walk with the Lord. It will distract us, causing us to stumble and fall.

Call out to the Lord to remove all pride from your life.

........................................................................................................

*Lord Jesus, help me to recognize and overcome pride in my life. Today I acknowledge You are my source of truth and life. Guide me and keep me this day, amen.*

# WEEK 14—WEDNESDAY

*He Is Still in the Saving Business*

*The LORD your God in your midst, the Mighty One, will save; He will rejoice over you with gladness, He will quiet you with His love, He will rejoice over you with singing.*

ZEPHANIAH 3:17

In His presence is peace beyond all comprehension. He calms the storms in our lives. He is mighty, ready, willing, and able to save.

No matter what we have done, no matter what we have been through, we can never be so far down sin's road that the nail-scarred hand of Jesus cannot reach us, pick us up, and make us new creatures. His ultimate desire is to save us. He is still in the saving business!

All of heaven rejoices when one lost sinner is saved. The gospel story of Jesus' death on the cross, burial, and resurrection never gets old. The Lord extends His invitation to all, but not everyone accepts His free pardon of sin. He calms our spirits, forgives our sins, and unveils new lives for us. He gives us a divine design for our lives. Love took Him to that cross for you and for me. We will never understand or comprehend that love fully, but we can trust Him.

If you have never trusted in Jesus, let today be the day of your salvation. Jesus is waiting on you to open your heart and let Him in. If that is your heart's desire, pray this prayer, and ask the Lord to come into your heart and life.

........................................................................

*Lord Jesus, I acknowledge that I am a sinner. Today I turn from my sin and turn to You. I come believing in the finished work at Calvary and an empty tomb. Thank You, Jesus, for hearing my prayer and saving me, amen.*

Brian Fossett, Fossett Evangelistic Ministries, Dalton, GA

# WEEK 14—THURSDAY
## *Carbon Copy*

*"My covenant was with him, one of life and peace, and I gave them to him that he might fear Me; so he feared Me and was reverent before My name. The law of truth was in his mouth, and injustice was not found on his lips. He walked with Me in peace and equity, and turned many away from iniquity."*

MALACHI 2:5–6

Obeying God's law is a show of respect. We should obey the Word of God because we have a desire to please the Father. This Bible describes a servant of God who did not lie, cheat, or steal, but one who lived a righteous life, pleasing to God.

Obeying the Word does more than just please God. It has a positive effect on our lives. It earns us respect from others. It makes us role models to others. It influences others to want to live like us. It causes others to turn from their sin and to trust in the Lord. Living according to the Scriptures gives us a good reputation, great influence, and a prosperous life full of integrity.

The process of sanctification is the process of becoming Christlike. While we will never be sinless walking daily with the Lord, following His ways, and obeying His Word, doing so will make us sin less frequently. If we say someone or something is a carbon copy of another, we mean that they look and behave exactly like him or her. We should have a desire to be a carbon copy of Jesus. We should desire for others to come to Him because they see Jesus in our lives.

*Lord Jesus, help me to live according to Your Word. Help me to walk in Your ways so others will see Jesus in me, amen.*

# Week 14—Friday

*Be a Blessing!*

*"You are the light of the world. A city that is set on a hill cannot be hidden. Nor do they light a lamp and put it under a basket, but on a lampstand, and it gives light to all who are in the house. Let your light so shine before men, that they may see your good works and glorify your Father in heaven."*

MATTHEW 5:14–16

The Lord did not save us to sit and sour, but to serve and shine. We are to be the light in this dark world. Being the light can mean many different things. It can mean being there for someone to bring comfort in sorrow, encouraging others through a difficult time, or affirming and praising believers in the work of the kingdom.

Being the light means to serve others—feed the hungry, clothe the naked, and evangelize the lost. Serve and share the gospel. Our heart's desire should be to add value to all those with whom we come in contact.

Many of us have done good works and ministered to others, only to realize later that we got a bigger blessing than the ones we were serving because the Lord never ministers through us without ministering to us.

Ask yourself: Am I letting my light shine? Whom can I help, encourage, and lift up?

........................................................................................................

*Lord Jesus, use me today. I want to let my light shine for You. Help me to be sensitive and recognize ministry opportunities. Help me to be a blessing to others and to add value to the lives of others, amen.*

Brian Fossett, Fossett Evangelistic Ministries, Dalton, GA

# Week 14—Weekend

*Be a Giver, Not a Taker*

*"And whoever compels you to go one mile, go with him two. Give to him who asks you, and from him who wants to borrow from you do not turn away."*

MATTHEW 5:41–42

Many times we just take and take and take the blessings of the Lord, always asking for more and never giving back—just taking and becoming a blessing hoarder. It is hard for most people to ask for help, but when they do, Christians and the church should be quick to respond.

We have always heard two kinds of people are in this world: givers and takers. The Lord wants us, His church, to be both. He wants us to take His many blessings with grateful hearts, and then give them away. To pass them on!

If we become blessing hoarders, we become stingy, selfish, and very much unlike Christ. We must be willing to get out of our comfort zones and to go the distance with people. If someone needs our time, talents, or treasures, we should be quick to help him or her.

The bigger we make the flow of more blessings from our own hearts to others, the greater the flow of blessings from Him to us. We should have a desire to help those in need and count it an honor to help people go through trials and struggles. All our resources come from Him anyway.

Be a generous and cheerful giver, and watch the Lord return the blessings.

................................................................................

*Lord Jesus, help me to become a cheerful giver, acknowledging that all good things come from You. Help me not to be selfish with my time, talents, and treasures. Thank You for pouring out Your blessings on me, amen.*

# WEEK 15—MONDAY

*Loving Your Enemies When You Don't Want To*

*"But I say to you, love your enemies, bless those who curse you, do good to those who hate you, and pray for those who spitefully use you and persecute you, that you may be sons of your Father in heaven; for He makes His sun rise on the evil and on the good, and sends rain on the just and on the unjust."*

MATTHEW 5:44–45

Becoming a Christian is easy, but being a Christian is hard. This is one of the hardest parts of the Christian life. Here Jesus tells us that we are supposed to do something that is so utterly counter to our common conceptions. We are supposed to love, bless, and do good to those who curse, hate, and seek to harm us.

How is it possible for us to accomplish Jesus' command? Only through His strength living, abiding, and acting in our lives. You see, we can live on one of three levels. We can live on the human level that repays good for good. We can live on the hellish level that repays evil for good. Or we can live on the heavenly level that repays good for evil.

Choose this day to live on the heavenly level. Make the decision now to grow in this area of your walk and witness for Jesus. Determine now to be like your Savior. Turn the other cheek. Go the second mile. Don't repay evil for evil, but rather love those who hate you. In doing so you'll be a strong witness of the One who redeemed you and lives in you.

........................................................................................................

*Lord Jesus, help me today to be like You. Help me to be kind to those who are not kind to me so I might point them to You, amen.*

Dr. Brad Whitt, Abilene Baptist Church, Martinez, GA

# WEEK 15—TUESDAY
### *Praying like Jesus Prayed*

*"In this manner, therefore, pray: Our Father in heaven, hallowed be Your name. Your kingdom come. Your will be done on earth as it is in heaven. Give us this day our daily bread. And forgive us our debts, as we forgive our debtors. And do not lead us into temptation, but deliver us from the evil one. For Yours is the kingdom and the power and the glory forever. Amen."*

MATTHEW 6:9–13

Evidently prayer was such an obvious priority in the life of Jesus that out of all the mighty works and miracles He performed, the one thing the Bible records His disciples asking Him to teach them was to pray.

We must realize that the Lord's Prayer isn't really meant to be a prayer that's recited so much as it is a guide to be followed. So how should we pray? We should pray with adoration, praising the person of God. We should pray with submission, surrendering to the will of God. We should pray with petition, asking for the provisions of God. We should pray with confession, seeking the forgiveness of God. We should pray for protection, looking for the deliverance of God. And we should pray with affirmation, bragging on the power and glory of God.

Determine today to model your life after the life of Jesus and make prayer the priority of your life.

........................................................................................

*Jesus, teach me to pray. Help me to pray as You prayed and to become such a person of prayer that prayer becomes the priority of my life, amen.*

# WEEK 15—WEDNESDAY
## Making an Eternal Investment

*"Do not lay up for yourselves treasures on earth, where moth and rust destroy and where thieves break in and steal; but lay up for yourselves treasures in heaven, where neither moth nor rust destroys and where thieves do not break in and steal. For where your treasure is, there your heart will be also."*

MATTHEW 6:19–21

W e live in a world consumed with and controlled by material things. How much time, money, effort, and energy do we waste by buying, worrying, guarding, and insuring things that one day will either turn to dust or be stolen by someone else? When we look at it that way, we realize that these are bad investments. Here Jesus tells us how to make an investment that lives forever. When we invest in heaven's economy—not hoarding it here, but storing it there—we show where our true hearts are.

I've known many people who have lived for this world, thinking that this present reality is what truly matters. Don't make that mistake. Determine today to plant your heart in heaven by storing your treasures there. I've done many, many funerals, and I've not seen one hearse pulling a U-Haul trailer with all that person's possessions. Remember, you can't take it with you, but you can send it on ahead of you. And when you do that, the appeal of this present world will become less and less, and you'll begin to look forward to heaven because your heart is already there.

*Jesus, help me not to live for this world, but for the world to come—heaven. Help me not to be consumed with material things, but to invest in spiritual things for Your glory and my good, amen.*

Dr. Brad Whitt, Abilene Baptist Church, Martinez, GA

# WEEK 15—THURSDAY

*The Key to Effective Prayer*

*"Ask, and it will be given to you; seek, and you will find; knock, and it will be opened to you. For everyone who asks receives, and he who seeks finds, and to him who knocks it will be opened."*

MATTHEW 7:7–8

How many times do we pray half-hearted, half-uttered, half-believing prayers? No wonder we don't see the heavens open and have our prayers answered.

When was the last time you were so desperate while praying that you kept praying and knocking and asking and seeking for God to answer your prayer? You see, the idea here isn't that of asking once, seeking once, or knocking once. No! It's the picture of knocking and knocking and knocking, urgently, fervently. It's the picture of a person who is so desperate that he or she doesn't care when, where, or how he or she gets the attention of God.

We should ask. That's our dependence. We realize that without God we are nothing. We should seek. That's our desire. We should continually seek the mind, heart, and will of God. We should knock. That's our desperation. We come to God realizing that without Him we have nothing and can do nothing.

Have you been praying for something or someone for a while? Keep asking. Keep seeking. Keep knocking, because God's Word says that kind of "effective, fervent prayer" will accomplish much.

......................................................................................

*Jesus, help me to be desperate in my prayers, realizing that I can't do anything without You. Help me to trust that in Your time, in Your way, You will answer.*

# WEEK 15—FRIDAY

*Jesus Draws the Net*

*"Enter by the narrow gate; for wide is the gate and broad is the way that leads to destruction, and there are many who go in by it. Because narrow is the gate and difficult is the way which leads to life, and there are few who find it."*

MATTHEW 7:13–14

I n this passage Jesus is concluding His masterful Sermon on the Mount. He's about to draw the net. But before He does that, He lifts His eyes from His disciples and begins to address the massive multitude that has gathered on that Galilean hillside to hear Him. He lays out before them the stark choice that faces every single person.

Are you on the broad, wide road that leads to destruction? If so, won't you do a U-turn and get on the narrow road that leads to life? If you choose to take the narrow road, there is a gate so narrow that only you can enter. You can't take your family or friends. You can't even take your desires or dreams.

Won't you enter through the narrow gate onto that narrow road that is the only way to heaven? Have you made that personal, life-changing decision? Remember that the door to eternal life is none other than Jesus. He is literally "the way" (John 14:6) that leads to eternal life. If you haven't made that decision, do so today.

............................................................................

*Jesus, I know that I'm a sinner and that You died on the cross for my sins. Today I turn from my sins, and I trust You and You alone for salvation, amen.*

Dr. Brad Whitt, Abilene Baptist Church, Martinez, GA

# WEEK 15—WEEKEND

## Rotten Fruit, Rotten Root

*"A good tree cannot bear bad fruit, nor can a bad tree bear good fruit. Every tree that does not bear good fruit is cut down and thrown into the fire. Therefore by their fruits you will know them."*

MATTHEW 7:18–20

In the first church I served as pastor was a precious young couple. They were faithful to church and served in a variety of capacities and ministries. One Sunday the young wife responded to the gospel and was saved. After the service I approached this young couple and expressed my excitement as well as a little shock. I told them how I thought that she was already a Christian. The husband looked at me and said, "Preacher, my wife was bearing fruit, but it was rotten." I've never forgotten that.

Jesus tells of a sure and certain way to know what kind of relationship a person has with Jesus—just check the fruit. If you see rotten fruit, you can bet there is a rotten root. Take a minute to let that soak in.

Too often Christians want to use this verse to judge others when they should be more deliberate in checking their own lives. What kind of fruit are you producing? Jesus tells us that trees that don't bear good fruit are cut down and thrown into the fire.

Take some time today and "examine yourself as to whether you are in the faith" (2 Corinthians 13:5). How can you tell? Jesus said it's by your fruit.

........................................................................................................

*Jesus, help me abide in You so I might bear good fruit—fruit that remains for Your name's sake, amen.*

# WEEK 16—MONDAY

*Fake Disciples*

*"Not everyone who says to Me, 'Lord, Lord,' shall enter the kingdom of heaven, but he who does the will of My Father in heaven."*

MATTHEW 7:21

The context of this verse is paramount to its meaning. Jesus is delivering the Sermon on the Mount, and His target audience is those who, for the most part, have become His followers. They're hanging on every word He says. However Jesus confronts them with this truth: just because someone claims to be a follower doesn't necessarily mean he or she has experienced salvation through faith in Christ. The same is true today: the church is full of members, but not all are saved by grace through faith.

The text suggests that even Jesus was concerned about the crowds who were following Him in those early days. Just because someone says he or she belongs to something doesn't necessarily make it so. I recently read where a decorated veteran of the army suspected a man he saw in an army uniform was in fact a fake because of how he was wearing the uniform. The decorated veteran turned out to be right, and the man masquerading as a soldier was exposed.

We don't have a "uniform" so to speak as Christians, or do we? We're living in a day when it's difficult to detect a true disciple from an imposter. Is there evidence in our lives that Jesus really is Lord of all we are and have? Only the Lord will ultimately know the real from the fake, and in the final judgment He will make the appropriate call.

..................................................................................................

*Dear Jesus, may Your lordship be a real thing in my life! Amen.*

Dr. Jim Phillips, North Greenwood Baptist Church, Greenwood, MS

# WEEK 16—TUESDAY
## Rock-Solid Obedience

*"Therefore whoever hears these sayings of Mine, and does them, I will liken him to a wise man who built his house on the rock: and the rain descended, the floods came, and the winds blew and beat on that house; and it did not fall, for it was founded on the rock."*

MATTHEW 7:24–25

I grew up in Oklahoma, and when I was a boy, my dad left early in the morning to service his customers by selling coffee and restaurant supplies out of a truck. Many nights he was not yet home from his workday before it was time for my sisters and me to be in bed. About the time I entered the fourth grade, I became convinced that if I were going to spend time with my dad I was going to have to get up early to engage him in conversation. He and my mom both worked, and I knew it took both of them to provide for our needs. I realized he could not alter his schedule and stay on track, so I altered mine.

Over the course of many mornings, I gleaned wisdom from him that I could then apply to my life. How he spoke over my life is how I have in turn spoken over the lives of my sons.

Jesus made it clear to His disciples that His words were life. He spoke to build up the lives of those who would listen. With every lesson He delivered, He expected His followers to build upon His words a rock-solid belief system that then could be experienced in everyday living.

........................................................................................................

*Dear Lord, speak to me today and give me the courage to apply what You say, amen.*

# WEEK 16—WEDNESDAY
## Hearing and Doing

*"But everyone who hears these sayings of Mine, and does not do them, will be like a foolish man who built his house on the sand: and the rain descended, the floods came, and the winds blew and beat on that house; and it fell. And great was its fall."*

MATTHEW 7:26–27

Our verse today picks up where we left off yesterday. Jesus admonished His followers to do what He said and not just listen to what He said. He knew that in the crowd, and in any crowd where God's Word is shared, there will be those who accept His wisdom and those who reject it. Here Jesus painted a very visual image of a life or a home that stands or falls based on the application of foundational truth.

Both houses to which Jesus referred in the text experienced storms. Whether houses are built on the sand or on the rock, storms are inevitable. Most people are not homeowners very long before they discover that the quality of their home's construction determines its capacity to withstand the elements.

Jesus wisely knew that some of His listeners would apply what He said and others would take shortcuts. Many of us learn the hard way that it truly is best to do what the Lord says to avoid the heartbreak of loss and destruction. A sure sign of a maturing Christian may just be how long it takes us to apply what God's Word says without having to test what it says. Just do it!

*Lord, help me to base my life on the rock of Your Word, amen.*

Dr. Jim Phillips, North Greenwood Baptist Church, Greenwood, MS

# WEEK 16—THURSDAY
## *The Power of Confession*

*When Jesus heard that, He said to them, "Those who are well have no need of a physician, but those who are sick. But go and learn what this means: 'I desire mercy and not sacrifice.' For I did not come to call the righteous, but sinners, to repentance."*

MATTHEW 9:12–13

N o situation is as frustrating as trying to help someone who won't admit that he or she needs help. I've spent countless hours through the years trying to help people get their lives back on track after some moral failure or stumble into sin. I was able to help only when they were willing to acknowledge they had made a decision that put them in a dangerous place.

Jesus showed interest in Matthew the tax collector. Matthew partnered with the Roman government in collecting taxes (and a profit) from his own countrymen. Consequently his own family and friends saw this as the ultimate betrayal. Jesus offered Matthew a way out. Not much longer after Matthew had been touched by the grace of the Lord did the other tax collectors and sinners seek Jesus. That immediately caused the Pharisees to sit in judgment of the whole situation.

The Pharisees were the ones most in need of what Jesus could do, but their self-righteousness blinded them. As long as they were unwilling to admit their need, not even the Great Physician could touch their lives. Matthew, on the other hand, found salvation that day.

........................................................................................

*Dear Lord, I admit there are areas in my life that are lacking due to my unwillingness to ask for help. Today I acknowledge the following needs: (fill in the blank).*

# Week 16—Friday

*The Lord of the Harvest*

*But when He saw the multitudes, He was moved with compassion for them, because they were weary and scattered, like sheep having no shepherd. Then He said to His disciples, "The harvest truly is plentiful, but the laborers are few. Therefore pray the Lord of the harvest to send out laborers into His harvest."*

Matthew 9:36–38

I n a very real sense, Jesus spent much of His ministry preparing to hand it off to His disciples. Gradually His disciples came to understand that He was going back to the Father, and then they would go forth into all the world with the gospel. Jesus taught them what they would be doing in His absence.

Jesus taught, preached, and healed as He and the disciples moved from place to place. Every time Jesus saw a need, He went out of His way to address that need. Though He was God in the flesh, He was limited as to where He could be and how He could address all the needs that He saw. The time would come when His followers would likely feel the same way about discovering their own limitations when faced with the ever-increasing needs around them.

It doesn't take long in ministry to discover that many days don't seem to have enough hours in them to help those who need us. Jesus taught us in Matthew 9:36–38 that when those times come, we're not necessarily to work harder, but smarter. He tells us that only the Father can grow similar burdens out of the hearts of others who then can come alongside us to share the labor of the harvest.

..................................................................................................

*Father, may I find my place in your harvest, amen.*

Dr. Jim Phillips, North Greenwood Baptist Church, Greenwood, MS

# Week 16—Weekend

### Sharing Our Load

*"Take My yoke upon you and learn from Me, for I am gentle and lowly in heart, and you will find rest for your souls. For My yoke is easy and My burden is light."*

MATTHEW 11:29–30

People say things they assume are in the Bible. One of those common statements is, "God won't put more on you than you can handle." It sounds close to 1 Corinthians 10:13, but not quite, for the verse says that *He* "makes the way of escape." Though the following statement is not in the Bible specifically either, it better illustrates the truth being sought: "God won't put more on you than *He* can handle."

When we make Jesus Christ the Savior and Lord of our lives, we agree to allow Him to use circumstances and experiences in our lives for His glory and our good. At times our pain and heartaches may seem out of place or even unnecessary, while at the same time fitting perfectly into God's will for our lives. In moments like these, the challenge for us is not to ask, "What's the meaning of this?" Rather, we should ask, "What's the meaning in this?" Jesus offers to carry our heavy burdens and help us see His good no matter the circumstances.

*Jesus, help me realize when my load is too great only because I didn't let You help, amen.*

# WEEK 17—MONDAY

*His Process*

*Then Jesus said to His disciples, "If anyone desires to come after Me, let him deny himself, and take up his cross, and follow Me. For whoever desires to save his life will lose it, but whoever loses his life for My sake will find it."*

MATTHEW 16:24–25

D id Jesus mean what He said in this verse? If any person wants to come after Jesus, he must deny himself and pick up a wooden cross? These were harsh words for Jesus to state in the first century or even now. Nevertheless they are the right words for faithful discipleship. No, our cross is not wooden as His was, but our cross is burdensome

Being more like Jesus is our ultimate goal, but the natural process of becoming like Him—now that's another story. If we find ourselves struggling with this issue, we should take heart. We are not alone. That is why the Lord promises us the Holy Spirit to help us when we are weak. As we begin this new week, let's ask the Lord to strengthen our resolve to trust the process.

The process of dying to yourself is not easy for anyone, but with the help of the Holy Spirit and the Word of God, you can make it. As you start this week, know that He is with you and He is ready to help you fulfill His plans for your life. The Holy Spirit is ready and willing to lift you up and encourage you along your journey in becoming like the Lord.

........................................................................................

*Dear Lord, help me draw closer to You as I learn more of Your Word and Your way. Show me by the power of the Holy Spirit how to die to myself and to trust the process of transformation that You have developed for me. In the name of Jesus, amen.*

Bishop A. B. Vines Sr., DMin, New Seasons Church, Spring Valley, CA

*Then Jesus called a little child to Him, set him in the midst of them, and said, "Assuredly, I say to you, unless you are converted and become as little children, you will by no means enter the kingdom of heaven. Therefore whoever humbles himself as this little child is the greatest in the kingdom of heaven. Whoever receives one little child like this in My name receives Me."*

MATTHEW 18:2–5

U nless you become as a little child." What is Jesus saying? When He called the child to Himself, the child listened. The child responded to the call of Christ. With childlike faith, he accepted the sincerity, warmth, gentleness, care, and love of Christ, so he felt free to trust Christ's call.

The child also surrendered himself to Christ. He willingly gave up what he was doing to go to Christ; he was ready to surrender whatever it was that occupied his mind and behavior.

The child submitted to Christ. He obeyed and did what Christ requested. At least thirteen adult men stood nearby, and the child had to walk into the midst of these men. That could have been uncomfortable for a child to do. But despite the difficulty it might have been, he obeyed merely because Christ asked him.

Finally, the child was humble before Christ. Another thing: little children do not push themselves forward. They are not interested in fame, power, wealth, or position. Children crave love! Guess what? So do we!

........................................................................................

*Lord, help me to see how You meet all my most profound needs. In the name of Jesus, amen.*

# WEEK 17—WEDNESDAY

*His Promise*

*"Assuredly, I say to you, whatever you bind on earth will be bound in heaven, and whatever you loose on earth will be loosed in heaven. Again I say to you that if two of you agree on earth concerning anything that they ask, it will be done for them by My Father in heaven."*

MATTHEW 18:18–19

This amazing promise in today's verse is dependent on two conditions. Those who pray must be unified in belief under the name of Christ (Matthew 18:20) and believe that He hears and answers their prayers. Also, for the Lord to answer our prayers, we must believe that the Lord hears the prayer of the righteous. The Bible teaches clearly: "Ask, and it shall be given you; seek, and ye shall find; knock, and it shall be opened unto you" (Matthew 7:7).

In the absence of those conditions, Christians should not expect the Lord to act on their behalf. Could this be the reason many prayers are not answered, because Christians have forgotten their model prayer requirement?

Biblical unity is a humbling responsibility among the body of Christ. We must strive for this unity always. Today ask the Lord to grant you the spirit of a peacemaker. When you are at peace with other Christians, you can rest in assurance that you are at peace with God. Together with other Christians you can come before God and expect Him to hear your petitions.

. . . . . . . . . . . . . . . . . . . . . . . . . . . . . . . . . . . . . . . . . . . . . . . . . . . . . . . . . . . . . . . . . . . . . . . . . . . .

*Dear Lord, help me to pray with faith that You answer my prayers. I also know that when I pray in unified belief with other Christians you hear the prayers of our hearts, amen.*

Bishop A. B. Vines Sr., DMin, New Seasons Church, Spring Valley, CA

# Week 17—Thursday

*His Position*

*Jesus said to him, "'You shall love the LORD your God with all your heart, with all your soul, and with all your mind.' This is the first and great commandment. And the second is like it: 'You shall love your neighbor as yourself.'"*

W hich is the greatest commandment in the law? Jesus' answer was an eye-opener to people immersed in man-made religion: "Love God as your very own God." The word *your* connotes a personal relationship, not a long-distance association. God is not impersonal, distant and removed.

God is personal, ever so close, and we are to be involved with God personally on a face-to-face basis. Understand this fact: the command is to "love the LORD your God." Loving God is an act that is alive and active. We are, therefore, to maintain a personal relationship with God, who is alive and active.

Second, loving our neighbors involves having a giving and surrendering relationship with others. This means we must be willing to give ourselves away, to surrender ourselves to others, and not to take and conquer. Furthermore, a loving relationship also involves knowing and sharing. The desire should be for our learning, growing, working, and serving closely together as a family of believers.

...........................................................................................................

*Dear Lord, forgive me for the barriers I have created between You and me. Deliver me from the pride of my opinion and my way of seeing things. Grant me the power to live in such a way that brings out the best in other people so their lives may rise to new levels of serving You. In Jesus' name, amen.*

# WEEK 17—FRIDAY

*His Plan*

*"Go therefore and make disciples of all the nations, baptizing them in the name of the Father and of the Son and of the Holy Spirit, teaching them to observe all things that I have commanded you; and lo, I am with you always, even to the end of the age."* Amen.

MATTHEW 28:19–20

The passage you just read is called the Great Commission and was given to us by our Lord and Savior, Jesus Christ. Nevertheless, it often seems this verse has significance only to specialized ministers or leaders in the local church. The shocking truth is that this commission from our Lord is given to everyone who believes in the name of Jesus!

Are you aware of that? Are you developing relationships with family, friends, coworkers, and others with whom you can share about Jesus and His effect on your life?

Evangelism and baptisms are at an all-time low in America, and that means disciples of Jesus are not sharing the gospel of Jesus, which indicates disciples have gone into hiding, quivering in their boots and crying about this corrupt and gloomy world, instead of being lights in dark places. Remember the Sunday school song that proclaims, "This little light of mine, I'm going to let it shine, let it shine, let it shine, let it shine!"

........................................................................................

*Lord Jesus, please let me have the courage to be strong, surrendered, and strategic about sharing the good news of Jesus Christ to my world. In Jesus' name, amen.*

Bishop A. B. Vines Sr., DMin, New Seasons Church, Spring Valley, CA

# WEEK 17—WEEKEND
## Our Problem

*"Yet it shall not be so among you; but whoever desires to become great among you shall be your servant. And whoever of you desires to be first shall be slave of all. For even the Son of Man did not come to be served, but to serve, and to give His life a ransom for many."*

MARK 10:43–45

I n this world of selfies, Instagram, Facebook, Twitter, and whatever else is out there to broadcast one's self, Jesus says the way to greatness is to serve.

Are you kidding me? When people are so consumed with the need to advance their agenda, it's refreshing to see someone help someone else. This is true greatness: living a life for the cause of others. Jesus is and will always be the most inspiring example of that lifestyle in the world.

As we close this week, let's remember we are disciples of Jesus Christ. We are supposed to live lives that glorify Him. I know this is difficult, but through the power of the Holy Spirit we can do this by His might and not our own.

What are you doing today so somebody else can be inspired, improved, or impacted by your sacrifice? Jesus said in Luke 9:23: "If anyone desires to come after Me, let him deny himself, and take up his cross daily, and follow Me." We *must* take up our crosses daily in order to be disciples of Jesus.

This question is still relevant today: Will we follow the One who lived and died for our sins?

........................................................................................................

*Lord Jesus, help me encourage and serve my community today, so people will see that You are still transforming the lives of people in this world, amen.*

# WEEK 18—MONDAY

*Faith and Forgiveness*

*"Therefore I say to you, whatever things you ask when you pray, believe that you receive them, and you will have them. And whenever you stand praying, if you have anything against anyone, forgive him, that your Father in heaven may also forgive you your trespasses. But if you do not forgive, neither will your Father in heaven forgive your trespasses."*

MARK 11:24–26

The context of this passage is crucial. Jesus has just cleared the temple and cursed the fig tree. Now he exhorts Peter and others to true religion, which has two components: have faith in God and extend forgiveness.

Faith is the title deed of things hoped for (Hebrews 11:1). The prayer life of a disciple demands faith. Mountain-moving prayer is faith filled. God can answer any prayers we have, no matter how impossible they seem. Today I encourage you to believe God for the impossible. He is able!

Jesus reminds us we are not to have anything against another. If we find hatred or bitterness in our hearts, we must forgive. Matthew 5:23–24 tells us to leave our offering and go make it right with someone whom we have wronged. And when Peter asked how often we must forgive, Christ's response was seventy times seven (Matthew 18:21–22). In other words, we must always keep forgiving others.

........................................................................................

*Lord, I ask You to grant me strength to forgive. I ask for my faith to increase that I might walk in Your ways, amen.*

Dr. Ted Traylor, Olive Baptist Church, Pensacola, FL

# Week 18—Tuesday
## *Listen*

*"'And you shall love the LORD your God with all your heart, with all your soul, with all your mind, and with all your strength.' This is the first commandment. And the second, like it, is this: 'You shall love your neighbor as yourself.' There is no other commandment greater than these."*

MARK 12:30–31

The passage from Deuteronomy in the Old Testament begins with the Hebrew word for hear. All of God's children should hear these words. The Jews took the admonition literally, to bind these words as a sign on the hand and forehead. So they placed the writing in small leather boxes called phylacteries and strapped them to their hands and heads.

Foundational principles are here. First, the Lord is one. Jehovah is the only God. He is above all. There is no other god, and we are not to have any gods before him. Second, we are to love Him entirely with every part of our being. He is Lord, and we are to recognize Him as such. We are to give Him first place in our lives.

In addition to this, we must heed the admonition of Mark 12:31. We are to love our neighbors as ourselves. We are to put other's needs as high as our own. We must not only look out for ourselves, but for the well-being of others.

Teach these verses to your children and grandchildren. Memorize them together.

........................................................................

*Lord, I acknowledge You as the one true God. I love You with all I am. Help me to pass this devotion to my children and my children's children. I am listening today, amen.*

# WEEK 18—WEDNESDAY
## More Than Religion

*So the scribe said to Him, "Well said, Teacher. You have spoken the truth, for there is one God, and there is no other but He. And to love Him with all the heart, with all the understanding, with all the soul, and with all the strength, and to love one's neighbor as oneself, is more than all the whole burnt offerings and sacrifices." Now when Jesus saw that he answered wisely, He said to him, "You are not far from the kingdom of God."*

MARK 12:32–34

In today's reading Jesus dialogues with a scribe who was a very religious man. The scribe knows the Old Testament intimately. Jesus is very complimentary of this individual. Jesus goes as far as saying the scribe is not far from the kingdom of God. What got this man so close to God's kingdom?

The scribe says that loving God unreservedly is more important than all the burnt offerings and sacrifices. Those were the rituals of Judaism. Heart religion is more important than mere ritual.

And we must never forget our neighbors. We are to love them as we love ourselves. If anyone says he loves God yet hates his brother or sister, he is a liar (1 John 4:20). In his epistle, John goes on to ask how we can love the invisible God if we do not love our visible neighbors.

Today I encourage you to seek out your neighbors and show them the love of God.

. . . . . . . . . . . . . . . . . . . . . . . . . . . . . . . . . . . . . . . . . . . . . . . . . . . . . . . . . . . . . . . . . . . . . . . . . . . . . . . . . . . . . . .

*Father, thank You for loving me. As I look to my right and left, help me see my neighbors as You see them. Show me ways to show Your love to them, amen.*

Dr. Ted Traylor, Olive Baptist Church, Pensacola, FL

# WEEK 18—THURSDAY
## *Christmas Every Day*

*So it was, that while they were there, the days were completed for her to be delivered. And she brought forth her firstborn Son, and wrapped Him in swaddling cloths, and laid Him in a manger, because there was no room for them in the inn.*

LUKE 2:6–7

These verses are not just good for the holiday season. The birth of Jesus is a game changer. Some Christmas thoughts are good for any day of the year.

Bethlehem is the city. The meaning of Bethlehem is "house of bread." The Bread of Life was delivered on this day in the city of David.

The birth was miraculous. While every birth may seem this way, Christ's birth truly was different. Mary was a virgin. The conception was of the Holy Spirit. Jesus had no sin. Matthew 1:23 quotes Isaiah's prophecy: "Behold, the virgin shall be with child, and bear a Son, and they shall call His name Immanuel." When Jesus came, God was with us in the flesh.

Mary cared for the baby. The young mother wrapped him and laid him in a feeding trough. While Mary was not divine, she was special. She told the angel in Luke 1:38: "Let it be to me according to your word." That is a great prayer for all of us.

There was no room for Mary, Joseph, and Jesus in the guesthouse. So they turned the stable into a Motel 6. Perfection came down and man rejected Him. Do not reject Him today. Make room for Jesus in your life.

*Dear Lord, thank You for coming to earth to save me from my sins, amen.*

# Week 18—Friday

*Judge Not*

*"Therefore be merciful, just as your Father also is merciful. Judge not, and you shall not be judged. Condemn not, and you shall not be condemned. Forgive, and you will be forgiven. Give, and it will be given to you: good measure, pressed down, shaken together, and running over will be put into your bosom. For with the same measure that you use, it will be measured back to you."*

Luke 6:36–38

Luke 6 is a powerful teaching from Jesus. In our portion for today, our Lord exhorts His followers to: Be merciful. Not judge. Forgive. Give.

I want to focus on what I see as one of the most misunderstood teachings of Christ: "Judge not." No doubt our Lord told us to be merciful and non-judgmental. When we condemn others, we fall into negativity and hypocrisy. To "judge not" is a good reminder.

However, we must remember that judgment calls are a part of life. And some of those have to do with making a call on the actions of others. Jesus also uses the illustration that we must take the beam from our own eyes before we can take a speck from a brother's eye (Matthew 7:3–5). Yet that speck calls for a judgment. In Galatians 6:1 Paul exhorts the spiritual individual to restore the one who has fallen into sin. This calls for judgment.

The judgment Jesus condemns is the attitude of superiority that crushes another person. We must ever be seeking to restore and lift others rather than tear them down in judgment.

........................................................................................

*Lord, give me grace to be discerning with others and their faults. Teach me to deal with my own sin first, and then to be a spiritual person of restoration with others, amen.*

Dr. Ted Traylor, Olive Baptist Church, Pensacola, FL

# Week 18—Weekend
## The Value of a Firm Foundation

*"Whoever comes to Me, and hears My sayings and does them, I will show you whom he is like: He is like a man building a house, who dug deep and laid the foundation on the rock. And when the flood arose, the stream beat vehemently against that house, and could not shake it, for it was founded on the rock."*

LUKE 6:47–48

W hat is the hardest thing you have ever faced? How did you handle it? In our text today Jesus promises storms will come. The storms with wind and rising water come to each of us.

The promise of Jesus is that the one who hears God's Word and acts on it has a sure foundation. He will be like the man who dug deep and laid the foundation on the rock. He will not be shaken and destroyed. Rather he will stand.

Jesus tells us three action steps for laying such a foundation.

*You must come to Him.* Seek the Lord today. Ask Him to save you. Go after Him like a man seeking buried treasure in a field.

*You must hear His words.* This calls for consistent personal intake of the Scriptures. Read the Word. Participate in a small group with others seeking to know God. And attend a church where the Bible is faithfully preached.

*You must act on what you know.* Faith without works is dead. Have you been baptized? Have you forgiven the one who wronged you? Are you a tither? If you perform these actions, you will find your foundation to be sure.

*Father, as the storms of life come, teach me to believe and stand on Your promises. Show me the difference in solid rock and sinking sand. Thank You that You are my firm foundation, the solid Rock, and chief cornerstone, amen.*

# Week 19—Monday

*Follow Him*

*But Jesus said to him, "No one, having put his hand to the plow, and looking back, is fit for the kingdom of God."*

Luke 9:62

"Follow Me" (Luke 9:23). With those words Jesus invited His disciples to a new way of living and to a new life altogether. Their priorities, their schedules, their habits—everything about their lives was going to change. In following Jesus they had a new aim and a new destination.

Following Jesus is not a casual assent to His teaching. It is not a respectful acknowledgement of importance. It is complete, total obedience and an abandonment of an old way of life.

Some professed their willingness to follow Jesus. In Luke 9:57 they stated, "I will follow You wherever You go." But Jesus knew that many of them had no idea what they were promising. In the end Jesus reminded them (and us) that the choice to follow Him meant no turning back.

The choice to follow Jesus is complete. We are to put our hand to the plow and refuse to look back. We are to lock the door to sin and willful rebellion and throw away the key. The choice is every day. It is all-consuming. It is leaving an old way of life behind and following Him.

And this begs the question, "Can a person be a follower of Jesus if he or she is not following Jesus?" Choose to follow Him today.

......................................................................................................

*Father, today I choose to follow You. With Your help I choose to renounce sin, to embrace the cross, to love others, to serve others, to share the truth, and seek in all I do to honor and glorify You. This day I want to follow Jesus, amen.*

Dr. Willy Rice, Calvary Church, Clearwater, FL

*"If anyone comes to Me and does not hate his father and mother, wife and children, brothers and sisters, yes, and his own life also, he cannot be My disciple. And whoever does not bear his cross and come after Me cannot be My disciple."*

LUKE 14:26–27

Jesus was never afraid to call for an absolute commitment. Jesus certainly did not call people to hate anyone, especially their own family. Repeatedly Jesus called people to love, and He exemplified true love everywhere He went.

In this passage Jesus used a familiar rhetorical device where an extreme statement is used to drive home a powerful truth. He reiterated what He said in Matthew 10:37: "He who loves father or mother more than Me is not worthy of Me." This is not a call to hate anyone, but the call is still radical just the same.

Jesus' words are the New Testament version of the first commandment given through Moses: Do not have other gods besides me (Exodus 20:3). Our greatest love, highest loyalty, our truest worship is reserved for God and God alone. Jesus clearly equated Himself with God when He asked for such unyielding allegiance. Only God could ever make such a request.

Jesus called us to love Him above everything and everyone in our lives. And if we do, and when we do, He transforms us to love others truly.

......................................................................................

*Father, help me to love You above everything: my possessions, my ambitions, my life—even those I love the most. Show me that only in true worship can I know real love and be transformed to love others, amen.*

# Week 19—Wednesday
## *The Character of God*

*"I say to you that likewise there will be more joy in heaven over one sinner who repents than over ninety-nine just persons who need no repentance."*

LUKE 15:7

W hat is God really like? Jesus' greatest critics were religious leaders. They saw His hanging out with sinners, and it angered them. They criticized Him and derisively called Him a friend of sinners. So He told some stories to help them see what God is really like.

Luke 15 tells the story of a shepherd. When this shepherd counts his sheep, he realizes he has lost one. Ninety-nine sheep remain in the fold, but somewhere out in the wilderness one sheep is lost. What does the shepherd do? He leaves the ninety-nine and begins to search for the one that is lost.

The value of each sheep is equal to this shepherd, which shows his loving character. No sacrifice is too great to find the missing sheep. Each one matters.

What does this say about God? Plenty. What does it say about you? Plenty. God cares for each person, even those trapped in sin. Jesus came to seek and save the lost.

The religious crowd had missed the character of God. They didn't understand His love. They didn't understand His mission, and that is why they didn't understand Jesus.

．．．．．．．．．．．．．．．．．．．．．．．．．．．．．．．．．．．．．．．．．．．．．．．．．．．．．．．．．．．．．．．．．．．．．．．．．．．．

*Father, remind me today what is important in heaven. Remind me what brings You the greatest joy: seeing the lost rescued and saved. This is why Jesus came, and this is why we, your church, are here. Help me to be on mission today and value that which is most treasured in heaven, amen.*

Dr. Willy Rice, Calvary Church, Clearwater, FL

# Week 19—Thursday
## *Blind Spots*

*And when Jesus saw that he became very sorrowful, He said, "How hard it is for those who have riches to enter the kingdom of God! For it is easier for a camel to go through the eye of a needle than for a rich man to enter the kingdom of God."*

Luke 18:24–25

B lind spots. We all have them. Many things blind us to spiritual truth, and one of the biggest and most dangerous is earthly wealth. The Bible does not say that money is evil. Many times in the Bible earthly riches are a result of God's blessings. In addition Paul urged those who were wealthy to give generously (1 Timothy 6:17–18).

The real danger is that earthly wealth can blind us to spiritual truth. It can dull our spiritual senses and cause us to love this world and the blessings we enjoy more than the world to come.

In the familiar story of the rich young ruler (Luke 18:18–23), Jesus spoke to a man who enjoyed status, privilege, and wealth. He was also under the delusion that his good works and morality could get him into heaven. His wealth blinded him to his spiritual need for a Savior. What he had wasn't the problem—it was what had him.

The truth is you can't enter the kingdom of heaven on your own. It is impossible. That is why Jesus said in Luke 18:27, "The things which are impossible with men are possible with God."

We all need a Savior. The rich young ruler did, and so do we.

*Father, give me eyes to see. Give me wisdom not to be blinded by the things of this world and miss the importance of the one to come, amen.*

# WEEK 19—FRIDAY

*Two Kingdoms*

*Then they asked Him, saying, "Teacher, we know that You say and teach rightly, and
You do not show personal favoritism, but teach the way of God in truth: Is it lawful for
us to pay taxes to Caesar or not?" But He perceived their craftiness, and said to them,
"Why do you test Me? Show Me a denarius. Whose image and inscription does it
have?" They answered and said, "Caesar's." And He said to them, "Render therefore to
Caesar the things that are Caesar's, and to God the things that are God's."*

LUKE 20:21–25

They thought they had Him trapped. What seemed like a simple question
about taxes was really a clever trap laid by the religious leaders. If Jesus
rejected the paying of taxes, He could be accused of treason or insurrection.
If He encouraged paying taxes, many of the Jewish people would characterize
Him as a disloyal Roman collaborator.

But Jesus turned the trap designed to ensnare Him into a truth that can
liberate. Jesus recognized the reality of human governments and financial
obligations. They are an important part of our world, but they don't encompass everything.

We are citizens of two kingdoms, two worlds. One is physical and the
other is spiritual. Our lives, our souls, our consciences—they belong to God
because they bear the image of God through creation. If we surrender to God
what is His, we will find great wisdom, peace, and freedom in dealing with
the kingdoms of man.

......................................................................................................

*Father, teach me the difference between the kingdoms of man and the kingdom
of God. May I live as a citizen of Your kingdom and live in such a way that those
in the kingdom of man will know Your truth and see Your love, amen.*

Dr. Willy Rice, Calvary Church, Clearwater, FL

# WEEK 19—WEEKEND
## *The Sacrifice*

*Now it was about the sixth hour, and there was darkness over all the earth until the ninth hour. Then the sun was darkened, and the veil of the temple was torn in two. And when Jesus had cried out with a loud voice, He said, "Father, 'into Your hands I commit My spirit.'" Having said this, He breathed His last.*

LUKE 23:44–46

N ever was a day like that day—the day Jesus died. That was the day God's own Son offered Himself up as a sacrifice for sin. Sometime that afternoon Jesus cried out and breathed His last. The world fell into the darkness, a sign of God's judgment upon sin.

Jesus' death was voluntary. He willingly gave Himself for our sins. His life was not taken from Him; it was given by Him.

Jesus' death was vicarious. He died in our place. Jesus bore our sins and became our sins. God judged the sins of mankind and accepted Jesus as a sacrifice in our place.

Jesus' death was victorious. Upon His death the veil in the temple was torn in two. The veil was the thick curtain that separated the Holy Place from the Holy of Holies in the Jewish temple. This veil symbolized the separation between God and man because of sin. Jesus' death literally tore that curtain and made a way for us to be forgiven and know God's love and forgiveness.

Never was a day like that day, and because of that we can know God and live forever.

*Father, thank You for the death of Jesus. Through Your sacrificial love I am forgiven. Help me to live today in Your presence as I walk in fellowship with You, amen.*

# WEEK 20—MONDAY

*The Glory of Jesus Gets Personal*

*He was in the world, and the world was made through Him, and the world did not know Him. He came to His own, and His own did not receive Him. But as many as received Him, to them He gave the right to become children of God, to those who believe in His name: who were born, not of blood, nor of the will of the flesh, nor of the will of man, but of God.*

JOHN 1:10–14

One of the most amazing things in the Scriptures is the nativity of the Son. Jesus, who is described by the writer of Hebrews 1:3 as the "brightness of His glory," brought God's immortal glory for mortal man to experience. Jesus' glory was personal to John, who was an eyewitness to it. He saw it displayed through an overwhelming catch of fish, the feeding of thousands with a small lunch, and the transfiguration.

Even though we are not eyewitnesses like John, Jesus' glory still touches us. Those who have no glory of their own are radically changed. Through the glory of Jesus' death and resurrection, He gives those who believe in His name the right to be the children of God.

........................................................................................................................

*Father, thank You for giving our world the privilege to see Your glory. May I never cease to praise You for giving me, who had no glory of my own, the right to be Your child, amen.*

Dr. Fred M. Evers, Northside Baptist Church, Tifton, GA

# Week 20—Tuesday

## *It Is Not About Us*

*John bore witness of Him and cried out, saying, "This was He of whom I said, 'He who comes after me is preferred before me, for He was before me.'" And of His fullness we have all received, and grace for grace. For the law was given through Moses, but grace and truth came through Jesus Christ.*

John 1:15–17

Jerusalem's inhabitants had never seen anyone quite like John the Baptist. He was not a preacher of a local synagogue or from the high surroundings of the temple precinct. His message was an impassioned call to turn from sin. Although he had his critics, he drew the crowds. Jews, tax collectors, and even hardened Roman soldiers came to hear him preach. He called his listeners to a deeper walk with God and baptized them as a sign of repentance from their sins.

John the Baptist had a following the likes of which would make any leader swell with pride. But John understood his mission was to be the forerunner of Jesus. His duty was not to magnify himself but to proclaim the importance of the one "who comes after me."

In the economy of God's work, our service is important and willed by God. But none of us should ever be enthralled by the deceptive temptation of personal greatness. It is not about us—no matter who we are.

........................................................................................................

*Father, thank You for giving me the privilege to serve You. Let me always seek for Your light to shine through me, and may I not be guilty of thinking too much of myself when You place me in leadership, amen.*

# WEEK 20—WEDNESDAY
*Who Is God?*

---

*"For God so loved the world that He gave His only begotten Son, that whoever believes in Him should not perish but have eternal life. For God did not send His Son into the world to condemn the world, but that the world through Him might be saved."*

JOHN 3:16–17

Who is God? This is a question of universal discussion. This oft-quoted passage is a summation of the gospel—He is the God who gives. God proves His love to us by the lavish gifts He gives.

Who is God? He is the God who gave us His Son. Jesus left heaven to walk among men. To eat our food, smell our sweat, feel our pains, and embrace our hardships.

Who is God? He is the God who gives eternal life to those who have no hope of escaping death. Death's shadow will fall across the face of every human being, but those who believe have the promise of everlasting life.

Who is God? He is the God who looks at the squalor of a sinful world and gives it hope instead of condemnation. Scripture teaches the judgment of sin, but by His gifts those who are irrevocably and eternally lost become cleansed from the stains of all their failures.

Who is God? God is a deity far better understood by the action of His gift than by postulations of His being. No finite person can understand the depth of His glory, but everyone can feel the touch of His love.

..........................................................................................................

*Father, thank You for the gift of Your love. Help me always to celebrate Your love and give thanks for the eternal life You have provided, amen.*

Dr. Fred M. Evers, Northside Baptist Church, Tifton, GA

# WEEK 20—THURSDAY
## God's Light Shines on Sin

*"For everyone practicing evil hates the light and does not come to the light, lest his deeds should be exposed. But he who does the truth comes to the light, that his deeds may be clearly seen, that they have been done in God."*

JOHN 3:20–21

G od loved the world so much He gave His Son to die for it. But to reject the gospel is to stand under the condemnation of God. Jesus speaks to Nicodemus, a teacher of the Jews, an upright and moral man, and warns him of those who fear the light of Jesus' truth (John 3:18–21). Jesus peels back the thin veneer of inner religious posture and instead speaks directly to the outward actions of religious practice. For those who embrace the gospel, the discovery of grace covers all sin. On the other hand, those who reject the gospel find only condemnation of their sin.

A person who knows nothing of art might visit an art gallery filled with masterpieces of exquisite beauty, the lifework of artistic geniuses. Upon leaving he might feel that he got nothing out of it; the art was nothing more than old paintings of people who died long ago. The reality is the paintings have already stood the judgment of time and are no longer on trial. Instead judgment is passed upon the one who could not comprehend their greatness.

Jesus also speaks of how His light exposes sin. In the same way roaches scatter when the light comes on in a toolshed, those who reject the gospel have grave difficulty allowing the light of Jesus to shine upon the faults of their lives. They don't want to admit that they have done the works of darkness.

*Father, convict me of all sin that would keep me from a vibrant relationship with You. Let me stand in the warmth of Your light, amen.*

# Week 20—Friday

*Point to Jesus*

*"For He whom God has sent speaks the words of God, for God does not give the Spirit by measure. The Father loves the Son, and has given all things into His hand."*

JOHN 3:34–35

A s a child attending church, sitting in the pews, I listened to my pastor. I often wondered about the appearance of God, and I thought that God must look like my pastor. My pastor was the individual pointing me in the direction of the Lord. In my childish immaturity it was easy to place him on a pedestal far higher than I should.

The honor of John the Baptist is without question. Jesus said, "There has not risen one greater than John the Baptist" (Matthew 11:11). As a prophet, he had the anointing of the Holy Spirit. Honor is a good thing to give those who lead us spiritually, but we must be careful to give our greatest honor to the One they are pointing toward—the Lord. In the same manner, spiritual leaders should use their gifts to point toward the One who is far greater than themselves.

In this passage John's disciples were concerned that Jesus had risen to a higher level of popularity than John. But John said that the anointing of the Spirit in Jesus could not be measured. In addition to this unmeasurable anointing, the Father had placed all things in His hand. John's honored position as a messenger of God was not to keep his followers for himself but to point them to Jesus, the Son of God.

*Father, help me to know that any gift You place in my hand is not to proclaim my own significance but to point to the greatness and glory of Jesus, amen.*

Dr. Fred M. Evers, Northside Baptist Church, Tifton, GA

# WEEK 20—WEEKEND
## Thirsty

*Jesus answered and said to her, "Whoever drinks of this water will thirst again, but whoever drinks of the water that I shall give him will never thirst. But the water that I shall give him will become in him a fountain of water springing up into everlasting life."*

JOHN 4:13–14

A divine appointment took place in the life of a thirsty woman at a well. Her life story would have been the subject for the most sordid of gossip. Although Jesus saw her sin and made it known that her lifestyle was wrong, He was far more interested in redemption than in judgment.

The Samaritan woman had experienced five failed marriages. Trapped in the cycle of moving from one dysfunctional relationship to another had left her with hurts far too deep to be touched by human hands. Jesus wanted her to know that she had been looking to fulfill the desires of her life by drinking from wells that gave little promise of quenching her thirst.

A relationship with Jesus not only gives hope for eternity but gives meaning to life. His love quenches our deepest thirsts. By drinking His living water, we discover a rich hope that springs forth to fulfill our deepest needs. Being a follower of Jesus does not promise to cure all fractured relationships, but these relationships have the hope of redemption that only Jesus can give.

*Father, thank You for the hope Jesus gives me. May I always remember that when I am hurt from the failures of my relationships, You are the greatest resource for my needs, amen.*

# WEEK 21—MONDAY

*The Place of Worship*

*"But the hour is coming, and now is, when the true worshipers will worship the Father in spirit and truth; for the Father is seeking such to worship Him. God is Spirit, and those who worship Him must worship in spirit and truth."*

JOHN 4:23–24

I n this passage Jesus spoke with a Samaritan woman with whom He purposed to have a divine appointment. When Jesus began to have a spiritual conversation with her, she immediately diverted the conversation to where her people, the Samaritans, worshipped. She reminded Jesus that while the Jews worshipped in Jerusalem, the Samaritans worshipped on Mount Gerizim.

The woman was talking about religious places, and Jesus pointed out she needed a personal relationship with the Father, which could only come by Him, the living water. This still often happens when we ask people about their relationship with Jesus—they want to tell you what church they belong to.

Jesus lifted the Samaritan woman's mind above earthly temples and the mountain shrines on which she was so focused. Temples get destroyed, shrines fall, churches decay. Jesus taught her—and us—that places of worship made by human hands will not have the same relevance in His kingdom. He told her plainly that true worship of the Father will be "in spirit and truth."

The truth is we are the places of worship, and in our spirits we can have church every moment of every day. This is not to say we shouldn't worship in a particular place with other believers. Rather our lives should be places where worship overflows with rivers of living water.

*Lord, please help me to worship You in spirit and truth, amen.*

Roy Mack, Grace Fellowship Church, Warren, OH

# WEEK 21—TUESDAY
## *They Are All Around Us*

*"Do you not say, 'There are still four months and then comes the harvest'? Behold,*
*I say to you, lift up your eyes and look at the fields, for they are already white for*
*harvest! And he who reaps receives wages, and gathers fruit for eternal life, that both he*
*who sows and he who reaps may rejoice together."*

JOHN 4:35–36

J esus' divine appointment with the Samaritan woman at the well was interrupted by the return of the disciples from getting lunch. She then raced
into town to tell about a Man, who in her words, "told me all things that I
ever did. Could this be the Christ?" (v. 29). Yet the disciples were interested in
lunch, not the harvest of souls all around them.

I imagine them standing before Jesus, reaching into their fast-food bags.
Perhaps Peter said, "Who has the one with extra onions?"

James called out, "I had no pickles and mustard."

Philip said, "Which smarty-pants put bacon on mine?"

During that scene, Jesus stared beyond the disciples, watching scores of
people make their way to Him because of a woman the disciples had ignored.
The disciples had just passed by a harvest of people in town without a mention of who Jesus was. As the disciples stood with food in their mouths, Jesus
spoke the words that we need to examine and reexamine to set our priorities
in order: "Look at the fields, for they are already white for harvest!"

........................................................................................

*Lord, help me to lift my eyes to see Your harvest all around me today. I want to*
*be a part of reaping and rejoicing over it, amen.*

# WEEK 21—WEDNESDAY
## *Dead Man Walking*

*"Most assuredly, I say to you, he who hears My word and believes in Him who sent Me has everlasting life, and shall not come into judgment, but has passed from death into life."*

JOHN 5:24

Most people think about death as something that comes at the end of their lives. However, Jesus told us when we are without Him as our Savior, we are in fact dead right now—though we think we are alive. Only when we hear His Word and believe in Him do we pass from "death into life."

Many people today are dead men walking, like condemned prisoners, yet unaware of it. People who are without Christ are dead right now and are unaware of their dangerous predicaments. Like the verse says, those who hear and believe will have everlasting life. Hearing and believing make the difference. Life is only found in the One who said, "I am the way, the truth, and the life. No one comes to the Father except through Me" (John14:6).

I am reminded of the band that kept playing while the Titanic sank. The musicians on the ship were dead men walking, yet kept playing. This world has hit a fatal iceberg of sin and is sinking fast. To be living only for this world is like going first class on the Titanic. Get in the lifeboat while there is still time!

........................................................................................

*Lord, thank You for dying for me so I can pass "from death into life," amen.*

　　　　Roy Mack, Grace Fellowship Church, Warren, OH

# WEEK 21—THURSDAY
## *Hidden Words*

*Jesus therefore answered and said to them, "Do not murmur among yourselves. No one can come to Me unless the Father who sent Me draws him; and I will raise him up at the last day."*

JOHN 6:43–44

W e have all played a word search puzzle. The words are seemingly hidden in plain sight. Some words are diagonal, others are vertical or horizontal. We stare at the puzzle and some words just jump out at us, while others we just can't see at first. In like manner have we ever tried to share something with someone and they just couldn't get it or understand? Like the words in a puzzle, they just couldn't see it?

Salvation is of God. Often we forget this simple and profound statement. Until God shows us His Words of salvation by having His Spirit draw us to Himself, we cannot see it, try as we might. I have witnessed to many people who simply looked at me with a puzzled look as if I were speaking a foreign language. When we share our faith story, we must remember the gospel is not an argument to win: it is truth to be shared.

Our duty is to share the gospel in love and live it out daily as an example to a lost world. There is a time for apologetics and a place for defending the gospel. However, there are far more times we should simply share our stories and trust that God is at work drawing people to Himself.

......................................................................................................

*Father, please draw people to Yourself and reveal Your words of life through me today, amen.*

# WEEK 21—FRIDAY
*Appetizer or Main Dish*

*"Most assuredly, I say to you, he who believes in Me has everlasting life. I am the bread of life. Your fathers ate the manna in the wilderness, and are dead. This is the bread which comes down from heaven, that one may eat of it and not die. I am the living bread which came down from heaven. If anyone eats of this bread, he will live forever; and the bread that I shall give is My flesh, which I shall give for the life of the world."*

JOHN 6:47–51

I recently sat down with my family to eat at a steakhouse. The hour was late, and we were hungry. A big basket of hot rolls and butter was served immediately, and I ate three of them. As a result, I greatly curbed my appetite for the main dish. When we order our meals, we normally choose a meat or main dish, and then we order some side dishes. The bread is often brought out just to appease us until our meal arrives.

In biblical times the bread was often the main dish. Bread was considered the element that sustained life; bread was synonymous with life. The meal was built around the bread. With His words in today's passage, Jesus declared Himself the most important part of life. Jesus said He was the main dish that everything else in our lives should be built around.

Is Jesus our main course? Or is He just what bread is to us today, an appetizer to nibble on at church until we can go do something else that is more important?

......................................................................................................

*Lord, may I be completely satisfied with You as the Bread of Life, amen.*

Roy Mack, Grace Fellowship Church, Warren, OH

# WEEK 21—WEEKEND
## *Darkness Must Flee*

*Then Jesus spoke to them again, saying, "I am the light of the world. He who follows Me shall not walk in darkness, but have the light of life."*

JOHN 8:12

L ight was the first thing God created in Genesis. Light exposed and dispersed darkness. Jesus spoke the words in today's passage one morning when the Pharisees brought a woman who had been caught in adultery. The Pharisees had a dark and devious plan to trap Jesus. They said to Him, "Teacher, this woman was caught in adultery, in the very act. Now Moses, in the law, commanded us that such should be stoned. But what do You say?" (John 8:4–5).

Jesus drew in the dirt, seemingly ignoring the question. Then He stood up and did what light does. He exposed the darkness in their hearts and dispersed the darkness from His presence with a simple statement: "He who is without sin among you, let him throw a stone at her first" (John 8:7).

The Pharisees were so blinded by their own hatred and darkness that they were also blinded by the light of the real presence of God, Jesus Christ. The glorious light of God had never shined over this temple as it did in the tabernacle or Solomon's original temple. But the real glory of God had come in the person of Jesus Christ, the true Light of the World, and He exposed the darkness of the Pharisees that day.

......................................................................................

*Lord, help me today to walk in Your light, amen.*

# WEEK 22—MONDAY
## Set Free

*Then Jesus said to those Jews who believed Him, "If you abide in My word, you are My disciples indeed. And you shall know the truth, and the truth shall make you free."*

JOHN 8:31–32

It is amazing today how our American culture has bought into the ideas of what must happen if one is to be happy: "If you go to the right school, get the right degree, land the right job and make the right money, drive the right car, marry the right person, live in the right neighborhood, then you will be happy."

Not so! Money and possessions don't bring happiness. On the other hand, they often bring unhappiness. Jesus said that one of the sure ways of knowing that we belong to Him is if we continue in His Word. This means that we not only read His Word regularly, but that we obey His Word. When this takes place, our lifestyles change, our speech is cleaner, our behavior is pleasing to God, and He redirects our purpose in life. This will give us true joy. Jesus did not come into this world to make us happy. He came into this world and into our lives to make us over.

The mark of a genuine disciple is not only one who hears the Word but also one who obeys the Word. Obedience is confirmation that we belong to Jesus. He is the truth and He makes us free.

......................................................................................................

*Heavenly Father, Your Word is truth. May I continually be influenced by the truth of Your Word. Strengthen me that I may be disciplined in my approach to your Word as well as in my living. May my lifestyle reflect to all those around me that I am Your child. I pray this in the name of Jesus, amen.*

Dr. Mike Whitson, First Baptist Church Indian Trail, Indian Trail, NC

# WEEK 22—TUESDAY
## Are You Really a Christian?

*"But because I tell the truth, you do not believe Me. Which of you convicts Me of sin? And if I tell the truth, why do you not believe Me? He who is of God hears God's words; therefore you do not hear, because you are not of God."*

JOHN 8:45–47

What would you say about someone who goes to the doctor but never follows through with taking the prescribed medication? The patient might say, "I believe I am sick. I believe the doctor is right. I believe the medicine would cure me." But does this person really believe?

Many people today go to church regularly. They sit week after week and hear the Bible preached and would agree with everything they have heard: the Bible is true, there is a heaven to gain and a hell to shun, and Jesus is the only solution to the malady of sin. Yet they remain unchanged.

In reality they don't really believe because the Scripture says if they did they would obey the words of the Lord. God's Word is very clear that for the soul to be healed of sin, one must repent of sin and place his or her faith in Jesus Christ. This will lead to obeying His Word. That is God's prescription for salvation.

*Heavenly Father, I know Your Word is true and relevant. Your Word says that anyone who calls on Your name will be saved. I ask You to forgive me of my sin. I place my faith in You, and with Your help I will live for You the rest of my life, amen.*

# WEEK 22—WEDNESDAY

*Saved, Secure Sheep*

*"My sheep hear My voice, and I know them, and they follow Me. And I give them eternal life, and they shall never perish; neither shall anyone snatch them out of My hand."*

JOHN 10:27–28

Three characteristics define Jesus' sheep. His sheep listen to the Shepherd's voice—not other shepherds—but only the Lord's voice. The second characteristic is that the sheep are known by the Shepherd. And, third, they follow the Shepherd. They don't have to be begged, conjured, or bargained with. Proof that one is a follower of Christ is that he or she consistently follows Him.

Today so many identify themselves as Christians but don't follow Christ. Their claims don't match how they live. Church attendance, tithing, and witnessing are rare or non-existent in their lives. Jesus said that His sheep unconditionally follow Him. They go the distance. They pay the price. There is a followership among God's true people!

Look at the nature of God's gift to His sheep: eternal life. We have it because He gave it. God didn't look from heaven and see us and discover how sharp we are. He knew we would brag about our righteousness if we could earn it. But we are saved by grace through faith.

He said we will "never perish." His gift of salvation is forever! And to top it off, He said that we are kept in His hand and nothing can ever take eternal life away from us. His strength enables us to have eternal salvation.

.......................................................................................

*Father, I will never be worthy of Your special gift of salvation. Give me the strength to be a good listener and strong follower of You, amen.*

Dr. Mike Whitson, First Baptist Church Indian Trail, Indian Trail, NC

# WEEK 22—THURSDAY

## *One with the Father*

*"My Father, who has given them to Me, is greater than all; and no one is able to snatch them out of My Father's hand. I and My Father are one."*

JOHN 10:29–30

The day that the Lord saved me remains a vivid memory. After church that Sunday, a lady came up to me and congratulated me and told me she was proud of me. My reply to her was one she was totally prepared for, and I praise the Lord she was because it really left an eternal impression on my heart. I said, "Thank you, ma'am, but I know me, and I will have to do it again before long." She then showed me in the Bible where my salvation is eternally secure. For the first time in my twenty years of life, someone opened the Scriptures and explained to me that I was secure in Christ. No one shall take me out of my Father's hand.

I have heard others say, "Well, I can take myself out of God's hand." I ask them, "Did you put yourself there? The verse says 'no one' and that includes you." Aren't you thankful to be kept by the hand of Jesus rather than by your own performance?

Over and over in the Bible Jesus proclaimed Himself to be God. The reason for that is—He is God! Jesus is one with God. He always has been and always will be.

*Heavenly Father, I give you praise and thanksgiving for doing for me what I cannot do for myself. Thank You for forgiving my sins and saving my soul. You were able to do this because You are one with the Father, amen.*

# WEEK 22—FRIDAY
*Christ's Compelling Challenge*

*Then Jesus said to them, "A little while longer the light is with you. Walk while you have the light, lest darkness overtake you; he who walks in darkness does not know where he is going. While you have the light, believe in the light, that you may become sons of light." These things Jesus spoke, and departed, and was hidden from them.*

JOHN 12:35–36

Dr. C. E. Matthews was a pastor from Texas in the mid-twentieth century. God used him mightily to grow a great church as the head of evangelism for a large denomination. When his daughter was about twelve years old, she told him that all the girls at school wore white knee socks and she would like for him to buy her a pair. For whatever reason, that day he said no. A short time later her life was suddenly over. At the family visitation Dr. Matthews noticed his wife had arrayed their daughter in white knee socks. As he wept, all he could think was how he wished he had said yes to her the day she asked for those socks.

Jesus said for all of us to trust and believe in Him while we have the opportunity. There will come a time, unbeknownst to us, when our opportunity will pass and we will never have another chance to be saved.

Don't let your opportunity slip past. Today step out of the darkness of sin and into the light of God's wonderful grace and forgiveness and become His child.

Pray this prayer from your heart and really mean it:

*Heavenly Father, today I willingly receive You as my Lord and Savior. Please forgive me of all my sins and help me to live for You the rest of my life. In Jesus' name, amen.*

Dr. Mike Whitson, First Baptist Church Indian Trail, Indian Trail, NC

# WEEK 22—WEEKEND
## *Love Shows*

*"A new commandment I give to you, that you love one another; as I have loved you, that you also love one another. By this all will know that you are My disciples, if you have love for one another."*

JOHN 13:34–35

R ecently a choir member in my church developed an aggressive form of brain cancer. We all observed his faithfulness as he lifted both hands in praise to the Lord during worship. As the disease progressed, he could only raise one hand. He sang and glorified the Lord until no strength was left.

His Life Group raised the funds to pay off his family's mortgage. One Saturday thirty-five members of his Christian family did a complete makeover on his house. Neighbors driving by stopped and asked what was happening. They were met with the message of the gospel being lived out. The love that was demonstrated that day impacted a whole community.

One of the true marks of being a disciple of Christ is that we have deep, abiding love for others. It is one thing for us to say that we love others, but it is another for us to show that love. How many ways do our lives show others that we love the Lord? Can others see Jesus in us by the way we love?

Look at how Jesus demonstrated His love to us. He said that is the way that we are to love others. Sometimes that is hard to do, so we must ask the Lord to love through us.

*Father, sometimes I find it very difficult to love. When I face those times, please let Your Holy Spirit do through me what I cannot do myself. In Jesus' name, amen.*

# Week 23—Monday

*Oh, What a Day!*

*"Let not your heart be troubled; you believe in God, believe also in Me. In My Father's house are many mansions; if it were not so, I would have told you. I go to prepare a place for you. And if I go and prepare a place for you, I will come again and receive you to Myself; that where I am, there you may be also."*

John 14:1–3

The longer we live, the more convinced we become that this life is ever so short and death is not the end. King Solomon said that God has put eternity in our hearts (Ecclesiastes 3:11), meaning that deep down we know that death is a launching pad into another life that is everlasting. Having peace with God about what the future holds begins with receiving Jesus Christ as our risen Lord and Savior.

When Jesus saw the concern on the faces of His disciples, He encouraged them to put their faith in Him forever. He promised that He would go ahead of them and would personally prepare a place for them in His Father's house. Moreover, this is still His promise for every one of His disciples today.

Imagine the moment when you will look upon the blessed face of your Savior and immediately know by the look in His eyes that you are finally and forever home with Him in the place He's prepared just for you. In the words of a familiar hymn, how wonderful it will be when you see Jesus! Remember you're living now on your way to living forever!

........................................................................................

*Lord, thank You for Your gift of saving grace and a home with You forever in heaven. Help me to remember that my home is with You, amen.*

Dr. Bryan E. Smith, First Baptist Church, Roanoke, VA

# WEEK 23—TUESDAY
## *One Way!*

*Thomas said to Him, "Lord, we do not know where You are going, and how can we know the way?" Jesus said to him, "I am the way, the truth, and the life. No one comes to the Father except through Me."*

JOHN 14:5–6

S ome people don't mind asking questions and admitting they don't have all the answers. Thomas opened the door for one of the most incredible statements of our Lord's earthly ministry. Jesus declared without any ambiguity or confusion that there is simply no other way to heaven but through Him. Whether it's regarding life, truth, or the way to heaven, the answer is ultimately and surely found in the Lord Jesus Christ.

His words forever distinguished Him from every other person throughout history. Who would dare make such an audacious claim? What evidence or reason would others have for believing Him? It would be His own resurrection that would ultimately provide indisputable proof that Jesus had every right to declare Himself to be "the way, the truth, and the life" and the only way to God.

Our world today accuses Christians of being hateful, arrogant, and insensitive because we believe that Jesus is the only way to heaven. Yet our Savior's declaration is also His wonderful and personal invitation for all people to call upon Him for salvation. In doing so Jesus has promised that they will be with God the Father and Jesus Christ the Son in heaven forever.

.................................................................................

*Lord, thank You for saving me and showing me the way to be with You in heaven forever. Help me to tell others this week that You are the way, the truth, and the life, amen.*

# Week 23—Wednesday
## Make Time to Pray!

*"Most assuredly, I say to you, he who believes in Me, the works that I do he will do also; and greater works than these he will do, because I go to My Father. And whatever you ask in My name, that I will do, that the Father may be glorified in the Son. If you ask anything in My name, I will do it."*

John 14:12–14

What is your prayer life like these days? Many Christians usually feel a twinge of guilt when they think about how little time they spend talking to God in prayer. We know that we should pray, but often we fail to do so. When we consider these words of Christ, then it should be no surprise that our adversary would work so hard to keep us from praying.

Prayer is our personal connection with God. Through prayer, God's power is enacted to radically transform our lives in ways that the world will never understand. The Bible tells us the Holy Spirit helps us when we pray and guides us in our prayers.

Jesus promised His disciples they will do "greater works" because He will be in heaven ready to answer the prayers offered in His name. Jesus' use of "anything" refers to those works that are within the framework of Christ's work here on earth. In other words, Christians are responsible for obeying God's Word. When they do this, their prayers will be heard and answered.

Are you setting aside a daily quiet time with God so you can read His Word and seek Him in prayer? If so, then you will experience a wonderful new level in your relationship with God.

.......................................................................................................

*Lord, help me to pray to You in faith and in the authority of Your name, amen.*

Dr. Bryan E. Smith, First Baptist Church, Roanoke, VA

# Week 23—Thursday
## The Spirit of Truth

*"If you love Me, keep My commandments. And I will pray the Father, and He will give you another Helper, that He may abide with you forever—the Spirit of truth, whom the world cannot receive, because it neither sees Him nor knows Him; but you know Him, for He dwells with you and will be in you."*

John 14:15–17

It's easy to say the words "I love you," but putting them into practice is a different matter. Jesus said that love requires both good words and good works: "If you love Me, keep My commandments." In other words, loving Jesus means obeying Him. Obedience reveals the true measure of our words.

Jesus then said, "And I will pray the Father, and he will give you another Helper." What wonderful news! Even in our efforts to obey Him, Jesus promised to help us. As Christians we are truly never alone for the Holy Spirit is helping us to know and follow our Lord's commands. Our bodies are temples in which He dwells this very moment. The Holy Spirit isn't just with us, but inside of us.

Jesus said the Holy Spirit is the "Spirit of truth." He is the One who opens the eyes of our hearts to recognize the truth of Scripture—the truth of the Son and what is true in life. But to see truth one must first receive Christ, who is truth personified. That is why the unsaved do not recognize Him: in rejecting Jesus they've also rejected the Holy Spirit.

.................................................................................................

*Help me, Lord, to love You with my whole heart and live out Your truth in my life today, amen.*

# WEEK 23—FRIDAY

*Loving God*

*"He who has My commandments and keeps them, it is he who loves Me. And he who loves Me will be loved by My Father, and I will love him and manifest Myself to him."*

JOHN 14:21

One of the blessed privileges that comes with the Christian life is having, knowing, and understanding Christ's commandments. But simply knowing what God says isn't enough. We're responsible for keeping His commands as evidence of our love for Christ.

Keeping our Lord's commandments isn't limited to a single experience but also means that we should continue keeping them. Striving for obedience should be ongoing. We either validate or invalidate our love for Christ by our obedience to Him. Francis Schaeffer, the Christian apologist spoke of love as the final apologetic.[2] Love is the defense for which there is no defense.

When our daughter was young she carried a birthmark on her forearm. It gradually faded away with age, as the doctors said it would. As a Christian, you have been blessed with a beautiful birthmark by which you should be easily recognized by others: a first love for Jesus Christ demonstrated by obedience to Him and wrapped up in the heavenly Father's love. But if you fail to obey Christ as the Lord of your life, then the birthmark will also begin to fade.

Is your love for God fading due to the darkness of disobedience? Does it seem as if God is far away? Then confess your sin and renew your love for Christ by obeying Him in the light of His glory and grace.

........................................................................................................

*Lord, thank You for loving me. Help me to love You and obey You today in all areas of my life, amen.*

Dr. Bryan E. Smith, First Baptist Church, Roanoke, VA

# Week 23—Weekend
### *The Blessing of Abiding*

*"If you abide in Me, and My words abide in you, you will ask what you desire, and it shall be done for you. By this My Father is glorified, that you bear much fruit; so you will be My disciples."*

John 15:7–8

The word *abide* simply means to remain in constant fellowship with Him. Don't ignore, forget, or forsake the Lord Jesus Christ in your daily life but continue to love Him first and obey Him foremost. Your relationship in Christ is secure, but your fellowship with Him will be interrupted by unconfessed sins.

When you seek to let His words abide in you through your obedience and faith, then your prayers, like your fellowship, will be both strong and effective. When His words abide in you, then you can pray in the will of God and with the mind of Christ. You can pray with confidence that your prayers will be answered in the carrying out of God's will for every petition.

The ultimate aim in your abiding in Christ is the glory of God and the bearing of much fruit. Spiritual fruit bearing is one of the wonderful blessings of the Christian life. When you walk with Him, abide in Him, talk to Him, and worship Him, then the Spirit will bring forth His fruit in your life.

So focus on your relationship with Christ today by loving Him above all others. He will take care of the fruit-growing process Himself.

.........................................................................................

*Teach me, Lord, to abide in You so I might bring You glory in my prayers and in my life, amen.*

# WEEK 24—MONDAY

*Steadfast Love*

*"As the Father loved Me, I also have loved you; abide in My love. If you keep My commandments, you will abide in My love, just as I have kept My Father's commandments and abide in His love."*

JOHN 15:9–10

Have you ever noticed that people were created for relationships? In the book of Genesis, one finds a tremendous teaching about mankind and his relationship with God. As the crown of God's creation, we were different from all things created. We see the difference in the fact that God intended man to be devoted and dedicated to Him. One must never miss that God desires for us to be in relationship with Him. He longs for our fellowship. He created us with the capacity to love Him as He loves us. However, man's sin severed that relationship.

His love for us and that relationship can only be seen as steadfast. He was committed to us and brought Jesus into this world, which resulted in the greatest display of His love. Our Savior's atoning work on Calvary illustrated that love. Through His sacrifice on the cross, we can enter this covenant relationship with God. Sinful man became reconciled with holy God. In this love relationship God fulfilled His commitment through His Son, Jesus.

When we enter this relationship by trusting Jesus, we devote our love to Him. Just as God is faithful in His commitment to us, we are to love Him by being faithful to His commandments. In the believer's life the fruit of the Spirit comes alive. The first fruit is love. Because we love Him, we obey Him. Steadfast love always marks this love relationship.

........................................................................................

*Lord, may my life always demonstrate my commitment to You through my obedience, amen.*

Dr. Frank Cox, North Metro First Baptist Church, Lawrenceville, GA

# WEEK 24—TUESDAY
## Intimacy

*"But when the Helper comes, whom I shall send to you from the Father, the Spirit of truth who proceeds from the Father, He will testify of Me. And you also will bear witness, because you have been with Me from the beginning."*

JOHN 15:26–27

I n this covenant relationship with God is a powerful gift given to the people of faith. Like any love relationship there is the need for intimacy. Part of this intimacy involves knowing Jesus and His ways, so we live as Jesus in this world.

The believer will face rejection in this world. Just as the world was hostile toward Jesus, so will the world be hostile to a follower of Christ. In fact Jesus reminds us of this hostility. He says, "If the world hates you, remember that it hated Me first" (John 15:18). We pay a cost in dedicating our lives to the Lord.

Here is great news. God provides for all our needs in this environment. He promises to the believer the indwelling of the Holy Spirit. This indwelling happens at the moment we trust Jesus. The Holy Spirit has proven to be one of our greatest gifts from God. He is our Guide to the holy life and the stimulus for intimacy with our heavenly Father.

The helper also illuminates the Word. The Holy Spirit brings His teaching alive, so we can know the ways of God and live obediently. Through this living and intimate relationship, the helper empowers us to be His witness in this world.

.....................................................................................................................

*God, thank You for the ministry of Your Holy Spirit. May He draw me intimately closer to You. Teach and equip me to bear Your name to my world today, amen.*

# WEEK 24—WEDNESDAY
## The Gift of the Holy Spirit

*"Nevertheless I tell you the truth. It is to your advantage that I go away; for if I do not go away, the Helper will not come to you; but if I depart, I will send Him to you. And when He has come, He will convict the world of sin, and of righteousness, and of judgment."*

JOHN 16:7–8

We are living in what many are calling a "post-Christian" nation. According to facts and trends, the majority of Millennials claim to be "nones." They have no religious connection of any kind. As a result, maybe we are a "pre-Christian" nation, where the freshness of the gospel can be heard once again.

One constant we can count on is the gift of the Holy Spirit. Jesus told us that when He returned to glory, He would send the presence of the Holy Spirit. The power of the Holy Spirit would be seen in many ways. He would make us aware of our sin condition and our need for Jesus. He would convict men of the righteousness of God along with the judgment to come. His presence would draw men and women to seek relief and forgiveness through the mercy of God that can only be found through Jesus.

As believers we must recognize God is at work in our culture through His wonderful gift of the Holy Spirit. His convicting presence is felt even today. Remember, God is for us and desires to pour out His mercy!

........................................................................................................................

*Lord, allow me to join Your Holy Spirit as He draws men and women to Your mercy, amen.*

Dr. Frank Cox, North Metro First Baptist Church, Lawrenceville, GA

# WEEK 24—THURSDAY

## Blessed by the Holy Spirit

*"I still have many things to say to you, but you cannot bear them now. However, when He, the Spirit of truth, has come, He will guide you into all truth; for He will not speak on His own authority, but whatever He hears He will speak; and He will tell you things to come. He will glorify Me, for He will take of what is Mine and declare it to you. All things that the Father has are Mine. Therefore I said that He will take of Mine and declare it to you."*

JOHN 16:12–15

While walking down the aisle of my church, I asked one of my members how he was doing. Without hesitation he said, "I'm blessed!" His response was one I have heard many times before, but on this day my mind absorbed his response like a sponge soaking up water. This man's family had faced many afflictions in recent days, yet they were blessed.

Why should that surprise us as believers? The ministry of the Holy Spirit is multifaceted. However, one of His main ministries is to teach us about Jesus. His teaching creates the Master's life within us. He will not teach us the deeper things of science and math, but He will teach us the mercy, grace, strength, healing, wisdom, and knowledge of the One who saves and changes our lives. He takes the attributes of Jesus and writes their truth into our lives. He guides us into all truth from the Word and lifts Jesus. He instills within the believer the kingdom life that brings glory to Jesus. Therefore, no matter what we face, we can be sure we are blessed by the Holy Spirit.

......................................................................................................

*Spirit of God, write upon the pages of my life, so I can glorify You, amen.*

# WEEK 24—FRIDAY

*The Joy of Heaven*

*"Therefore you now have sorrow; but I will see you again and your heart will rejoice, and your joy no one will take from you. And in that day you will ask Me nothing. Most assuredly, I say to you, whatever you ask the Father in My name He will give you. Until now you have asked nothing in My name. Ask, and you will receive, that your joy may be full."*

JOHN 16:22–24

R eal joy is the desire of every believer. However, the truth is we all go through pain in this world. Our Lord went through a great deal of tribulation and suffering. No one escapes this life without sorrows because we live in a fallen world. The disciples of Jesus' day did not realize the cross was just hours away. Jesus reminded them that just as sorrow was on its way, so was true joy. What they would experience was joy that could never be taken away. Real joy birthed in heaven would be theirs. Christ followers, then and now, would delight in the joy of their salvation that was made possible through the pain of Calvary. In the same way, the joy of wisdom comes through the pains we experience. The journey of this life teaches us that joy rises from the ashes of sorrow.

Believers understand that in the midst of the sorrow we rejoice, because we want the joy that can only come from Christ. If we ask for God's will to be in our lives, our joy will be complete. As C. S. Lewis noted, "Joy is the serious business of Heaven." [3]

*Jesus, in my sorrow, I ask that You make my joy complete according to Your will for my life, amen.*

Dr. Frank Cox, North Metro First Baptist Church, Lawrenceville, GA

# Week 24—Weekend
## *Our Conquering Lord!*

*"These things I have spoken to you, that in Me you may have peace. In the world you will have tribulation; but be of good cheer, I have overcome the world."*

John 16:33

In 1933, Alfred Ackley wrote a wonderful song that has encouraged many Christians: "He Lives!" In the lyrics of the song, he proclaims that Jesus lives in this world today. Just that one thought brings great comfort to those who are traveling through life. We need to claim this truth each day for the experiences we will face.

Some real benefits are found in walking with Jesus. One is peace. I have never met a person who embarks upon his or her day desiring trouble, much less turmoil. Trouble arrives through discouragement, stress, conflict with others, and maybe sickness. Like hurricane-force winds it blows into our lives to defeat us. Yet our wonderful Savior promises us that during the storms He brings peace.

The second benefit is prayer. Before Jesus' death the disciples asked Jesus to meet the needs that arose in their lives. But after His resurrection Jesus gave us prayer. We ask in the name of Jesus for our needs. Ackley sang that when we need Him, Jesus is always near. When we pray, we connect with God.

The third benefit in our relationship with Jesus is power. Each morning I ask the Lord to fill me with His resurrection power. The same power that raised Jesus and gave us the empty tomb lives today in the believer. That is the reason we can be of good cheer. Our Savior is the victorious Overcomer; therefore, so are we.

....................................................................................

*Jesus, be my victory today. Fill me each hour with Your resurrection power! Amen.*

# WEEK 25—MONDAY

*Sanctified by Truth*

*"But now I come to You, and these things I speak in the world, that they may have My joy fulfilled in themselves. I have given them Your word; and the world has hated them because they are not of the world, just as I am not of the world. I do not pray that You should take them out of the world, but that You should keep them from the evil one. They are not of the world, just as I am not of the world. Sanctify them by Your truth. Your word is truth."*

JOHN 17:13–17

I n the world, but not of the world." Two dangers exist for followers of Christ. On the one hand a separatist mentality beckons us to hide ourselves from the intrusions of a depraved culture. Rather than being salt and light *in* the world, we often feel much safer hiding *from* the world. On the other hand, conforming to the shortcomings of society is a real temptation when we engage our world in a meaningful way.

Believers who are indistinguishable from their surroundings, however, fall short of God's intentions for them. Thus Jesus prayed that His joy would manifest itself in our lives, keeping our hearts anchored to heaven and protecting us from the evil one. When God's truth sanctifies us, we can effectively reach those in the world without becoming like them. Neither retreat nor compromise should describe a born-again Christian. Jesus not only offered this remarkable prayer for His first disciples, but also for every believer who followed (John 17:20).

......................................................................................

*Lord, sanctify me with Your truth so I can be a witness for You in this world, amen.*

Dr. Adam B. Dooley, Sunnyvale First Baptist Church, Dallas, TX

# WEEK 25—TUESDAY
## What Is Truth?

*Pilate therefore said to Him, "Are You a king then?"*

*Jesus answered, "You say rightly that I am a king. For this cause I was born, and for this cause I have come into the world, that I should bear witness to the truth. Everyone who is of the truth hears My voice."*

*Pilate said to Him, "What is truth?" And when he had said this, he went out again to the Jews, and said to them, "I find no fault in Him at all."*

JOHN 18:37–38

W hat is truth?" Pilate's sincere question captures the fallen predicament of every person in the world. We search for truth through a variety of means, many of which confuse us even more, but the internal pull of our conscience compels us to discover reality's North Star.

Perhaps Pilate's question reveals the profound influence of his wife, who struggled with the cruelty levied toward Jesus (Matthew 27:19). Or maybe the Roman prefect scoffed at the notion that Jesus bore witness to the truth because his sensual, materialistic, and intellectual pursuits left him jaded.

We do know that the answer we seek resonates in the voice of Jesus because He is truth (John 14:6). Every worldview has its beliefs. The atheistic, naturalistic position leaves no room for the supernatural. The agnostic skeptic assumes God refuses to interact with His creation. The Christian, however, not only accepts that God is real but also acknowledges that He has spoken.

Are you searching for life's meaning? Open your Bible and heed the words of the Lord. God is still speaking if only you will listen.

.....................................................................................

*Father, give me ears to hear and a heart to obey all that You have said, amen.*

# WEEK 25—WEDNESDAY

## What Happened to Repentance?

*Then Peter said to them, "Repent, and let every one of you be baptized in the name of Jesus Christ for the remission of sins; and you shall receive the gift of the Holy Spirit. For the promise is to you and to your children, and to all who are afar off, as many as the Lord our God will call."*

ACTS 2:38–39

Repentance has fallen on tough times. Despite its repeated emphasis throughout the Bible, many erroneously divorce the concept of faith from the need to repent. The two are separate sides of the same coin, making it impossible to have one without the other. Obedience through baptism and receiving the Holy Spirit are the natural results of walking through the doorway of repentance and faith. Why, then, do these verses seem to equate baptism with our need to repent in order to be saved?

The Bible uses the components of repentance, faith, confession, and baptism to celebrate the presence of salvation. Calls to repentance throughout Acts seldom list all the accompanying realities we associate with being born again. Yet refusing baptism after receiving Christ would have been scandalous to first-century believers because they associated the ordinance with their spiritual rebirth. This does not mean baptism has the power to save us, but it does underscore its importance as an expression of our repentance.

Peter's invitation remains for those of us who are "afar off" today. Through repentance and faith any person can enter into a relationship with Jesus.

*Lord, help me to live by faith and turn away from my sins. In Jesus' name, amen.*

Dr. Adam B. Dooley, Sunnyvale First Baptist Church, Dallas, TX

# WEEK 25—THURSDAY
## *No Other Name*

*Let it be known to you all, and to all the people of Israel, that by the name of Jesus Christ of Nazareth, whom you crucified, whom God raised from the dead, by Him this man stands here before you whole. This is the "stone which was rejected by you builders, which has become the chief cornerstone." Nor is there salvation in any other, for there is no other name under heaven given among men by which we must be saved.*

ACTS 4:10–12

Salvation. No other word clarifies the mission of Jesus so succinctly; and no other word gives us more hope. The apostle Peter uttered these words before the Sanhedrin after what was the first of his many arrests. With Psalm 118 as a backdrop, the fiery preacher boasted Jesus as the new way to salvation. After a clear declaration of the gospel, Peter maintained that Jesus not only fulfilled Israel's messianic expectations, but also served as the foundation of their faith from this point forward. Thus he insisted that a genuine encounter with Jesus necessitated their affirming the exclusivity of Jesus.

The same is true for us today. Faith in Jesus Christ must be more to us than a way to heaven; we must acknowledge Him as the only way to heaven. In a world of ecumenical pluralism and religious syncretism, Jesus refuses to be added to our pantheon of gods. Our choice is to worship Christ alone or not follow Him at all.

Have you trusted in Christ alone to save you? If so, does the pattern of your life reveal heartfelt devotion to Him or to the false gods of this world?

........................................................................................................

*Father, thank You for sending Your Son to die for me. I confess Him as the only true Savior. Protect me from idols that compete for my complete devotion to Jesus, amen.*

# WEEK 25—FRIDAY

## No Exceptions

*Then Peter opened his mouth and said: "In truth I perceive that God shows no partiality. But in every nation whoever fears Him and works righteousness is accepted by Him. The word which God sent to the children of Israel, preaching peace through Jesus Christ—He is Lord of all."*

ACTS 10:34–36

N o exceptions. Those two words are sometimes painful and isolating. No ticket, no entry. No money, no food. No degree, no job. The exclusivity of these claims allows for no exceptions. Ironclad realities with fixed results are not always negative, though. Every person who calls on the name of the Lord will be saved. No exceptions. God loves all people. No exceptions. The gospel is for everyone. No exceptions.

After meeting Cornelius and a large group of Gentiles, the apostle Peter broadened the trajectory of the gospel beyond the Jewish people. In every nation, among every people group, God is able and willing to save those who fear Him and live for Him through Jesus Christ. Regardless of skin color, nationality, education, income level, or location, the gospel reveals that God shows no partiality among the people of the earth. No one is beyond the reach of His grace. All categories of people, without exception, will be present before the throne of God in eternity (Revelation 5:9).

Have you given up on someone who needs to be saved? Do you wonder if God can change certain kinds of people? Do you harbor any racial, social, or economic hatred toward any group? God does not show partiality and neither should you.

........................................................................................................

*Thank You, Lord, that Your grace has no boundaries. I worship You for saving me. Use me to lead others to Christ by sharing Your gospel, amen.*

Dr. Adam B. Dooley, Sunnyvale First Baptist Church, Dallas, TX

*Concerning His Son Jesus Christ our Lord, who was born of the seed of David according to the flesh, and declared to be the Son of God with power according to the Spirit of holiness, by the resurrection from the dead.*

ROMANS 1:3–4

W hy do you have faith? Sometimes people celebrate finding their purpose, living a fulfilled life, and creating a better society as the primary reasons they should believe what the Bible says about Christ. Though these outcomes are often legitimate byproducts of genuine salvation, they are poor substitutes for the heart of Christianity.

Paul speaks vividly about the monumental impact of Christ's resurrection from the dead. By identifying God's Son as the "seed of David according to the flesh," the apostle helps us appreciate that Jesus met all the Bible's messianic expectations and requirements. What was formerly obvious only to students of Old Testament prophecy, Jesus' resurrection from the dead declared openly to all people. After His victory over sin and death Jesus exchanged His lowly posture as a sacrificial Lamb for an exalted kingship over heaven and earth. Witnesses who saw Him could no longer deny Jesus as the Son of God.

Apart from the resurrection, Christianity collapses like a house of cards. On the coming day when every eye shall see Him, none will deny who Jesus is and what He has done for us. Even those who reject Christ will mourn because of Him (Revelation 1:7).

........................................................................................................

*Father, thank You for sending Your Son to die on the cross for me. I long for the day when Jesus reigns over all the cosmos. Lord, help me remain faithful to You until that day comes, amen.*

# WEEK 26—MONDAY

*Ready to Preach the Gospel*

*I am a debtor both to Greeks and to barbarians, both to wise and to unwise. So, as much as is in me, I am ready to preach the gospel to you who are in Rome also.*

ROMANS 1:14–15

T he apostle Paul was not without his critics. Some hated him because of his stand for Christ, and some hated him because of the success of his ministry. Some were jealous of him and sought every opportunity to discredit him. In their perverse way of thinking, they believed if they could bring Paul down they would exalt themselves.

Some scholars believe these envious opponents of Paul declared that he would preach in small communities but that he was afraid to come to Rome, the most notable city in the known world. Of course this was not true, and Paul sent word to the church in Rome that he was ready to visit and had tried on several occasions to come there (Romans 1:13). He was not reluctant to go anywhere, because he was indebted to the Lord Jesus. Thus he was indebted to people everywhere to share the gospel with them.

All Christians share that same indebtedness, and we should all be ready, even eager, to proclaim the gospel wherever we go.

......................................................................................................

*Father, make me ready to share the gospel with those around me, and keep me from being intimidated by anyone. Make me bold in my witness, amen.*

Dr. Robert C. Pitman, Bob Pitman Ministries, Muscle Shoals, AL

# WEEK 26—TUESDAY
## *Unashamed of the Gospel*

*For I am not ashamed of the gospel of Christ, for it is the power of God to salvation for everyone who believes, for the Jew first and also for the Greek. For in it the righteousness of God is revealed from faith to faith; as it is written, "The just shall live by faith."*

ROMANS 1:16–17

M ost of us can look into our pasts and remember things of which we are ashamed. Even the apostle Paul had those things in his past that were not very becoming. Thank God for His grace and forgiveness! However, Paul was certainly not ashamed of the gospel. He was unashamed of the person of the gospel, Jesus Christ. The good news of the gospel is Jesus, the Son of God, the Savior of the world. Jesus is the Christ, the Messiah of the Old Testament. He is God in the flesh.

Paul was also unashamed of the power of the gospel. The gospel is powerful enough to save anyone, anywhere, at any time. Regardless of race, gender, or ethnic background, the gospel is relevant to every situation and powerful enough to change lives when it is received into the heart.

Christians are persecuted in many places in the world, and even in America the tide seems to be turning against followers of Jesus. In troublesome times remember that the faith we have in Christ is a faith for all people, and we need not be ashamed of it.

*Father, may I never be ashamed of Christ or the salvation He provides to everyone who trusts Him as Savior, amen.*

# WEEK 26— WEDNESDAY

## We Are All Important

*Glory, honor, and peace to everyone who works what is good, to the Jew first and also to the Greek. For there is no partiality with God.*

ROMANS 2:10–11

Christians do not have all the same talents, abilities, skills, or even spiritual gifts, but all Christians are important. We are all in the same family of God, and we are all part of the same body of Christ. All believers really are precious in His sight.

God grants to every one of His children three wonderful things. First, He grants us glory. The main idea found in that glory is dignity. Second, He gives His children honor. Honor has to do with value or worth. We are bought with the precious blood of Christ, and that gives value and worth to the child of God. Third, God blesses us with peace, the peace that passes all understanding. The world cannot understand it nor figure it out.

God wants us to experience all three of these qualities both here and in heaven. The world does not give us these three qualities nor does the world affirm them. But the world cannot take them from us, because God gave them to us. We should affirm the dignity and worth of every Christian and do everything we can to enhance the peace God grants to brothers and sisters in Christ.

*Father, thank You for saving me out of the world and placing me in Your glorious family. Thank You that in Christ is dignity, worth, and sweet peace for every believer, amen.*

Dr. Robert C. Pitman, Bob Pitman Ministries, Muscle Shoals, AL

*For all have sinned and fall short of the glory of God, being justified freely by His grace through the redemption that is in Christ Jesus.*

ROMANS 3:23–24

These two verses provide a summary of salvation. In them we see man at his worst and God at His best. Man is a sinner, and because of that he comes short of the glory of God, which is Jesus Christ. When we compare ourselves to other people, we might feel good about ourselves, but other people do not provide God's measuring stick. The standard by which we are judged is Jesus Christ and Him only. Not everyone commits the same sins, but everyone is a sinner and falls short, far short, of the Lord Jesus Christ.

Because man is a sinner he is completely without hope in his own merit or standing. But two great gospel words in this text give hope to the hopeless.

The first word is *justified*. It means to be declared righteous in the sight of God and to be rendered not guilty of all sin. This is God's work in our lives. Note that it is bestowed freely and is based on His grace.

The second great gospel word is *redemption*. This word means to be rescued or to be set free. As Christians we have been set free from the bondage of sin and rescued from the penalty of sin. Redemption always involves the payment of a price, and the price of our redemption is the shed blood of Jesus (1 Peter 1:18–19).

........................................................................................

*Father, thank You for justifying us and redeeming me. Hallelujah, what a Savior! Amen.*

# WEEK 26—FRIDAY

*The Principle of Faith*

*But to him who does not work but believes on Him who justifies the ungodly, his faith is accounted for righteousness, just as David also describes the blessedness of the man to whom God imputes righteousness apart from works: "Blessed are those whose lawless deeds are forgiven, and whose sins are covered; blessed is the man to whom the LORD shall not impute sin."*

ROMANS 4:5–8

Two basic views exist concerning salvation. First, many believe that salvation is a reward to be earned. Those who hold to this view believe that if a person is good enough, kind enough, prays enough, gives enough, and works enough, then he or she will earn the right to go to heaven. An old song representing this view says, "If working and praying has any reward, then surely some morning I'll meet my dear Lord. If anyone makes it, precious Lord, surely I will."

The second view—the correct one—declares that salvation is a gift to be received. Salvation cannot be earned or bought. It is never merited or deserved. Salvation is a gift from God that is received by grace through faith. On the basis of faith God forgives us and covers our sins and never lays them to our charge again. Therein is the blessedness, the happiness, of the child of God. Another hymn proclaims: "Marvelous grace of our loving Lord, grace that exceeds our sin and our guilt; yonder on Calvary's mount outpoured, there where the blood of the Lamb was spilt. Grace, grace, God's grace, grace that will pardon and cleanse within. Grace, grace, God's grace, grace that is greater than all our sin." That's my song!

........................................................................................................

*Father, thank You for the gift of faith, amen.*

Dr. Robert C. Pitman, Bob Pitman Ministries, Muscle Shoals, AL

# WEEK 26—WEEKEND
## *You Can Trust God*

*He did not waver at the promise of God through unbelief, but was strengthened in faith, giving glory to God, and being fully convinced that what He had promised He was also able to perform.*

ROMANS 4:20–21

When Abraham was ninety-nine years old and his wife, Sarah, was eighty-nine years old, God reaffirmed His promise to give them a son. The son was not going to be an adopted son but a naturally born son. This seemed to be an unbelievable promise, and even Sarah chuckled when she heard it. I don't know many ninety-nine-year-old men and eighty-nine-year-old women looking for a house close to a school! But Abraham believed God, whose promises are not based on human rationale but on His ability to perform. Nothing is too hard for God.

Abraham had great faith in God, and he trusted the Lord would provide. Note four evidences of this in his life. First, he did not waver through unbelief. He had no struggle, no hesitation, to believe God. He did not succumb to faithlessness. Second, he was strengthened in faith. He waxed strong, he flexed his spiritual muscle, and he refused to be distracted. His faith was firm. Third, he gave glory to God. He praised God for what He said was going to happen before it happened. Fourth, he was fully convinced of the ability of God. He had full assurance that God always does what He says He will do.

The Bible is full of divine promises. Believe them, claim them, and stand on them. Friend, you can trust God.

.................................................................................

*Father, thank You for always giving me a sure word. It is a joy to trust You in everything You say, amen.*

# WEEK 27—MONDAY
*Faith*

*Therefore, having been justified by faith, we have peace with God through our Lord Jesus Christ, through whom also we have access by faith into this grace in which we stand, and rejoice in hope of the glory of God.*

ROMANS 5:1–2

F aith is the foundation and strength of our belief in Jesus Christ, for "without faith it is impossible to please Him, for he who comes to God must believe that He is" (Hebrews 11:6). Faith and belief are integral and necessary in our relationship with God.

Today's passage reinforces this truth as we see that faith in Christ brings peace and through God's grace, we are made right in His sight. Peace with God produces hope within us as we grow closer to Him.

You may wonder where this faith originates and how it is activated. Scripture declares that God has given everyone a measure of faith (Romans 12:3). God is involved in activating faith (John 6:44). Your responsibility is to nurture that faith and help it grow strong as you face the challenges each day brings.

You nurture your faith through prayer and studying God's Word. As you internalize the promises of God, and then take hold of His promises in your everyday walk, your faith grows and your relationship with Him deepens. This process continues as long as you keep your eyes fixed upon Him.

*Thank You, Lord, for providing me with what it takes to be in relationship with You. Help me to be faithful with the gift You have deposited within me to know You better. Guide my steps and guard my heart so I do not stray from Your path, amen.*

Tim DeTellis, New Missions, Orlando, FL

# WEEK 27—TUESDAY
*Hope*

*And not only that, but we also glory in tribulations, knowing that tribulation produces perseverance; and perseverance, character; and character, hope. Now hope does not disappoint, because the love of God has been poured out in our hearts by the Holy Spirit who was given to us.*

ROMANS 5:3–5

A mong the blessings that come with the gift of faith is hope. Without hope we wilt and our lives become drudgery as we plod from day to day, trying to get along. But with hope active in our lives, we discover we can face any obstacle as well as trust for a good outcome.

Hope is the result of character that develops by persevering through tribulations and trials. The gritty truth of life is that trials and tribulations will come. Through Christ you can face these challenges with an uplifted spirit and be willing to step into the fray to overcome the obstacles before you.

You may feel at this moment that the challenges you face are overwhelming with no good outcome possible. You may feel defeated and find it difficult even to put one foot in front of the other. Read again the promise in today's passage: "Hope does not disappoint, because the love of God has been poured out in our hearts by the Holy Spirit who was given to us."

On the other hand, you may find your life cruising along well with no significant challenges facing you. If so, then praise God. Nevertheless you must remain faithful to the life to which God has called you. Continue to pray and study God's Word so you can stay connected.

........................................................................................................

*Lord, help me to see through the tribulations to the victory ahead, amen.*

# WEEK 27—WEDNESDAY
## Salvation

*Moreover the law entered that the offense might abound. But where sin abounded, grace abounded much more, so that as sin reigned in death, even so grace might reign through righteousness to eternal life through Jesus Christ our Lord.*

ROMANS 5:20–21

U nless a person knows he or she needs to be saved, it is very difficult to help this individual. With the advent of reality television, seeing people in great danger is common in living rooms around the world. Some of these people are unaware of how close they are to losing everything.

People have always been unaware. Notice in today's passage how "the law entered that the offense might abound." In other words, when the law was given, people could see how they violated it every day. Until they knew what the law was, they were unable to obey it. Like the people on reality television, they didn't know the danger they faced.

Everyone on the planet has that same problem. We are all just one breath away from facing eternity, and many of us are unaware that we need saving. Thank God that Jesus came to help us find safety in the loving arms of our heavenly Father through grace.

You may know someone who has never received the gift of eternal life, or maybe you have not yet received it. Because it is a gift, you don't have to earn it or work for it. Simply believe Jesus and invite Him to be Lord of your life (John 3:16–17).

........................................................................................................

*Jesus, I believe You are the Son of God and have come to bring me eternal life. I invite You now to become the Lord of my life as I place my trust in You. Thank You, Lord, for this gift of love, amen.*

Tim DeTellis, New Missions, Orlando, FL

# WEEK 27—THURSDAY
## *Life*

*Or do you not know that as many of us as were baptized into Christ Jesus were baptized into His death? Therefore we were buried with Him through baptism into death, that just as Christ was raised from the dead by the glory of the Father, even so we also should walk in newness of life.*

ROMANS 6:3–4

E ternal life with God sounds amazing, but at what cost? Notice in today's passage how eternal life comes to us only because of the death of both Christ and us. How can that be?

Some of us may have difficulty understanding how and why we must die in order to live—and why Jesus had to die at all. To our human minds and sensitivities, this makes no sense and can even seem brutal and mean. What we often fail to grasp is how brutal and mean we already are in our natural, sinful state.

Scripture declares that "without shedding of blood there is no remission" (Hebrews 9:22). The word "remission" simply means to cancel a debt, a charge, or a penalty. In our unredeemed state, we are in debt, under charges, and face the death penalty because we regularly sin and violate God's law.

Jesus' death on the cross and resurrection paid our debt, cleared our charges, and removed the penalty of death from our lives. We simply have to receive salvation by believing Christ and turning our lives over to Him. Doing so unlocks eternal life and showers us with newness of life in Christ.

................................................................................................................

*Thank You, Lord, for removing the stench of death from me and replacing it with the fragrance of new life in Christ. I submit my life to You, Lord, and give You praise for Your sacrifice for me, amen.*

# Week 27—Friday
*Sanctification*

*But I see another law in my members, warring against the law of my mind, and bringing me into captivity to the law of sin which is in my members. O wretched man that I am! Who will deliver me from this body of death? I thank God—through Jesus Christ our Lord! So then, with the mind I myself serve the law of God, but with the flesh the law of sin.*

ROMANS 7:23–25

M ind and flesh—two parts of our humanity that often are at war with each other. People today are bombarded by countless advertisements designed to sell products touted to make them slimmer, more beautiful, more appealing, with a better complexion, no bad breath, and brighter teeth.

People watch these ads and decide that they will begin a diet, an exercise program, or some other regimen to become the perfect self they imagine. Then doubt sets in and the diet goes out the window . . . and exercise? No way! This is a simple example of the mind saying one thing and the flesh saying something else. Today's passage is more about sin and how we often vow to stop something that we know is sinful but continue to engage in it.

You may have a habit or behavior that you know is not good but that you find difficult to overcome. When you fail, the voice of guilt and shame sweeps over you and makes you feel even worse as you are confronted by your weakness. Sanctification is the process of working through those areas in your life that are at odds with your Christian walk. Take heart! Christ will deliver you as you move forward.

．．．．．．．．．．．．．．．．．．．．．．．．．．．．．．．．．．．．．．．．．．．．．．．．．．．．．．．．．．．．．．．．．．．．．．．．．．．

*Thank You, Lord for helping me overcome the issues of my flesh, amen.*

Tim DeTellis, New Missions, Orlando, FL

# WEEK 27—WEEKEND
## *Righteousness*

*For what the law could not do in that it was weak through the flesh, God did by sending His own Son in the likeness of sinful flesh, on account of sin: He condemned sin in the flesh, that the righteous requirement of the law might be fulfilled in us who do not walk according to the flesh but according to the Spirit.*

ROMANS 8:3–4

Jesus promised that after He ascended into heaven, the Holy Spirit would come and live within people who have made Jesus the Lord of their lives (John 16:7–15). He said that this would be an advantage because the Spirit would help us to remember Jesus' words and to live righteous lives.

As we discussed in yesterday's devotion, trying to overcome the flesh by ourselves is futile and usually leads to frustration, shame, and guilt. The Holy Spirit, however, is here to help us overcome those desires so our sanctification can be complete. This promise is of such great importance that Jesus refers to it several times in the gospels. The simple truth is that in and of ourselves, we are powerless to overcome the sinful urges of our flesh. Only God can help us succeed.

The apostle Paul talks about the Holy Spirit often in his epistles: "For He made Him who knew no sin to be sin for us, that we might become the righteousness of God in Him" (2 Corinthians 5:21). God knows that we cannot be righteous on our own. Therefore, He sent Christ who became our sin so we could become His righteousness!

......................................................................................

*Holy Spirit, work in and through me to make me whole. Help me overcome my weaknesses to be strong in Christ, amen.*

# WEEK 28—MONDAY
## Good Out of Bad

*Now He who searches the hearts knows what the mind of the Spirit is, because He makes intercession for the saints according to the will of God. And we know that all things work together for good to those who love God, to those who are the called according to His purpose.*

ROMANS 8:27–28

We find in Romans 8:28 one of God's most powerful promises. It's one of the most well-known verses in the Bible. It's also one of the most misunderstood. Pay close attention to what it says: "We know." That means, we're not hoping. We can be confident that this is what God does!

What know "all things work together for good to those who love God, to those who are called according to His purpose." The verse does not say all things are good. A lot of evil is in the world. But God can work good out of all things.

Can God really bring good out of bad? How about the crucifixion? The death of His Son was a horrible event. Men tortured Him, and then they crucified Him. Did God bring good out of that? Only the salvation of the world! God specializes in bringing good out of bad.

This promise, however, is not for everybody: "All things work together for good to those who love God, to those who are called according to His purpose." This promise applies to Christians. When we love God, that means we obey Him (John 14:15). When we are called according to His purposes, we trust Him (Proverbs 3:5–6). Then we can trust Him to take the pieces of our lives and put them together in order to create a masterpiece.

............................................................................................................

*Dear Lord, thank You for working all things for my good, amen.*

Chris Dixon, Liberty Baptist Church, Dublin, GA

# WEEK 28—TUESDAY
## The Image of His Son

*And we know that all things work together for good to those who love God, to those who are the called according to His purpose. For whom He foreknew, He also predestined to be conformed to the image of His Son, that He might be the firstborn among many brethren. Moreover whom He predestined, these He also called; whom He called, these He also justified; and whom He justified, these He also glorified.*

ROMANS 8:28–30

P aul tells us in these verses that God's greatest desire is for us "to be conformed to the image of His Son." Throughout the New Testament we are taught God uses trials, difficulties, and circumstances to develop our character, our endurance, and our faith. God uses the things we face in life to mold us and shape us into the image of His Son.

The picture that comes to my mind is that of a potter. This person will take a lump or mess of clay and begin to apply water and pressure. The clay has been worked and wedged to make it moldable. Only then it is thrown onto the wheel. When it is centered on the wheel, the potter can shape it into a form. The potter's water lubricates more than softens. That is exactly what God does in our lives with "all things." Like the potter's water, the Spirit of God begins to soften us toward the Word of God and the plan of God. Then as the pressures of life are applied, God shapes us into Christ's image.

It is important as a Christ follower that you look for God in every circumstance in life. Remember, God is working to make you more like Jesus.

..............................................................................................................

*Lord, continue to mold me into the image of Your Son, amen.*

# WEEK 28—WEDNESDAY

*Who Can Be Against Us?*

*What then shall we say to these things? If God is for us, who can be against us? He who did not spare His own Son, but delivered Him up for us all, how shall He not with Him also freely give us all things?*

ROMANS 8:31–32

If God is for us, who can be against us?" Paul makes this statement in full confidence. The people of God have nothing to fear because God is on their side. If you ever feel that God does not care about you or that He does not listen to your prayers, these two verses should greatly encourage your heart. When God the Father gave His Son, Jesus Christ, to save you, He demonstrated His love for you (Romans 5:8).

Paul wants to convey that God will do whatever is necessary to care for us. God gave His best to give us eternal life, and He will continue to work to give us abundant life here on earth.

How amazing and overwhelming it is to know that God deeply loves us. We can live confident that even though the world is challenging and life is full of tribulation, God has already delivered eternal life and He is working with us and for us on the abundant life.

*Dear Lord, thank You so much for being on my side. I know I have nothing to fear because of Your love for me, amen.*

Chris Dixon, Liberty Baptist Church, Dublin, GA

# WEEK 28—THURSDAY

*More Than Conquerors*

*Yet in all these things we are more than conquerors through Him who loved us. For I am persuaded that neither death nor life, nor angels nor principalities nor powers, nor things present nor things to come, nor height nor depth, nor any other created thing, shall be able to separate us from the love of God which is in Christ Jesus our Lord.*

ROMANS 8:37–39

When we read Romans 8:35, Paul lists seven struggles we can all face in life. We all know about the struggles of life. We have all felt the pressure, the stress, the frustration, and the despair that comes from trials. However Paul follows up with those amazing words: "We are more than conquerors." It really means we are "super conquerors."

The Bible says we are conquerors, but most of the time we don't feel like it. But the Bible says it, so it must be true. But something seems to be missing.

Romans 8:37 says, "Through Him (Christ) who loved us." Our strength, our endurance, our hope, and direction all come from Him. Life has never been about the seven things Paul mentions in Romans 8:35 or the ten things he mentions in Romans 8:38–39. It has always been what we as Christ followers find in the middle of those things: Jesus Christ.

And if you will look for Him during your challenges, you will find Him there. You can conquer life and death because of Him. Victory is fixing your eyes on Jesus and following Him. He has already won!

........................................................................................

*Lord, help me to live with the mindset of a conqueror, amen.*

# WEEK 28—FRIDAY

*How Can I Be Saved?*

---

*If you confess with your mouth the Lord Jesus and believe in your heart that God has raised Him from the dead, you will be saved. For with the heart one believes unto righteousness, and with the mouth confession is made unto salvation.*

ROMANS 10:9–10

It is important for us to know we can't make ourselves righteous. Heaven is a perfect place. There's no sin in heaven. But here's the problem: we are imperfect, and God can't allow sinful people into heaven because then it would be full of sin. Romans 3:23 says, "For all have sinned and fall short of the glory of God." The only people who think they can keep God's laws are those who don't know them. God's laws are perfect, and none of us is perfect.

God sent Jesus to pay for our sins. He said, "I'll send my Son, Jesus, to pay the penalty. He will take your place so you don't have to pay the penalty and spend eternity in hell. You can be with me forever." Jesus traveled to earth and never sinned, but He took the penalty for our sins so we would never have to. That means everything we've ever done or will ever do wrong has already been paid for by Jesus Christ on the cross. We can be made right with God.

So what must we do? We must accept by faith what God did for us. To be made right with God, we must believe and accept by faith what Jesus did on the cross when He paid for our sins. We must put all of our trust in the fact that Jesus Christ took the wrath and penalty for our sins. We can all be saved no matter who we are, what we've done, or where we've been. If you need to put your trust in Christ, simply cry out to Him for forgiveness today and put all your trust in Him as your only hope of heaven.

...............................................................................................................................

*Dear Lord, thank You for providing a way to salvation for me, amen.*

Chris Dixon, Liberty Baptist Church, Dublin, GA

# Week 28—Weekend
## *A Living Sacrifice*

*I beseech you therefore, brethren, by the mercies of God, that you present your bodies a living sacrifice, holy, acceptable to God, which is your reasonable service. And do not be conformed to this world, but be transformed by the renewing of your mind, that you may prove what is that good and acceptable and perfect will of God.*

ROMANS 12:1–2

What a great passage to close our week. In the last couple of days we have seen how much God loves us, what He has done for us, and how He is working in and around us. Then we see the response God desires from us in these two powerful, well-known verses.

God asks Christians to lay down their lives on His altar as a "living sacrifice." If you are a Christ follower, your life is not your own. As a result God asks you to live for Him as a living sacrifice. Every day you are to offer Him your attitude, perspective, time, energy, resources—everything you have. He doesn't want only your spare time or your leftovers. He wants you to live for Him by offering Him everything!

How can you do this? You consistently, persistently, and relentlessly set your mind, affection, and attention on Him every day. What you say, where you go, and what you do is all up to His wisdom and direction.

.......................................................................................

*Dear Lord, help me to devote myself as a living sacrifice for You, amen.*

# WEEK 29—MONDAY

*Christian Love 101*

*Let love be without hypocrisy. Abhor what is evil. Cling to what is good. Be kindly affectionate to one another with brotherly love, in honor giving preference to one another.*

ROMANS 12:9–10

I am of the deep conviction that the greatest trait of the Christian disciple today is to display the love of God. True Christian love focuses on the needs of others and the welfare of the one needing love. True Christian love is neither quick nor easy, but it is essential for the believer. What legacy are you creating for the next generation? What are you leaving in the minds of those who will outlive you so their lives are deeper, richer, better than yours has been?

Take a few moments now and imagine standing beside your own casket, invisibly attending your own funeral. Your life on earth has ended. Your family is sitting nearby, brokenhearted and in tears. Your friends are there recalling your life and sharing stories. What are your family and friends remembering? They are probably not talking about your financial portfolio.

One area where we should never stop growing is true Christian love. Our love also must be without hypocrisy. True Christian love does not have "two faces." It only has one, and that one face is the face of God. True Christian love is not hypocritical. Do not pat someone on the back, and then say something that you do not mean. Evil is the enemy of God and the enemy of love, and it is to be totally avoided by every disciple of Jesus Christ.

..................................................................................................

*Dear Jesus Lord, please forgive me for my hypocritical relationships. In Jesus' name, amen.*

Tim Anderson, Clements Baptist Church, Athens, AL

# WEEK 29—TUESDAY

*Kindness or Meanness—Which Do You Prefer?*

*Be kindly affectionate to one another with brotherly love, in honor giving preference to one another; not lagging in diligence, fervent in spirit, serving the Lord; rejoicing in hope, patient in tribulation, continuing steadfastly in prayer; distributing to the needs of the saints, given to hospitality.*

ROMANS 12:10–13

We can show the love of God to the people we meet on a regular basis in many ways. In today's passage Paul highlights eight qualities to help us express God's love in ways so others can experience it:

Devoted affection—This term is drenched with tenderness and kindness. Today's world could use a revival of kindness.

Honor—The word means "value" or "respect." Honoring someone means allowing someone else to have his or her way in nonessential matters.

Passion—This enthusiasm is characterized by active optimism and energetic zeal that cannot be contained; it is the very opposite of lethargy and indifference.

Patience—If we can have patience with one another, nothing can divide us.

Generosity—Love is never stingy; it freely shares.

Hospitality—God shows love to everyone, even strangers.

Graciousness—Returning good for evil should be our desired response.

Sympathy—True love never stands alone. It rejoices and grieves when a situation arises.

.................................................................

*Dear Jesus, please help me to show these virtues in my everyday life, amen.*

# WEEK 29—WEDNESDAY
## *Is Loving Our Enemies an Option?*

*Bless those who persecute you; bless and do not curse. Rejoice with those who rejoice, and weep with those who weep. Be of the same mind toward one another. Do not set your mind on high things, but associate with the humble. Do not be wise in your own opinion.*

ROMANS 12:14–16

Options—we all like options. America is not only the land of the free and the home of the brave, but America is also a nation of wonderful options. Think about the options we have in cars: Ford, Chevrolet, Jeep, Chrysler, Mazda, Toyota, Nissan. Then there are many clothing lines: Ralph Lauren, Tommy Hilfiger, Columbia, Eddie Bauer. Lastly, what type of phone do we choose? Apple, Samsung, Sony, Nokia, or LG? Yes, the list could go on and on.

At times we might wish we could have as many options when it comes to obeying the Scriptures. But we don't. The only two options we have are to obey or disobey. Romans 12:14 is a verse that I wish came with an option: "Bless those who persecute you; bless and do not curse." Wow! Who wants to do that when we have been wronged? It goes against every instinct we possess. Grace in response to sin is a quality unique to God, and this ability can only come from Him and be enabled by Him.

Lastly, be sensitive to those around you. Some need affirmation, while others need a shoulder to cry on. Choose to be humble instead of proud!

................................................................

*Dear Jesus, please help me to treat others with the same grace You show me, amen.*

Tim Anderson, Clements Baptist Church, Athens, AL

# WEEK 29—THURSDAY
## Never Right Your Own Wrongs

*Repay no one evil for evil. Have regard for good things in the sight of all men. If it is possible, as much as depends on you, live peaceably with all men.*

ROMANS 12:17–18

R est assured, the closer we get to Jesus, and the deeper our commitment to Him becomes, the more enemies we discover we have. Jesus had enemies on earth, and so shall we. But, sadly, many believers have enemies because they do not possess kindness. Without exception the Christian must not seek to play God and try to avenge himself with his enemies. Our forgiving, gracious behavior toward our enemies should be an example of Christ's love to them and to others who witness that behavior.

The statement in verse eighteen is conditional in that it partly depends on our response to our enemies: "If it is possible, as much as depends on you, live peaceably with all men." Our responsibility is to make sure that our side of the relationship is right, that our inner desire is genuinely to be at peace with all men, even the meanest and most undeserving of people. We should be willing to go to great lengths to build peaceful bridges to those who hate us and harm us.

Admittedly, some people are extremely difficult to get along with. But we must ditch any grudge or settled bitterness and fully forgive from the heart all who harm us. Having done that, we can seek true reconciliation. I once read a statement about revenge; "Don't do it. If you defend yourself, then the Lord cannot defend you. Leave it in His hands."

........................................................................................

*Dear Jesus, please allow me always to take the first step in reconciliation with everyone, especially my enemies, amen.*

# Week 29—Friday

## Leave It in God's Hands

*Beloved, do not avenge yourselves, but rather give place to wrath; for it is written, "Vengeance is Mine, I will repay," says the Lord. Therefore, "If your enemy is hungry, feed him; if he is thirsty, give him a drink; for in so doing you will heap coals of fire on his head." Do not be overcome by evil, but overcome evil with good.*

ROMANS 12:19–21

Never take revenge into your own hands; always give God room to work in other people's lives. God's wrath is always just and never retaliatory or spiteful. During this age of grace, the wrath of God pursues sinners, cuts off their escape, confronts them with the consequences of sin, chastises them, and makes their continued sin miserable. God does this to bring them to repentance, to give them grace, to redeem our enemies as He has redeemed all believers. Thus we must feed our enemy and give water to our enemy. That's what Jesus did.

What does it mean to "heap coals of fire on his head"? Many believe it refers to an ancient custom sign of contrition. However, I have come to believe that it refers more to good, old-fashioned humility. Charles Swindoll said: "Whatever the exact origin of the phrase, the meaning is clear. The purpose of kindness is to allow the conscience of the enemy to do its job. Hopefully, our good conduct, our humility, will bring about humility and repentance in return."[4] I agree! In God's divine time, the wrath of God will come, and just reckoning awaits the unforgiven.

............................................................................................................

*Dear Jesus, please let me wait on Your timing for justice. It's always better than my timing, amen.*

Tim Anderson, Clements Baptist Church, Athens, AL

# WEEK 29—WEEKEND

## Love and Our Debt

*Owe no one anything except to love one another, for he who loves another has fulfilled the law. . . . Love does no harm to a neighbor; therefore love is the fulfillment of the law.*

ROMANS 13:8, 10

M any people don't feel as if they owe God anything these days. It would be wonderful if all of us could live debt free. People have asked, "Is our church in debt?" "Yes," I reply, "and it's a debt so God's people can respectfully manage by God's grace." "But, Pastor, *why* is our church in debt?" I reply, "Because some Sundays it rains on our church building. Paying money over time in a mortgage allows us to have adequate facilities while serving the needs of the people God sends to us. And, yes, there is always balance between liability and assets."

The command to avoid owing anything extends beyond money to include intangible things. The only exception is love. Paul's point is simple. Be a person of honor. Fulfill your obligations. Don't make creditors track you down; seek them out; be completely honest and forthright, pursuing arrangements to pay off what you owe. The less we must do out of obligation, the more we are able to give freely. Keeping our list of obligations short allows us more room to give grace.

........................................................................................

*Dear Jesus, may I never allow the preciousness of Your love to become common to me, amen.*

# Week 30—Monday
## No Matter What

*For if we live, we live to the Lord; and if we die, we die to the Lord. Therefore, whether we live or die, we are the Lord's. For to this end Christ died and rose and lived again, that He might be Lord of both the dead and the living.*

ROMANS 14:8–9

I n *Mere Christianity* C. S. Lewis wrote, "The Son of God became a man to enable men to become sons of God." [5] That's what Jesus did for us! The apostle Paul penned for us in Romans 14 our proper response back to Him. If "we live or if we die," we do it for the Lord Jesus.

When Paul says, "For to this end," he is explaining Jesus' endgame—what it was, and what it still is. An endgame summarizes the point of something. John 10:10 tells us that Satan's endgame is to steal, kill, and destroy, but Jesus' endgame is to give abundant life. Paul emphasizes that from the very beginning, Jesus' endgame in coming to earth was to die and rise again. That is why He came, and He did it so we could make Him our Lord.

The key to peace, no matter what happens in your life, is to live in an atmosphere of complete trust in God—no matter what. It's about making Him Lord of all. In other words, may His kingdom come and His will be done (Matthew 6:10). When that happens, something dynamic takes place.

........................................................................

*Jesus, today I want to thank You for life and the life I have in You. Thank You for coming to this place to bring life and life abundantly. Today I also want to thank You for Your death and resurrection. I want to surrender my life to Your kingdom and Your will no matter what, amen.*

Dr. Alex Himaya, theChurch.at Churches, Broken Arrow, OK

# Week 30—Tuesday
## *Freedom to Respond*

*For the kingdom of God is not eating and drinking, but righteousness and peace and joy in the Holy Spirit. For he who serves Christ in these things is acceptable to God and approved by men. Therefore let us pursue the things which make for peace and the things by which one may edify another.*

ROMANS 14:17–19

F reedom in Christ is so much more than freedom from dietary regulations. Primarily our freedom is to respond to the promptings of the Holy Spirit. Righteousness and peace and joy are namely for those who walk in the freedom of such responsiveness to the Spirit. In this passage Paul responds to the conflict of being a stumbling block in front of a weaker brother. Paul summarizes the solution to the problem around the word peace.

And that's so important today because we get it wrong. We think of peace as this unattainable ideal—the absence of any conflict or the absence of any troubles in our lives, but peace is not the absence of trouble. Peace is the presence of Jesus amid our troubles.

So we can have peace on earth no matter what, because Jesus is with us.

................................................................................

*Lord Jesus, thank You for the gift of righteousness. I know that in and of my own doing, I am not righteous, but I know that I get to wear Your righteousness. Thank You for that gift. Thank You for the gifts of peace and joy. Today I choose joy and peace regardless of what life looks like. I choose joy and peace. Thank You, Lord.*

# WEEK 30—WEDNESDAY
## Now to Him Who Is Able

*Now to Him who is able to establish you according to my gospel and the preaching of Jesus Christ, according to the revelation of the mystery kept secret since the world began but now made manifest, and by the prophetic Scriptures made known to all nations, according to the commandment of the everlasting God, for obedience to the faith.*

ROMANS 16:25–26

P aul declares that God is the source of strength for all believers. This gospel that Paul preaches both comes from and points to Jesus. Paul's use of the personal pronoun "my" in front of the word gospel shows how personal the good news is to him. It is not just something that he has heard—it is now his own.

Do you view the gospel that way? Do you see it as yours or something given personally to you? Is your relationship with Jesus and the good news so intimate that you would refer to it as "mine"?

Paul goes on to equate the gospel with a mystery that was once held back. Paul's use of "mystery" implies that the gospel was not something that was hidden, but something that we could never reason out on our own. We could only know it through the revelation of God. That mystery has since been made known. In fact God commanded that it be made known to all nations.

Do you hear that personal call of God on your life to make the good news known to the nations?

.........................................................................................................

*Thank You, Lord Jesus, for being the source of all revelation and the author of my salvation. Thank You that salvation is mine. Thank You for loving me intimately and personally. Help me see how to share the gospel with someone in my life today, amen.*

Dr. Alex Himaya, theChurch.at Churches, Broken Arrow, OK

# WEEK 30—THURSDAY
### *Spirit or Soul?*

*But the natural man does not receive the things of the Spirit of God, for they are foolishness to him; nor can he know them, because they are spiritually discerned. But he who is spiritual judges all things, yet he himself is rightly judged by no one. For "who has known the mind of the LORD that he may instruct Him?" But we have the mind of Christ.*

1 CORINTHIANS 2:14–16

The presence or absence of the Holy Spirit of God makes all the difference in the world. In this passage Paul talks about the spirit of a man, which is the essence of who he really is. The spirit is where we relate to the Holy Spirit.

As spiritual beings, we must operate with the Holy Spirit out front. We must let the part of us that the Holy Spirit indwells call the shots. In our spirits is where the completed work of salvation exists. In Philippians 2:12 Paul also writes that we should work out our salvation. We know that he is not instructing us to work for our salvation. Rather, he is telling us to allow what has been done and completed in our spirits to work itself out into our souls and bodies. Paul tells us in Philippians 2:5 that we should have the mind of Christ. You and I both know that there are times when we seem to know the heart of God and other times when we seem to conflict with the heart of God.

*Lord, I surrender to You fully. Bless my spirit, that part of me where You live, Holy Spirit. Spirit of God, I tell my soul and body to fall in line with what You are doing, amen.*

# Week 30—Friday

*Steward What?*

*Let a man so consider us, as servants of Christ and stewards of the mysteries of God. Moreover it is required in stewards that one be found faithful.*

1 Corinthians 4:1–2

When Paul writes "consider us," he is specifically referring to himself and other church planters, but he intends for you and me to be included in those he calls "stewards of the mysteries of God." A steward is not an owner of something, but the one given the responsibility of something. We are called to be stewards of the mysteries of God. The mystery of the gospel, Paul proclaims over and over, is something that has been revealed. We could never "reason" ourselves into an understanding of the gospel. God had to reveal it to us, and He has chosen to use Christians to reveal the gospel to others.

Paul goes on to say we must "be found faithful." In our stewardship of the gospel, we must be faithful to proclaim the message properly and effectively.

.................................................................................................

*Lord Jesus, may You find me faithful today as a steward of Your good news. You own it because You bought it and paid for it. I am a grateful recipient of it. Please give me opportunities today to share the good news with those around me. Give me the insight to recognize these opportunities and the courage to take advantage of them. May all who come behind me find me faithful. Amen.*

Dr. Alex Himaya, theChurch.at Churches, Broken Arrow, OK

# Week 30—Weekend
## *Imitate Christ*

*I do not write these things to shame you, but as my beloved children I warn you. For though you might have ten thousand instructors in Christ, yet you do not have many fathers; for in Christ Jesus I have begotten you through the gospel. Therefore I urge you, imitate me.*

1 Corinthians 4:14–16

In today's verse Paul was not trying to shame the Corinthians, but to admonish them. Paul didn't want to embarrass them, but rather instruct them. When dealing with people, we should remember that we have never laid eyes on someone whom Jesus does not love. We should view people as the children of God and seek to uplift them with our advice.

"For though" introduces a conditional phrase that is not a reality. Although the Corinthians had some mentors, they certainly did not have ten thousand mentors. Paul goes on to remind them that he became their spiritual father by bringing them the gospel.

Much of what we oppose in our world, we could combat if we would simply share the gospel of Jesus Christ with people. If we would become the spiritual fathers we were meant to be, think how much greater our impact in our world could become.

Leading people to Jesus and then loving them as if they were our own children is the one-two punch that Paul presents. What if we imitate Paul in this regard?

*Lord Jesus, may my focus today be on leading people to You and lovingly encouraging them. Help me to focus on what really matters and what really lasts: people! Amen.*

# WEEK 31—MONDAY
## Working for the Man

*For if I preach the gospel, I have nothing to boast of, for necessity is laid upon me; yes, woe is me if I do not preach the gospel! For if I do this willingly, I have a reward; but if against my will, I have been entrusted with a stewardship. What is my reward then? That when I preach the gospel, I may present the gospel of Christ without charge, that I may not abuse my authority in the gospel.*

1 CORINTHIANS 9:16–18

Our society often measures success by the paychecks we bring home each week. We climb the ladder so we can bring home more, drive a nicer car, or put more away for retirement. While money is not evil, we often take the thing that was meant to allow us to provide for our families and allow it to overtake the joy of our work.

The same could be said for the Christian. Paul was more concerned with the opportunity to share the gospel and the gift of salvation through Christ than he was with gaining reward for his work as a proclaimer of the gospel. While vocational ministry is commendable, we must remember the reason we first fell in love with Jesus and share His message. Paul spoke of the "necessity" placed upon him; he was compelled to preach the good news of Christ because of what the gospel had done to transform his life. He sought the reward of sharing Christ with those whom he encountered.

........................................................................................................

*Father, please compel me to share the gospel with a heart that is pleasing to You, amen.*

Rev. David Richardson, First Baptist Church, Creedmoor, NC

# Week 31—Tuesday
### Training for the End

*Do you not know that those who run in a race all run, but one receives the prize?*
*Run in such a way that you may obtain it. And everyone who competes for the prize*
*is temperate in all things. Now they do it to obtain a perishable crown, but we for an*
*imperishable crown.*

1 Corinthians 9:24–25

A couple of years ago I lost a considerable amount of weight. It felt good to be able to move better and have an overall improved health. Since then I have fluctuated a bit here and there. One thing I learned during that process is that I know what I need to do to be successful at improving my health. My doctor instructed me, my wife helped me, and my church family even encouraged me. However, just like an athlete, I must make conscious decisions to make wise choices.

The same can be said of the Christian. Every day we face the choice either to be obedient or to compromise. We must run, or live the Christian life, in such a way that we will obtain the goal of being more like Jesus. We cannot expect to be faithful followers if we neglect time with the Father and if we do not accept accountability and are not sensitive to the leading of the Holy Spirit.

Sometimes I break down and have too much chocolate, and I must try harder to make better choices. The same can be said of our spiritual lives when we make mistakes. We must allow Christ to lead us as we run the race of life so we can reflect the image of the Father.

........................................................................................

*Father, help me make choices in my life every day that impact the kingdom positively, amen.*

# Week 31—Wednesday

*Fighting with Purpose*

*Therefore I run thus: not with uncertainty. Thus I fight: not as one who beats the air. But I discipline my body and bring it into subjection, lest, when I have preached to others, I myself should become disqualified.*

1 Corinthians 9:26–27

I have come to realize that I am a results-oriented person. I love to check things off my list and move to the next challenge to conquer. Sometimes in my effort to check things off the list, I find myself moving from one pile of things to do to the next without much thought or direction. At the end of the day, I find that if I had focused my energy and thoughts better, I might have accomplished much more.

In the Christian life we often drink from a fire hydrant. We want to impact the largest number of people, yet sometimes we need to be more focused on how we use our resources to make a meaningful impact on the world. Instead of looking like a hamster on a wheel, running with no end in mind, we should live the Christian life with discipline. We should land blows against Satan that count, not just throw punches in the air.

Be disciplined in your pursuit of Christ and the life He has for you. Be victorious on purpose.

........................................................................

*Father, help me focus with the end in mind. I want to run with endurance and purpose, amen.*

Rev. David Richardson, First Baptist Church, Creedmoor, NC

# WEEK 31—THURSDAY
## *It's a Long Way Down*

*Therefore let him who thinks he stands take heed lest he fall. No temptation has overtaken you except such as is common to man; but God is faithful, who will not allow you to be tempted beyond what you are able, but with the temptation will also make the way of escape, that you may be able to bear it.*

1 CORINTHIANS 10:12–13

I have often heard the saying, "The higher you are, the farther you can fall." Paul warns the Christian in this passage not to let spiritual pride set in because it makes him or her vulnerable to attack. I love to play the game Monopoly, but it's hard to find people who go at it with the level of zeal I do. When the game starts to intensify, I always turn my focus on the player who has the most to lose. If I focus on overcoming that player, then I will likely win the game.

The same concept can be said about how Satan often attacks the church. Satan would much rather focus on one who is impacting the world for the kingdom than the lazy Christian, because Satan destroys so much more by tempting the focused Christian to fall. Every soul matters to God; however, more hurt, heartache, and disgrace is brought to the name of Christ if one who is working for Christ falls—especially in a public way.

Paul's warning to us is to guard against becoming spiritually prideful and to watch our backs. Satan is right around the corner, waiting and watching for the opportunity to bankrupt us.

*Father, keep me close and clean. Help me not to bring disgrace to the message and work of the cross, amen.*

# WEEK 31—FRIDAY

*Maybe I Should've Had a V8?*

*Therefore, whether you eat or drink, or whatever you do, do all to the glory of God. Give no offense, either to the Jews or to the Greeks or to the church of God.*

1 CORINTHIANS 10:31–32

My wife has been focused on eating right and exercising lately. Her trainer has given her a very specific meal plan, one that I personally am not a big fan of—way too many root vegetables for my taste! Every morning she dutifully packs her breakfast and lunch, and off to work she goes to enjoy her leaves and carrots and whatever other green things she packed to eat. However, when dinner time rolls around we face the dilemma of whether or not to prepare two different meals so she can stay on track—as I find nourishment in a cheeseburger. Though she is perfectly fine eating her salad, she says it should make me feel a little guilty to enjoy a burger in front of her.

Our spiritual liberties are vast, yet we should be mindful of the brother or sister who may not have overcome the same things we have. Being mindful of the journey our fellow Christian is on brings glory to God when we become a supporter of our faith family instead of one who tempts and distracts from the cross.

Perhaps I should eat a few more salads, and perhaps we should be carrying the burdens of our fellow brothers and sisters a bit more.

........................................................................................

*Father, help me to be mindful of my fellow brothers and sisters and always lift them up in their journeys, amen.*

Rev. David Richardson, First Baptist Church, Creedmoor, NC

# WEEK 31—WEEKEND
## When I Grow Up I Want to Be . . .

*When I was a child, I spoke as a child, I understood as a child, I thought as a child;*
*but when I became a man, I put away childish things. For now we see in a mirror,*
*dimly, but then face to face. Now I know in part, but then I shall know just as I also am*
*known. And now abide faith, hope, love, these three; but the greatest of these is love.*

1 CORINTHIANS 13:11–13

As a kid I wanted to be a teacher. I thought it would be cool to decide what a class would play at recess. Now as an adult I am a member of our board of education, and I have quickly realized that teachers are tasked with much more than just planning the perfect recess with kickball and a healthy mix of freeze tag. School is about academic achievement, raising children to be productive citizens, and preparing a student to reach his or her greatest potential.

The same scenario played out in my head as a kid when I thought I could be the Pope—I had lots of ambitions! Today as a pastor I guide people through the messiness of life, such as marital issues and the loss of loved ones. I experience the joy of someone accepting the gift of salvation as well as teaching a child how the miracles of Jesus impact our lives. As a seasoned Christian I am learning how to impact the lost world for Christ. I am learning that the love of Jesus covers the multitude of sins in the world. That love was free, but it came with a great cost.

*Father, help me never to lose sight of the love that was exhibited at the cross for*
*me and the world, amen.*

# WEEK 32—MONDAY

*The Source of Our Success*

*But thanks be to God, who gives us the victory through our Lord Jesus Christ.*
*Therefore, my beloved brethren, be steadfast, immovable, always abounding in the*
*work of the Lord, knowing that your labor is not in vain in the Lord.*

1 CORINTHIANS 15:57–58

The apostle Paul wrote in 1 Corinthians 15 about the bodily resurrection that every follower of Christ will experience one day. The verses immediately preceding this passage tell us, "Death is swallowed up in victory" (v. 54), meaning that although we will all experience death if Jesus delays His return, death does not have the final word over our lives and the years we spent taking care of our families and serving the Lord.

Because Christ died and rose again His followers will follow Him right through the experience of death into eternal life—where there is no more death. Considering what Paul said, we can be "steadfast, immovable, always abounding in the work of the Lord." This means we can be firm, steady, and fruitful. These characteristics come to us because victory has been given to us, that is, victory over death and this life. We do not have to win it; Christ won it for us by His death, burial, and resurrection. Nor do we have to fight to maintain it because God has given victory to us. Once we realize that our lives are lived from a position of victory rather than trying to obtain victory, we become steady, immovable, and our work becomes fruitful and pleasurable.

Thanks be to God for supplying all our needs through Christ Jesus.

*Lord, I ask that You help me understand the success You have given me to spare me from a confused and empty life, amen.*

Dr. Phil Thomas, Shiloh Baptist Church, Fort Gaines, GA

# Week 32—Tuesday

*Nobody Knows the Trouble I've Seen*

*Blessed be the God and Father of our Lord Jesus Christ, the Father of mercies and God of all comfort, who comforts us in all our tribulation, that we may be able to comfort those who are in any trouble, with the comfort with which we ourselves are comforted by God.*

2 Corinthians 1:3–4

We may have been told some variation of "God won't allow more in your life than you can handle." But in verses eight and nine, Paul thought he might die from his troubles. So we're not the first to think we might not survive a situation. However, Paul also pointed out in verse six that whatever trouble he had was for the benefit of others.

But back to verses three and four. God is the "Father of mercies and God of all comfort." He comforts us in all our troubles. We may find ourselves having troubles due to bad decisions on our part or sin in another's life. Still God comforts us in "all our tribulation" regardless of the source of our troubles.

We're to comfort others the way God comforts us. Often people stay away from church when trouble comes along, but church is the place to find help. God helps others who can help us. Someone likely has experienced the same situation as us and can help us through it.

We have two responsibilities concerning troubles in life. When we find ourselves in a bad situation we're to seek out someone who can help us. And when we encounter someone who has troubles that we've been through, we're to offer them the comfort we received from God.

*Lord, please don't let my trouble be for nothing. Show me how to help others, amen.*

# WEEK 32—WEDNESDAY
## The Smell of Jesus

*Now thanks be to God who always leads us in triumph in Christ, and through us diffuses the fragrance of His knowledge in every place. For we are to God the fragrance of Christ among those who are being saved and among those who are perishing.*

2 CORINTHIANS 2:14–15

To diffuse something is to spread it around. This verse refers to the knowledge of Jesus. We're told that God uses us to spread the knowledge of Jesus "in every place." Therefore no place exists where the knowledge is not to be spread around. The apostle Paul refers to the influence we have as an "aroma." And the fact is we can't smell like something or someone that we're not around.

To spread the knowledge of Jesus, we talk freely about Him and live holy lives that are on display for all to see. We may meet a person from time to time who tells us we look or act like our parents. We cannot help what we look like, but we can help our actions, and those actions spread the knowledge of Christ around. When we mimic God's mercy and grace in our dealings with others, we act like our Father in heaven and spread the knowledge of Christ to all.

Verse sixteen tells us that not everyone responds to us in the same way. To some we bring pleasure and peace and to others conviction of sin. Two questions we need to ask ourselves: Do people respond favorably to the aroma we give off? Also, what kind of people do we attract? We need to make sure we are giving off the right aroma and attracting people to the Lord.

........................................................................................................

*Please, Lord, help me to give off the kind of fragrance that causes others to want to know Christ, amen.*

Dr. Phil Thomas, Shiloh Baptist Church, Fort Gaines, GA

# WEEK 32—THURSDAY
## *Christian Transformation*

*Now the Lord is the Spirit; and where the Spirit of the Lord is, there is liberty. But we all, with unveiled face, beholding as in a mirror the glory of the Lord, are being transformed into the same image from glory to glory, just as by the Spirit of the Lord.*

2 CORINTHIANS 3:17–18

When we are first saved we know instinctively that some things in our lives must change. So we make an effort to do just that: to change things in our lives. But we often find that we fall back into old habits. We repent and in time we find ourselves back where we started. We feel guilty and maybe even question our salvation. And so the cycle continues. The problem is that we try to change our habits, and we attempt to act like Christians but all we manage to do is to change appearances. We never really change our hearts, nor are we able to do so.

The apostle Paul wrote to the church at Corinth to tell them that the change, or the transformation, that needs to occur within us as Christians comes from inside of us and is accomplished by the Spirit of the Lord. The "liberty" Paul refers to is the liberty of being set free from legalism, that is, man-made rules designed to make us holy before God. Eventually we learn we can do nothing ourselves, and we let the Spirit do His work in our lives. Only then are we transformed into the image we see when we're looking at the glory of the Lord.

......................................................................

*Lord, please help me to give up my ideas of righteousness and allow You to transform me, amen.*

# Week 32—Friday

*The Purpose of Grace*

*Knowing that He who raised up the Lord Jesus will also raise us up with Jesus, and will present us with you. For all things are for your sakes, that grace, having spread through the many, may cause thanksgiving to abound to the glory of God.*

2 Corinthians 4:14–15

T he apostle Paul served the Lord with his eyes on the future rather than the circumstances in his life. He knew that God would raise him up with Jesus one day. And not just Paul alone, but all believers.

Without Christ there is no future to look forward to and no reason to celebrate. Those who die without Christ will be raised up one day to face judgment. Those who die in Christ, that is, those who accept His atoning sacrifice on their behalf, have already had their sins judged by the death of Jesus Christ. Paul also assured us that there is no condemnation for those in Christ (Romans 8:1). So death divides people, but Christ unites them. All believers will be raised up to be together with Christ.

God shows us grace in our lives, not just in the past for salvation, but for day-to-day living. The proper response to this grace is thanksgiving, so thanksgiving may abound toward God. Finally, all the grace God gives us is for His glory, not ours or another. He established His law to show His perfect standard; when we realize we can't meet these standards, He provides forgiveness through Jesus Christ, His Son. Even telling us the standard for judgment is a means of grace.

Spread God's grace to many, so He may receive more glory.

......................................................................................

*Lord, help me to be more thankful for Your grace and to tell others about it, amen.*

Dr. Phil Thomas, Shiloh Baptist Church, Fort Gaines, GA

# WEEK 32—WEEKEND
## *When Troubles Are Good*

*Therefore we do not lose heart. Even though our outward man is perishing, yet the inward man is being renewed day by day. For our light affliction, which is but for a moment, is working for us a far more exceeding and eternal weight of glory.*

2 CORINTHIANS 4:16–17

W e're getting old, and we don't like it. We find that our bodies don't work as well as they used to, and it frustrates us. We start to experience health problems to one degree or another and become anxious. Not only are we anxious about the condition of our bodies, we're concerned about who's going to take care of our house and other possessions. And this anxiety may lead to further medical problems. Even before we reach the age where we must address medical issues, we still experience troubles of some kind, such as financial or relational issues.

The apostle Paul felt his age and troubles, but he wrote to the Corinthians that he had not lost heart. Actually Paul used the term "we," meaning all of us have the same capability as him. When we're young and healthy and the world is before us, our desire for eternal things is small. But the older we get or the more troubles we have, the more we look forward to heaven. God does us a favor by allowing troubles in our lives. The way not to "lose heart" with our troubles here is to look forward to heaven. The time we have left here is short in light of eternity. Let's turn our eyes on heaven.

........................................................................................

*Lord, help me to see my troubles as temporary and necessary to make me look forward to seeing You, amen.*

# WEEK 33—MONDAY
## Confident in Any Circumstance

*So we are always confident, knowing that while we are at home in the body we are absent from the Lord. For we walk by faith, not by sight. We are confident, yes, well pleased rather to be absent from the body and to be present with the Lord.*

2 CORINTHIANS 5:6–8

S ir Percival Lowell strained through squinted eyes and a powerful telescope to see something no one else had. Lowell saw canals created by superior intelligence on the Red Planet. Lowell tediously and painstakingly mapped the canals he saw on Mars. Since then probes have landed on Mars, and there are no canals. It turns out Lowell had a unique eye condition that caused him to see blood vessels in the back of his eye instead of canals on Mars.

The point is that we cannot always trust what we see no matter how real our perceptions are. Paul knew not to put confidence in what he saw. He could see afflictions with his eyes, but he could see glory with his faith. What we see sometimes brings us fear and anxiety or gives us a false confidence. Living by sight is inferior to living by faith by miles. Our sight is so limited because we focus on what we feel, think, or experience. Faith is unlimited; it puts our focus on God, who is greater than our feelings, thoughts, and experiences. Sight sees what we can do; faith perceives what God can do in any circumstance.

*Father, You see my beginning and end. Nothing is hidden from Your sight. I trust that what You are doing is for Your glory. I do not have to walk in fear today because I walk in faith in You, amen.*

Scott Yirka, Hibernia Baptist Church, Fleming Island, FL

# Week 33—Tuesday

*What a Way to Live*

*Therefore we make it our aim, whether present or absent, to be well pleasing to Him. For we must all appear before the judgment seat of Christ, that each one may receive the things done in the body, according to what he has done, whether good or bad. Knowing, therefore, the terror of the Lord, we persuade men; but we are well known to God, and I also trust are well known in your consciences.*

2 Corinthians 5:9–11

Living by faith means aiming to live in a way that pleases the Lord Jesus. Aiming to please Him is what matters. If we please Him, it does not matter who else we displease; further, if we displease Him, it does not matter who else we please. Think about the day we will stand before the Lord to give an account of what we have done, what our lives were aimed toward. That day will be terrifying, not because we who are saved will face judgment, but because we will receive either commendation or the loss of rewards (1 Corinthians 3:12–13).

All the redeemed will give an account before God (Romans 14:10), not for sin since we have Jesus as our Advocate for sin, but for what we've done to build His kingdom. So living with an aim to be pleasing to the Lord Jesus today assures us of reward in that day. How we view the future results in our present testimonies before our Father and those who know us well. Who better can persuade others of the weight of judgment than the person whose main ambition is to please the Lord?

*Lord, I pray that by Your grace I will make it my aim to please You in every conversation and circumstance, amen.*

# WEEK 33—WEDNESDAY

## Reconciled and Reconciling

*Therefore, if anyone is in Christ, he is a new creation; old things have passed away; behold, all things have become new. Now all things are of God, who has reconciled us to Himself through Jesus Christ, and has given us the ministry of reconciliation.*

2 CORINTHIANS 5:17–18

Reconciliation is a sweet thought. When we reconcile with a friend, a burden is lifted. When enemies reconcile, we rejoice. But nothing compares to reconciling with God. Why are we now reconciled to God? God pursued us when we were enemies and reconciled us to Himself.

Now we have the ministry of reconciliation. God has sent us as ambassadors (2 Corinthians 5:20) to plead with everyone to be reconciled to God. For us everything has become new. How we see others is new. Paul says in 2 Corinthians 5:16, "We regard no one according to the flesh." We now see the world not as the enemy to be shunned, but as sinners needing reconciliation to God. A sure sign that we are indeed a new creation is that we are active in the ministry of pleading with sinners to be reconciled.

How do you see others outside of Christ? Do you see them as people needing to be reconciled to God? Today rejoice that God has saved you. Today pray that you will represent Him well by imploring others to be reconciled to God on the bus, at work, at school, in the dorm, on the field, in your neighborhood, and wherever people are far from God.

.................................................................................................................

*Father, thank You for pursuing me, saving me, and reconciling me to You. Embolden me to call others to reconciliation today. Make me a faithful ambassador for You, amen.*

Scott Yirka, Hibernia Baptist Church, Fleming Island, FL

# Week 33—Thursday
## Seen and Heard

*We give no offense in anything, that our ministry may not be blamed. But in all things we commend ourselves as ministers of God: in much patience, in tribulations, in needs, in distresses, in stripes, in imprisonments, in tumults, in labors, in sleeplessness, in fastings; by purity, by knowledge, by longsuffering, by kindness, by the Holy Spirit, by sincere love, by the word of truth, by the power of God, by the armor of righteousness on the right hand and on the left.*

2 Corinthians 6:3–7

F rankly, it took some time before I could even write after meditating on these verses. As ambassadors of Christ nothing else matters as much as powerfully pleading with people to be reconciled to God. What gives our pleading its power, however, is not our words of wisdom, doctrinal accuracy, or passionate delivery. No, our holiness before God is what gives our pleading its power.

Paul said we are to give no offense in anything. He is bluntly stating that the message of the gospel may offend, but our lives must not. The gospel cannot be proclaimed by silent witnesses piously living out our faith. The gospel must be proclaimed with boldness accompanied by piety. We are to be audio-visual Christians. We endeavor "by the Holy Spirit, by sincere love, by the word of truth, by the power of God, [and] by the armor of righteousness" to live so everything people witness about us is a witness to the Lord Jesus Christ.

*Father, thank You for saving me. Thank You for including me as Your ambassador in Your ministry of saving others. May I today live in the power of Your Spirit so those who see me will be exhorted to respond to Christ today, amen.*

# WEEK 33—FRIDAY
## *More Not Less*

*So let each one give as he purposes in his heart, not grudgingly or of necessity; for God loves a cheerful giver. And God is able to make all grace abound toward you, that you, always having all sufficiency in all things, may have an abundance for every good work.*

2 CORINTHIANS 9:7–8

God loves a cheerful giver. Imagine that: our Father loves when we give to Him. All parents love gifts their children give to them, even though parents likely provided the means to make the purchase. I think I have paid for most of the gifts my children have given me. But, then again, God has also provided the means for everything I have given to Him.

A cheerful giver does not give out of obligation or duty, but voluntarily as he purposes in his heart. Giving to God funds the work of the gospel at home through His church, and it helps to care for those in need. A cheerful giver is loved by God and loves to give to God.

How joyful is it to know you really cannot out give God. God loves to give. He has promised that the giver will be provided sufficiency in all things and abundance for every good work. There is no remorse in giving to God because when you give you receive more than you give.

........................................................................

*Lord, thank You for giving to me so lavishly. Thank You for allowing me to give to You and invest in Your kingdom. I ask You to grow my generosity so I may put to death covetousness, greed, and jealousy. Lord, please open the windows of heaven and fill me with the blessings of Your lavish generosity, amen.*

Scott Yirka, Hibernia Baptist Church, Fleming Island, FL

# Week 33—Weekend

*This Means War*

*For the weapons of our warfare are not carnal but mighty in God for pulling down strongholds, casting down arguments and every high thing that exalts itself against the knowledge of God, bringing every thought into captivity to the obedience of Christ.*

2 Corinthians 10:4–5

Unfortunately, times arise when means of discourse and diplomacy are exhausted and the only alternative for preservation is war. The truth of God is constantly under siege, and we are God's entrusted defenders against attackers. Does this sound serious? It is—eternity is at stake. Sometimes, as in the case in Corinth, we must go to battle for the truth. In Corinth the battle was not only outside the church, but within the church.

The apostle was ready to go to the battlefield, but the battle would be unfair. The weapons against truth were man's logic, understanding, opinions, and feelings. Paul's weapon was the truth from God's Word. That weapon is mighty in God. Attackers of truth were bringing a knife to a gunfight. Man's thoughts are no match for the truth of God.

Our war is not against flesh and blood (Ephesians 6:12), but as soldiers (2 Timothy 2:4), we fight the "good fight of faith" (1 Timothy 6:12) against the lies of the enemy. We confront lies with fierce love and eternal truth. To love is to tell the truth, and the truth wins every time.

......................................................................................................

*Lord, today I will have thoughts that are not true. I will hear lies. I will witness attacks on Your truth. On every occasion may I with love and patience confront those lies with truth, amen.*

# WEEK 34—MONDAY
## The Real Battlefield

*Now I pray to God that you do no evil, not that we should appear approved, but that you should do what is honorable, though we may seem disqualified. For we can do nothing against the truth, but for the truth. For we are glad when we are weak and you are strong. And this also we pray, that you may be made complete.*

2 CORINTHIANS 13:7–9

How do we change the hearts, minds, and ultimately the actions of carnal people? Do we admonish them because of their sin? Do we bring them before the church and exercise church discipline? Sometimes admonishment and church discipline are the only ways to get someone's attention. But there is a better way, a more effective way. And that way is prayer.

In this passage Paul prays for believers to stay away from evil, do what is right, stand for the truth, and grow in their faith. For whom are you praying? What is the evil they need victory over? What is the good thing they need to do? How can they stand for the truth? How do they need to mature in their faith? We accomplish more in the lives of those whom we love through prayer than any other means possible.

........................................................................................

*Dear God, today I pray I will become bolder and more specific in my prayers for others. Use my intercession to accomplish Your will in their lives, amen.*

Rocky Purvis, Northside, Lexington, SC

# WEEK 34—TUESDAY
## Confrontation

*But when I saw that they were not straightforward about the truth of the gospel, I said to Peter before them all, "If you, being a Jew, live in the manner of Gentiles and not as the Jews, why do you compel Gentiles to live as Jews? We who are Jews by nature, and not sinners of the Gentiles, knowing that a man is not justified by the works of the law but by faith in Jesus Christ, even we have believed in Christ Jesus, that we might be justified by faith in Christ and not by the works of the law; for by the works of the law no flesh shall be justified."*

GALATIANS 2:14–16

Confrontation is never easy. And it's certainly not fun. We should always check our motives and make sure we have good reasons before we ever confront someone, especially if that confrontation is public.

When Paul met with the leaders of the Jewish Christians, they had a productive meeting. They all agreed that salvation was by faith apart from obeying the Jewish laws. But Peter gave in to legalistic peer pressure and wouldn't eat with the Gentiles who had not been circumcised. Paul knew that this simple act would create confusion about salvation and divide the Jewish and Gentile believers. So he confronted Peter face to face in Antioch and in front of the other believers. The integrity of the gospel was at stake!

Times may arise in your life when you must take a stand and confront someone. When you do, do it for the right reasons and in the right spirit.

...................................................................................................................

*Dear God, give me the wisdom to know when and how to confront others for the sake of the gospel, amen.*

# WEEK 34—WEDNESDAY
## At Just the Right Time

*But when the fullness of the time had come, God sent forth His Son, born of a woman, born under the law, to redeem those who were under the law, that we might receive the adoption as sons.*

GALATIANS 4:4–5

W hen I was still a child, my dad taught me how to play chess. If you don't know, chess is a game of strategy in which each player tries to capture the opponent's king. Good players can think ahead and prepare for whatever move their opponents will make with a move of their own. But the great players move beyond that. They can get their opponents to make the moves that will put the great players in the position to win.

And that's what God did. When man entered into Satan's rebellion and sinned, God already had a plan in place to redeem man. And God patiently worked that plan for thousands of years, waiting for just the right time. He chose Abraham and David to be the lineage through which His Son would be born. He chose Bethlehem to be the city in which He would be born. He chose Mary to be the mother who would give birth to this special Son. And when the time was right for the Savior to be born, God sent His Son, born of a virgin, to redeem those under the law.

And just as God had a plan for the birth of His Son, God has a plan for your life. Trust Him!

........................................................................

*Dear God, thank You for sending Your Son, Jesus, at just the right time, amen.*

Rocky Purvis, Northside, Lexington, SC

# Week 34—Thursday

*Present Hope, Future Hope*

*For we through the Spirit eagerly wait for the hope of righteousness by faith. For in Christ Jesus neither circumcision nor uncircumcision avails anything, but faith working through love.*

GALATIANS 5:5–6

E veryone who is a follower of Jesus has both a present hope and a future hope. Our present hope rests in the reality that our sins have been forgiven, not based on what we have done or what we will ever do, but simply on the reality that we have placed our faith in Jesus. As Paul said in Ephesians: "For by grace you have been saved through faith" (Ephesians 2:8).

But we also have a future hope, a hope that goes beyond past forgiveness to future righteousness. A day is coming when we as followers of Jesus will not only have the penalty of sin forgiven, we will have the presence of sin removed! One day the struggles we have with our sinful flesh will be a distant memory. One day the thoughts that bring us shame will all be gone. One day the very hint of sin will be removed from our lives. And we, through the Spirit, eagerly wait for that hope of righteousness that is by faith!

......................................................................................................

*Dear God, thank You for my present forgiveness that was bought and paid for through the blood of Jesus, and thank You for the future hope I have of righteousness that will come through Your Spirit, amen.*

# WEEK 34—FRIDAY

*Free to Serve*

*For you, brethren, have been called to liberty; only do not use liberty as an opportunity for the flesh, but through love serve one another. For all the law is fulfilled in one word, even in this: "You shall love your neighbor as yourself."*

GALATIANS 5:13–14

One of the paradoxes of Scripture is we are slaves and yet we are free. We are no longer slaves to sin but we are slaves to righteousness. We aren't free to do everything, yet we are free to do anything. I know that doesn't make sense . . . unless we have discovered the freedom that only comes through Jesus.

And when we experience that freedom, something happens. Our desire is no longer to use our freedom to serve our sinful flesh but rather to serve one another. Dave Thomas, who was the founder of Wendy's, once appeared on the cover of their annual report dressed in a knee-length work apron while holding a mop and a plastic bucket. Here's how he described that picture: "I got my MBA long before my GED. . . . At Wendy's, an MBA doesn't mean Master of Business Administration. It means Mop Bucket Attitude."[6] Mop bucket attitude—the mind-set of a servant willing to do anything that will minister to and build up others.

That's how Christians should use their freedom! So how are you using yours?

......................................................................................................

*Dear God, today I pray I will use my freedom, not to feed my sinful desires, but to serve others, amen.*

Rocky Purvis, Northside, Lexington, SC

# WEEK 34—WEEKEND
## *Comparisons*

*For if anyone thinks himself to be something, when he is nothing, he deceives himself.*
*But let each one examine his own work, and then he will have rejoicing in himself*
*alone, and not in another. For each one shall bear his own load.*

GALATIANS 6:3–5

Comparisons. We all make them. We make them when it comes to the money we have, the homes we live in, the cars we drive, the bodies we work hard to maintain, and even the churches we pastor.

The truth is that pastors can be the worst. We're always comparing ourselves to other pastors and our churches to other churches. We tend to brag when things are going well and make excuses when things aren't. If another church is doing well, we typically can find something it's doing wrong or find something it's compromising on. That's just the way we are. Isn't it about time we stop?

I discovered a long time ago that if I spend time examining my own work, I will have enough examining to keep me busy. Remember that God created you to be you and accomplish what only you can accomplish. When you compare yourself to others, you're telling God you don't like what He created you to do. Think about it.

............................................................................................

*Dear God, forgive me for comparing myself, my marriage, my life, and my ministry with other people. Help me today to be the best me I can be for Your glory, amen.*

# WEEK 35—MONDAY
## Touched by God

*Blessed be the God and Father of our Lord Jesus Christ, who has blessed us with every spiritual blessing in the heavenly places in Christ, just as He chose us in Him before the foundation of the world, that we should be holy and without blame before Him in love.*

EPHESIANS 1:3–4

God is all-powerful, all-knowing, and all-loving. We ought to reverence His name in every way and always. Jesus taught us to do this when He taught us the Lord's Prayer. Without Him we can do nothing and we are nothing.

This passage in Ephesians takes every believer deep into the great and wonderful mystery of our God—way beyond any of our own understanding or comprehension. The apostle Paul describes God's master plan for our salvation in terms of the past (what He has done), the present (what He is doing), and the future (what He will do). Here we see God and the Son at work, active in love and in grace toward all who would believe in His name.

What about the believer who becomes exasperated that any sinful person could dare to bless the Lord? But David blessed God repeatedly in his psalms. And we sing with great gusto, "Bless the Lord, O my soul; and all that is within me, bless His holy name!" (Psalm 103:1). Apparently blessing God is not an option. It's an imperative based on God's providential grace.

This grace is the work of God, who is the divine and spiritual source of all blessings. And to think that the realm from which these blessings come is none other than the heavenly places, known only to God, because they are the very abode of God. This is God's saying, "From my heart to yours!"

......................................................................................

*Heavenly Father, I bless You! In Jesus' name, amen.*

Dr. Don Wilton, First Baptist Church, Spartanburg, SC

# WEEK 35—TUESDAY
## Touched by Trust

*That we who first trusted in Christ should be to the praise of His glory. In Him you also trusted, after you heard the word of truth, the gospel of your salvation; in whom also, having believed, you were sealed with the Holy Spirit of promise, who is the guarantee of our inheritance until the redemption of the purchased possession, to the praise of His glory.*

EPHESIANS 1:12–14

God has let us know that His glory is the supreme purpose of redemption. We are the redeemed. Let the redeemed of the Lord say so! We know this because we have not only heard the Word of truth, but we have become convinced and have believed. This means we know the gospel of our salvation is absolute truth. We know this gospel is about God's plan for our salvation and that this plan is made possible through Christ Jesus alone.

We also have every reason to praise His glory because the Holy Spirit has come to indwell every believer. This is the only means by which we are secured in Christ and preserved for eternal salvation. Once sealed, this seal can never be broken. No one can pluck us from the hand of God. God's seal is His official mark of identification and carries His full and complete authority. His authority is both unbreakable and final. It can never be altered or changed. The Holy Spirit is the guarantee of our inheritance and signifies God's pledge to all believers for all eternity. This is why we are touched by our trust in Him.

................................................................

*Dear God, thank You for saving me and securing me forever. In Jesus' name I pray, amen.*

# WEEK 35—WEDNESDAY
## Touched by Mercy

*But God, who is rich in mercy, because of His great love with which He loved us, even when we were dead in trespasses, made us alive together with Christ (by grace you have been saved).*

EPHESIANS 2:4–5

For many years the students from our church have sung in prisons across America. One song by the Rhett Walker Band, "When Mercy Found Me," inspired hundreds of incarcerated persons to find the mercy and love of God for the very first time.

This is who God is. He is rich in mercy, not because He has everything, but because He is everything. Out of His heart and holiness flows the richness of His grace and mercy in that, while we were yet sinners, Christ Jesus died for us (Romans 5:8). Through Christ our Savior and Lord, God has extended His love to us. And His salvation is for God's glory.

This is the very means by which God's glory is put on display. His mercy is the very extent of His boundless love for those who are spiritually dead in their trespasses and sins. Through His incomparable mercy we are made alive in Him because of the power of the resurrection of the Lord Jesus from the dead. God did this so we can be made alive.

How incredibly reassuring that "there is therefore now no condemnation" (Romans 8:1) for those who have become the recipients of His mercy. And this same power energizes every believer to live out the life of Christ.

.................................................................................

*Thank You, heavenly Father, for Your great mercy and love, amen.*

Dr. Don Wilton, First Baptist Church, Spartanburg, SC

# WEEK 35—THURSDAY
### *Touched by God's Call*

*I, therefore, the prisoner of the Lord, beseech you to walk worthy of the calling with which you were called, with all lowliness and gentleness, with longsuffering, bearing with one another in love, endeavoring to keep the unity of the Spirit in the bond of peace.*

Ephesians 4:1–3

Any effort to live out the Christian life can be costly. For example, Paul paid a considerable price. As long as he had persecuted the church and agreed with the world, he had favor with men. But this all changed on the road to Damascus. Jesus Christ changed his life from inside out.

His insatiable desire to teach others what it meant to be a disciple of Christ came from deep within his changed heart. His gratitude to the Lord for His mercy and grace was unlimited. He knew that following Christ meant taking up his cross, and this cross was neither comfortable to carry or painless to experience. He understood these truths firsthand and was instructed by the Holy Spirit to write them down for us.

In so doing, the apostle urged his readers to be everything the Lord desires and empowers them to be. The effectual call that saves is the same call to holy conduct. Walking worthy of Christ is not an option. It is an imperative to do in the power of the Holy Spirit. Thus the spiritual qualities of humility, gentleness, long-suffering, and the bearing with one another in love are laid down for every disciple of Christ. The result ought to be the Spirit-given oneness of all believers who are bound together by an unbreakable cord of God's peace and grace.

*Thank You, dear Father, for Your call on my life, amen.*

# WEEK 35—FRIDAY
## Touched by Serving

*And He Himself gave some to be apostles, some prophets, some evangelists, and some pastors and teachers, for the equipping of the saints for the work of ministry, for the edifying of the body of Christ.*

EPHESIANS 4:11–12

T he church is made up of people who have placed their faith and trust in the finished work of Jesus Christ. All believers are the recipients of God's grace, and God has no gift-less children. The Holy Spirit's presence indwells every believer, and all believers have been granted gifts according to the grace of God. We are not all designed to do the same things for God, but we are all designed to do things for God according to the gifts He has given us.

Christ possesses the authority to make these assignments. Our duty is to identify these gifts and go to work for the Savior. God's way of carrying out His work is through assigning these gifts. The apostles were uniquely set apart to lay the foundation of the church (Ephesians 2:20), to receive, declare, and write God's Word (Ephesians 3:2–5), and to confirm the Word through signs, wonders, and miracles (2 Corinthians 12:12). The prophets had the gift of prophecy and came to the local church in Antioch (Acts 11:27). The evangelists were people who proclaimed the good news of salvation to unbelievers (2 Timothy 4:5). A pastor was the shepherd of the flock, one who led, prayed for his flock, and explained the Word (1 Peter 5:2). A teacher was one who was much like a Sunday school teacher today.

This is how the Lord equips us to serve Him. This is how we are nurtured and edified as believers in a church.

.........................................................................................................

*Thank You, Jesus, for the gifts you have given me, amen.*

Dr. Don Wilton, First Baptist Church, Spartanburg, SC

# WEEK 35—WEEKEND
## Touched by Maturity

*That we should no longer be children, tossed to and fro and carried about with every wind of doctrine, by the trickery of men, in the cunning craftiness of deceitful plotting, but, speaking the truth in love, may grow up in all things into Him who is the head— Christ—from whom the whole body, joined and knit together by what every joint supplies, according to the effective working by which every part does its share, causes growth of the body for the edifying of itself in love.*

EPHESIANS 4:14–16

Every parent loves to see his or her children grow up to be strong, productive, and mature adults. Immature adults wreak havoc on the lives of others and suffer greatly for the choices they make. This is especially true in a world filled with trickery and deceit—a world in which the devil is out to destroy and even kill.

And what joy to see wisdom take hold of a person's life! What joy to seek the counsel of those who daily practice what they preach! Paul pleaded for this to be the case with believers. He had seen the devastation caused by immature believers in society, in homes, and in the church. He knew immature believers are inclined to go whichever way the wind blows. He knew that without spiritual maturity and discernment, great harm would come to not only the immature, but also the whole church.

The power for producing mature and equipped believers comes from those who lead spiritually within the church, and, most importantly, from the Head, Christ Jesus. He is the one who holds all Christians together. Proper church growth comes when every member uses his or her gifts accordingly.

*Heavenly Father, keep me growing in spiritual maturity! Amen.*

# Week 36—Monday
## Your Manner

*This I say, therefore, and testify in the Lord, that you should no longer walk as the rest of the Gentiles walk, in the futility of their mind, having their understanding darkened, being alienated from the life of God, because of the ignorance that is in them, because of the blindness of their heart; who, being past feeling, have given themselves over to lewdness, to work all uncleanness with greediness.*

EPHESIANS 4:17–19

When we are in Christ, we are new creations (2 Corinthians 5:17). Christ has equipped us for the work of the ministry (Ephesians 4:12), and we are no longer slaves to sin (Romans 6:6). Therefore, we "should no longer walk" as those who don't know Christ.

Paul says those without Christ walk in futility of mind. Through Christ we have purpose. Paul says the understanding of unbelievers is darkened. But we know the truth, and the truth sets us free. Those without Christ are separated from the life of God. But we are brought near and are adopted into His family.

Without Christ, people have ignorance and blindness in their hearts. If the Holy Spirit lives in you, then you have the ultimate Counselor and Guide. If you are in Christ, He cleanses you from all unrighteousness.

Do you feel purposeless, distant from God, trapped in sin? If you know Christ, no matter how you feel, you don't have to walk like you used to; you are a new creation! Return to God and live the way you ought.

........................................................................................................

*Father, thank You for making me new. Help me to walk in that newness daily, amen.*

Dr. Grant Ethridge, LibertyLive.Church, Hampton, VA

# WEEK 36—TUESDAY
## Your Mind

*That you put off, concerning your former conduct, the old man which grows corrupt according to the deceitful lusts, and be renewed in the spirit of your mind, and that you put on the new man which was created according to God, in true righteousness and holiness.*

EPHESIANS 4:22–24

L ike taking off a garment, there are some things we need to put off and other things we need to put on. Christ has given us a new shirt! We need to take the old shirt off and stop doing some things, and instead put the new shirt on and start doing other things.

Tucked in the middle of this passage is a key for doing this. Paul says, "Be renewed in the spirit of your mind." You are going to live the way you think. Even Solomon said, "As [a man] thinks in his heart, so is he" (Proverbs 23:7).

In Ephesians 4:17–18, Paul said we should no longer walk in the futility of our minds with our understanding darkened. When we don't understand God's good purpose for our lives and when we start thinking improperly, we act improperly.

In John 8:31–32, Jesus said, "If you abide in My word, you are My disciples indeed. And you shall know the truth, and the truth shall make you free." When we spend time in God's Word, we learn the truth. Lies we've believed are corrected, and our minds are renewed. The truth isn't meant for condemnation, but freedom! The renewing of our minds sets us free from our sinful ways.

........................................................................................

*Father, help me to be transformed by the renewing of my mind, so I may know Your will and walk in Your ways, amen.*

# WEEK 36—WEDNESDAY
## *Your Mouth*

*Therefore, putting away lying, "Let each one of you speak truth with his neighbor," for we are members of one another.*

EPHESIANS 4:25

"D eath and life are in the power of the tongue" (Proverbs 18:21). Your words either heal or hurt. Do you say things that are unacceptable, unkind, or unimportant? In today's verse Paul reminds us that we are all members of one another. When we lie, gossip, and speak harshly to one another, we destroy the unity of the body, the church.

When we sin with our tongue, we sin against the Spirit living both in us and in the listener. Not only do you sin against the Holy Spirit, but also against the Son who died for you, and the Father who forgave you. Before you speak, ask yourself three questions: Is it true? Is it necessary? Is it helpful? You must put away every sin that threatens the unity of the church.

In Ephesians 4:29, Paul says, "Let no corrupt word proceed out of your mouth, but what is good for necessary edification, that it may impart grace to the hearers." Are your words graceful or do they tear others down? Do they build up the body of Christ or cause division?

Out of the overflow of the heart the mouth speaks (Luke 6:45). Are you harboring bitterness, anger, malice, or resentment toward someone? Has your desire to be right, first, or on top caused you to embellish, distort, or hide the truth? If so, pray like David did: "Create in me a clean heart, O God" (Psalm 51:10), and decide today that you will not bring division to the body of Christ.

........................................................................................................

*Father, help my words to honor You. Create in me a clean heart and use me to edify those around me, amen.*

Dr. Grant Ethridge, LibertyLive.Church, Hampton, VA

*Your Money*

*Let him who stole steal no longer, but rather let him labor, working with his hands what is good, that he may have something to give him who has need. Let no corrupt word proceed out of your mouth, but what is good for necessary edification, that it may impart grace to the hearers.*

EPHESIANS 4:28–29

I n John 10:10 Jesus says, "The thief does not come except to steal, and to kill, and to destroy. I have come that they may have life, and that they may have it more abundantly." Stealing is the opposite of being Christlike. Jesus gives. He gives freely, sacrificially, repeatedly, and abundantly. When we steal, instead of building up, we tear down and destroy.

Any form of stealing is unacceptable for the believer: stealing property through burglary, shoplifting, inventory shrinkage; stealing time from your employer through long lunches, time on the internet, coming in late, leaving early; stealing someone's reputation through harmful words, stealing from the Lord through not tithing. And the list could go on.

There is joy in giving and in giving generously. Work is a gift and a blessing because it provides money that we can use to help others. Proverbs 13:11 warns: "Wealth gained by dishonesty will be diminished, but he who gathers by labor will increase." Our motive should not be to get rich, but to live generously.

........................................................................

*Father, thank You for giving freely and generously to me. Forgive me for ways I've taken from others. Help me to work honestly and to honor You through my giving. Help me to build up others with my words too, amen.*

# Week 36—Friday

*Your Mode*

*And do not grieve the Holy Spirit of God, by whom you were sealed for the day of redemption.*

EPHESIANS 4:30

Grief is a strong word. Anyone who has experienced loss knows the depth of this emotion. When we read that we can grieve the Holy Spirit, that should move something deep within us. When we do not "put off" our old ways and walk in a way that is pleasing to Him, there are consequences, yes, but our offense also causes The Holy Spirit sadness. He is grieved when we do wrong.

As we read yesterday, the Lord offers us life abundantly. Jesus paid the ultimate sacrifice so we might have it, and it was not free. When we choose our own way and live according to the sinful nature, we miss the abundant life. Sin always kills. When we sin, relationships are divided, people are hurt, and consequences are set in motion. The Bible says that our sin can hinder our prayers from being heard and cause our hearts to be hardened (Psalm 66:18; Hebrews 3:15). The Lord has better plans for us!

The Holy Spirit leads us and gives us power, comforts us, helps us pray, and helps us say no to sin. Following Him is the only way we can live an effective and abundant new life, and we need all of Him we can get. In Ephesians 5:18, Paul tells us to "be filled with the Spirit." We need to be filled daily. Our lives should welcome His presence, not push Him away.

*Father, thank You for the Holy Spirit. Please help me live a life that honors Him and welcomes Him. Teach me to listen to His still, small voice, amen.*

Dr. Grant Ethridge, LibertyLive.Church, Hampton, VA

# WEEK 36—WEEKEND

## *Your Mood*

*Let all bitterness, wrath, anger, clamor, and evil speaking be put away from you, with all malice. And be kind to one another, tenderhearted, forgiving one another, even as God in Christ forgave you.*

EPHESIANS 4:31–32

B itterness is a poisonous attitude that refuses reconciliation. Wrath and anger are outbursts of emotion. Clamor is an angry person's desire for everyone to hear his or her grievance. Evil speaking can involve blasphemy. We speak against God when we speak against His children who bear His image. Malice is meanness or hatefulness. We've all experienced each of these emotions at one time or another. Praise God through Christ we can deal with them.

Paul reminds us that Jesus is our example. He was wronged and hurt, but He chose forgiveness. Think about it. When Jesus hung on the cross, He did not harbor a grudge against Peter, who had denied Him, or the crowds, who had crucified Him. He forgave them and focused on what He had set out to accomplish. Be kind to people even when they are unkind to you, tenderhearted even when they hurt you.

Be forgiving even when they don't deserve it. Sometimes we feel like running, quitting, or giving up after we've been wronged, and that is the worst thing we can do. God won't let His servants run. There is work to do! The devil wants to use our problems to tear us down, but God wants to use them to build us up and grow us in spiritual maturity.

......................................................................................

*Father, help me deal with the strong emotions that come from being wronged. Help me to be kind and to forgive just like You did, amen.*

# Week 37—Monday

*Imitate God*

*Be imitators of God as dear children. And walk in love, as Christ also has loved us and given Himself for us, an offering and a sacrifice to God for a sweet-smelling aroma.*

EPHESIANS 5:1–2

I mitate God. It is not a demand to be God or be fully like God. No one can copy God in His power or knowledge or wisdom—that is an impossible requirement. So how can a Christian imitate God? We imitate God by walking in love. This love is totally unique to the Christian. Many believe this love is an impossible love; it is a love that only Jesus could possess. They are wrong.

First, this love is not reserved for God alone. Rather it is a love that flows from God through each of His dear children and out to Christians and non-Christians alike.

Second, it is a sacrificial love. Jesus is the great example. He willingly came to earth, humbled Himself, and lived as a man. He demonstrated how the family of God should love each other.

Jesus healed the sick, gave food to the needy, and loved the poor. He spoke out against evil and hatred, and He delivered those who were oppressed by the devil. Ultimately Jesus gave Himself as the great love offering to pay for the sins of the world. As a result, each person can know the saving love of God. That remarkable, powerful act of love in the life of Jesus was a sweet-smelling aroma to God.

........................................................................................

*Dear Father, by walking in this love, I can imitate you. Today make this my priority, amen.*

Dr. David Edwards, Church Project, The Woodlands, TX

# Week 37—Tuesday

## *The Ultimate Witness*

*But fornication and all uncleanness or covetousness, let it not even be named among you, as is fitting for saints; neither filthiness, nor foolish talking, nor coarse jesting, which are not fitting, but rather giving of thanks.*

Ephesians 5:3–4

E phesus was one of the most significant cities in the Roman Empire. It was devoted to the goddess Artemis and was home to the magnificent Artemisium, the temple built in her honor. Some limited form of temple prostitution existed in the worship of Artemis and would not have been perceived as impure or immoral since it was a sacred function.

The church at Ephesus was in constant struggle with the false gods, demons, and powers of the religion of Artemis. Paul understood this struggle and was determined the church would live as befitting saints; Christians must live in ways that honor the Lord Jesus and not yield to the immorality of the culture. Not only did he demand the church avoid fornication and all uncleanness, he insisted that type of behavior was not even to be named among them.

Christians face the same challenges today. As the society becomes more and more blatant in its immorality, filthiness, and coarseness, those who claim to love the Lord Jesus must be committed to living pure lives before God. Living a pure life is the ultimate witness even though it is not easy with all the temptations available. Christians must place the same demands on his or her life: fornication, filthiness, foolish talking, and coarseness cannot be accepted.

......................................................................................

*Lord, today I set my feet on Your path of purity. I commit to walk in a manner that honors You, amen.*

# Week 37—Wednesday
*Unending Challenge*

*For you were once darkness, but now you are light in the Lord. Walk as children of light (for the fruit of the Spirit is in all goodness, righteousness, and truth), finding out what is acceptable to the Lord. And have no fellowship with the unfruitful works of darkness, but rather expose them.*

Ephesians 5:8–11

The apostle Paul did not insist that Christians have been in darkness or that have done dark things. Rather he states, "You were once darkness." He wrote much the same when he declared earlier in Ephesians, "You . . . who were dead" (Ephesians 2:1). Then Paul immediately turns and dramatically declares, "But now you are light in the Lord!"

Before an individual received Jesus as Lord and Savior, he or she was darkness. When that same person was born again, he or she became light! After making that dramatic spiritual distinction, Paul presents a demand: Since you are now light, walk as a child of light. Where you once lived in the darkness of evil and sin, now live in the light of goodness, righteousness, and truth. In doing so you will discover what is acceptable to the Lord.

This is an unending challenge. Although the truth of a person's relationship with the Lord Jesus is settled at salvation, the ongoing, unending journey to learn fully where and how to walk in the light remains. That struggle is only overcome through the work of the Holy Spirit in a Christian's life. So yield to the Spirit and learn to walk in goodness, righteousness, and truth.

........................................................................

*Lord Jesus, thank You for bringing me out of darkness and into Your light. I want my desire for You to be greater than any other desire in my heart, amen.*

Dr. David Edwards, Church Project, The Woodlands, TX

# WEEK 37—THURSDAY
## *Christianity Is Warfare*

*For you were once darkness, but now you are light in the Lord. Walk as children of light (for the fruit of the Spirit is in all goodness, righteousness, and truth), finding out what is acceptable to the Lord. And have no fellowship with the unfruitful works of darkness, but rather expose them.*

EPHESIANS 5:8–11

Paul's challenge in this passage is personal. It is directed toward a never-ceasing search to ensure that each aspect of a Christian's life is built upon the clear knowledge of what is acceptable to the Lord. In fact every aspect of Christianity flows from that position. It is the basis of faith, the certainty of blessings, and the confidence that God will powerfully move to destroy the enemies that hope to destroy the Christian.

In order to discover what is acceptable, the Christian must pray, read and reread the Bible, and listen. God will speak. The answer may come through prayer, the Bible, a sermon, or a song, but God will speak. Once you discover the will of God, you must take the next step. Turn away from the darkness.

Christianity is warfare. But it is not a warfare that must be lost. The great weapons are the knowledge of the will of God and the aggressive exposure of the works of darkness. Each Christian must be involved, must be a warrior. No one can fight the battle for another. Others can assist and support, but ultimately the individual Christian must fully commit to live according to God's Word. The Christian who finds the will of God and lives it will win.

*Dear Lord, may I always remember that I am engaged in spiritual warfare. Lead me to victory. Amen.*

# WEEK 37—FRIDAY
## *Well Done*

*Bondservants, be obedient to those who are your masters according to the flesh, with fear and trembling, in sincerity of heart, as to Christ; not with eyeservice, as men-pleasers, but as bondservants of Christ, doing the will of God from the heart, with goodwill doing service, as to the Lord, and not to men.*

EPHESIANS 6:5–7

Some use this verse to insist the apostle Paul supported slavery. If these words were all that was known about Paul, such accusations would be correct. But these words are not the totality of what is known. Since Paul insisted that everyone is equally free (Galatians 3:28), how are Paul's words in today's passage to be understood, and what do the words mean today?

There is not room to deal with this verse in its full context, but it must be remembered that the position of a bondservant in Paul's day was not the same as the brutal, dehumanizing experience of American slavery.

That being clearly understood, the challenge in the verse can be interpreted properly. Without condoning slavery, the apostle established a philosophy of work that still stands. When a Christian works for another person, the Christian is to be a faithful employee who sees his or her work as for Christ. The Christian is to approach his or her work as doing the will of God, and it is to be work that comes from the heart.

Ultimately Paul made a remarkable demand. The Christian attitude toward his or her employer should be one of goodwill, not negativity which causes division. Whatever position the Christian holds, his or her work serves the Lord, not men.

...........................................................................................

*Dear Lord, let my work be for You and not for others, amen.*

Dr. David Edwards, Church Project, The Woodlands, TX

# WEEK 37—WEEKEND

*Only His Power*

*Finally, my brethren, be strong in the Lord and in the power of His might. Put on the whole armor of God, that you may be able to stand against the wiles of the devil.*

EPHESIANS 6:10–11

P aul, the apostle, possessed a warfare worldview. He saw the Christian in constant battle with a real enemy who was intent on stealing, killing, and destroying every aspect of life. The church in the opening days of Christianity was during persecution solely based on its faith in the Lord Jesus. Many of the new Christians were coming out of a society that offered them acceptance and protection. Rather than being on the inside, they were now the outsiders, the ones separated from their former cultures and religious ideas. Where were these new believers to find safety?

The apostle brought their problem into focus. Since their battle was not against flesh and blood, their strength could not come from human relationships. So Paul gave them the instruction: "Be strong in the Lord and in the power of His might." What a remarkable concept! Regardless of what they were facing or how daunting the attacks seemed, the believers' strength was found in their relationship with the Lord Jesus. Only His power could give them the promise of victory. This principle is still true today.

The secret of victory is putting on the whole armor of God, which begins with the helmet of salvation and ends with praying always in the Spirit (Ephesians 6:11–18). With that armor comes the promise of God's strength.

........................................................................................................

*Lord Jesus, help me to find my strength in You as I fight the spiritual forces of this world, amen.*

# Week 38—Monday

*Dressed for Battle*

*For we do not wrestle against flesh and blood, but against principalities, against powers, against the rulers of the darkness of this age, against spiritual hosts of wickedness in the heavenly places. Therefore take up the whole armor of God, that you may be able to withstand in the evil day, and having done all, to stand. Stand therefore, having girded your waist with truth, having put on the breastplate of righteousness.*

EPHESIANS 6:12–14

P aul assures us that a battle is taking place in the spiritual realm against these forces. And they are not just forces! These are spiritual beings that have been given great authority to interrupt, disrupt, and destroy the lives of believers.

But here is the good news: God has already given us exactly what we need to defeat every principality, power, ruler, and every human authority that is being used for evil. Paul calls it "the whole armor of God." Paul encourages us to array ourselves for the battle. However, Paul doesn't tell us just to array ourselves for battle and do nothing else. He tells us to put on the armor and stand. This means we must go to war.

God assures us that He will fight the battle for us in the spiritual realm if we are obedient in putting on the whole armor of God. What God fights in the spiritual realm, He helps us fight in the natural world. In another epistle Paul says, "I have fought the good fight, I have finished the race, I have kept the faith" (2 Timothy 4:7). We must prepare for battle!

.........................................................................................

*Lord, help me to be obedient to array myself with the spiritual armor of God so I may fight "the good fight" of faith, amen.*

Bryon J. Barmer, Bright Hope Community Church, Spring Valley, CA

# WEEK 38—TUESDAY

*God's Armor*

*Above all, taking the shield of faith with which you will be able to quench all the fiery darts of the wicked one. And take the helmet of salvation, and the sword of the Spirit, which is the word of God; praying always with all prayer and supplication in the Spirit, being watchful to this end with all perseverance and supplication for all the saints.*

EPHESIANS 6:16–18

One of the proudest moments of my life was the day I graduated from the Marine Corps boot camp. It meant that I had earned the right to serve my country in the military and to wear the uniform of a United States Marine. That uniform holds special meaning to those who serve in the Corps. From the high neck banded collar to the blood stripe on the trousers, every aspect of that uniform is significant.

So it is with the whole armor of God. Every aspect of God's armor is significant in the life of a Christian soldier. But unlike the dress uniforms of the military, the armor of God is never to be taken off. Paul admonishes that once we have taken up the shield of faith and put on the helmet of salvation, we are never to take remove them. Once we have picked up the sword of the Spirit, we are never to put it down. There are no provisions for removing it. Then Paul reiterates what Jesus once said: "Men always ought to pray and not lose heart" (Luke 18:1). Christians must be in a constant state of prayer.

Just as the soldier's equipment offers protection on the battlefield, God's armor offers protection from the evil of this world.

........................................................................................................

*Lord, may I never take off my Christian armor! Amen.*

# WEEK 38—WEDNESDAY
*Prayer for the Saints*

*I thank my God upon every remembrance of you . . . being confident of this very thing, that He who has begun a good work in you will complete it until the day of Jesus Christ.*

PHILIPPIANS 1:3, 6

E xperiencing life as a disciple of Christ is most rewarding and fulfilling. It can be very challenging. And often it is filled with burdens, disappointments, failures, and frustrations that lead us to seek God for help. But it is also filled with joy and satisfaction, contentment, and hope.

Every believer who puts forth the maximum effort to live a life of holiness and righteousness through Jesus Christ will attest to that fact. That is why it is so important to have an encourager in your life who will lift you up in prayer.

The apostle Paul had a fond relationship with the church at Philippi. He often remembered them in his prayers, and he told them about it in today's passage. Paul was aware of their devotion to God and their love for the work of Christ. He sought to encourage them by letting the church know that he was praying for them. Paul also let them know that the work started in them would be completed by God. Paul's prayer was that their work would remain until Christ returned to judge the world.

When you go through difficult challenges in life, it is always a blessing to have a friend to encourage you through the ministry of prayer. To know that someone else is taking your cares and concerns before God can be absolutely energizing! Praying also connects you with other believers in closer fellowship.

......................................................................................................

*Lord, I thank You for the ministry of prayer, amen.*

Bryon J. Barmer, Bright Hope Community Church, Spring Valley, CA

# WEEK 38—THURSDAY
## Spiritual Fruit and Gifts

*And this I pray, that your love may abound still more and more in knowledge and all discernment, that you may approve the things that are excellent, that you may be sincere and without offense till the day of Christ, being filled with the fruits of righteousness which are by Jesus Christ, to the glory and praise of God.*

PHILIPPIANS 1:9–11

The most powerful force in the universe is the power of prayer. E. M. Bounds once said, "The prayers of God's saints are the capital stock in heaven by which Christ carries on His great work upon earth." [7]

The apostle Paul prayed for the spiritual fruit and the spiritual gifts of the church at Philippi to be increased so that they would be administered without offense. Paul's prayer was also to promote greater harmony within the body of Christ. He offered this prayer because the church at Philippi tended to fall into disunity. Paul's desire was for the church to abound in love, knowledge, and discernment.

The true test of every believer is remaining faithful to Christ until He returns. Paul understood this test, and he lifted the church up in prayer because of it. Paul said that believers in Philippi were "being filled with the fruits of righteousness." Although God fills us with the fruit and the gifts of the Spirit when we believe, they must be developed by Christ as we mature. Paul's desire was for the church at Philippi to mature in Christ and live in harmony to the glory and praise of God.

..................................................................................................

*Lord, help me to live a Spirit-filled life, amen.*

# Week 38—Friday

*Boldness*

*But I want you to know, brethren, that the things which happened to me have actually turned out for the furtherance of the gospel, so that it has become evident to the whole palace guard, and to all the rest, that my chains are in Christ; and most of the brethren in the Lord, having become confident by my chains, are much more bold to speak the word without fear.*

PHILIPPIANS 1:12–14

The testimony of others can be an important factor in leading someone to Christ. When we have enough courage to share what we have gone through, God can use our experiences to reach into the hurt and pain of another life to save it. When Joseph's brothers sold him into slavery, that must have been the worst experience of his young life. How heartbroken he must have felt that all his older brothers conspired in this betrayal. He must have fallen into a state of deep depression, having been taken away from his family to live in a strange land.

But God was with him. As it turned out, it was all a part of God's plan. After God exalted him, Joseph told his brothers, "But as for you, you meant evil against me; but God meant it for good, in order to bring it about as it is this day, to save many people alive" (Genesis 50:20).

Paul told the church at Philippi that despite the evil things that had happened to him, it was for the furtherance of the gospel. Paul rejoiced in knowing that even his suffering served as a witness to his captors. Most importantly Paul's sufferings infused fellow believers with boldness in Christ.

...........................................................................................................

*Lord, help me to be bold for Christ, amen.*

Bryon J. Barmer, Bright Hope Community Church, Spring Valley, CA

# WEEK 38—WEEKEND

## *Sharing the Gospel*

*Some indeed preach Christ even from envy and strife, and some also from goodwill: The former preach Christ from selfish ambition, not sincerely, supposing to add affliction to my chains; but the latter out of love, knowing that I am appointed for the defense of the gospel. What then? Only that in every way, whether in pretense or in truth, Christ is preached; and in this I rejoice, yes, and will rejoice.*

PHILIPPIANS 1:15–18

O ne of the greatest joys I experience is sharing the gospel with someone, and then seeing this person surrender his life to Christ. The principle goal of standing behind a pulpit to proclaim God's Word is to point lost souls to Jesus. That is a responsibility that should not be taken lightly.

You would like to think that every person who is a preacher of the gospel has a sincere calling. God places high value on preaching the gospel because it involves the blood of His Son. However Paul made it clear that some preach the Word of God for other reasons. Perhaps some preach out of selfish motives or vanity. Others may do so because someone thought they would make a good leader.

The apostles of Christ were martyred for the sake of the gospel. They all died with the hope and understanding that an eternal reward awaited them in heaven. Paul wrote, "For we must all appear before the judgment seat of Christ, that each one may receive the things done in the body, according to what he has done, whether good or bad" (2 Corinthians 5:10). If believers remain faithful to the gospel, then they will receive their eternal rewards.

........................................................................................................

*Lord, forgive me if I have been selfish with Your Word. Help me to share Your Word out of love for all who will hear it. In Jesus' name, amen.*

# Week 39—Monday

*A Christ Follower's Confession*

*For to me, to live is Christ, and to die is gain. But if I live on in the flesh, this will mean fruit from my labor; yet what I shall choose I cannot tell. For I am hard-pressed between the two, having a desire to depart and be with Christ, which is far better. Nevertheless to remain in the flesh is more needful for you.*

PHILIPPIANS 1:21–24

Try this today. Say it out loud or write it down.

"For me, to live is _____." Now fill in the blank.

Consider carefully what you say or write, for it's a telling confession. If life is all about money, what happens if you lose your money? If your life is your work or health, what will it mean to be unemployed or in bad health? Defining your life by the earthly things you experience and own will always end in futility.

If you are a Christ follower, Christ is your life. Today's passage reminds readers of the difference between the temporal and eternal. Christ is eternal, and because He is in you, you have eternal life. As a disciple of Christ, you must learn to discern. Temporal, earthly things are not bad, but Christ is better! Enjoy the temporal, but value the eternal.

Christ will not be second place. He's not the back-up plan. When you try to let anything define your life apart from Christ, prepare for a major letdown. But when you choose to live for Christ, you will know there is no loss in Christ—only gain.

. . . . . . . . . . . . . . . . . . . . . . . . . . . . . . . . . . . . . . . . . . . . . . . . . . . . . . . . . . . . . . . . . . . . . . . . . . . . . . . . . . . .

*Lord Christ, I confess this out loud today: "For to me, to live is Christ." Help me put You first today as I keep sight of the ultimate goal—being in Your presence for eternity, amen.*

Jeff Crook, Christ Place Church, Flowery Branch, GA

# WEEK 39—TUESDAY
## *The Conduct of a Christian*

*Only let your conduct be worthy of the gospel of Christ, so that whether I come and see you or am absent, I may hear of your affairs, that you stand fast in one spirit, with one mind striving together for the faith of the gospel.*

PHILIPPIANS 1:27

Alexander the Great conquered and acquired the largest empire of the known world. The story is told that one of his soldiers, also named Alexander, was behaving badly. When the soldier was brought before him, the king asked the soldier's name.

The soldier replied, "Alexander, sir."

The ruler replied, "Then change your conduct or change your name."

We who follow Christ are called Christians. We are named after Christ; our daily conduct is to reflect Him. The best argument for Christianity is a Christian, and the worst argument against Christianity is a Christian. How well do we represent the One we are named after? Today's verse reminds us to be unified with other believers. When we are not, our conduct does not reflect the gospel of Christ.

In other words, believers are to behave! How we live in our homes, what we post on Facebook, how we behave at work or on vacation—it all matters. Christ lives in us. We share His name. Just as the soldier received the strong rebuke from Alexander the Great, we too need a strong reminder of whom we represent. If we have repented and trusted Christ, our names have been changed, and our conduct should change too.

..................................................................................

*Today and every day, I want to reflect You, Christ. May my conduct show others that I am a Christian, amen.*

# WEEK 39—WEDNESDAY

## A Season of Suffering

*For to you it has been granted on behalf of Christ, not only to believe in Him, but also to suffer for His sake.*

PHILIPPIANS 1:29

We often view suffering as something that is evil, either caused by Satan or resulting from a sin that's been committed. However, Christ suffered, and He was without any sin. The apostles suffered as well.

Paul wrote Philippians while he was suffering in prison. In the letter he spoke of suffering as a privilege. We suffer on behalf of Christ and for His sake. This shouldn't sound strange because suffering serves a great purpose in the life of a Christian. Suffering identifies us with Christ. It signifies that we belong to Him. It validates that we are true Christ followers.

Suffering also conforms us into Christlikeness. We cling closer to Christ when we suffer. The intimacy with Christ we experience transforms us. We begin to resemble Christ more. Suffering also allows us to be a powerful witness for Christ. We become emboldened in our testimony and talk more about Jesus Christ. Suffering also allows us to minister to others. Trouble can give you a tender heart. Pain can give you a platform. Use difficulties as an opportunity to love and minister to others.

........................................................................

*Thank you, Jesus, for the honor to identify with You in suffering. May You use suffering in my life to help me resemble You more and as an opportunity to minister to others, amen.*

Jeff Crook, Christ Place Church, Flowery Branch, GA

# WEEK 39—THURSDAY
## *Others over Ourselves*

*Therefore if there is any consolation in Christ, if any comfort of love, if any fellowship of the Spirit, if any affection and mercy, fulfill my joy by being like-minded, having the same love, being of one accord, of one mind. Let nothing be done through selfish ambition or conceit, but in lowliness of mind let each esteem others better than himself.*

PHILIPPIANS 2:1–3

The apostle Paul begins this passage by reminding us that since we belong to Christ, we are to esteem others better than ourselves. Babies are born self-focused. Children must be taught not to be selfish. Marriages can get in trouble because of selfishness. Friendships can be ruined, congregations can become divided, and relationships can be destroyed by selfish ambition and conceit. Nothing good comes from a selfish heart.

Jesus modeled this before the disciples as He washed their feet in the Upper Room. Jesus later said, "This is My commandment, that you love one another as I have loved you" (John 15:12). He demonstrated a selfless heart when He prayed, "Not My will" (Luke 22:42). While Jesus suffered on the cross, He prayed for others (Luke 23:34). Jesus always put others above Himself.

Love and selfishness cannot coexist in our hearts. Love overcomes selfishness. We shrink selfishness each time we put others over ourselves. Most importantly we exalt Christ when we die to self. It's a daily choice we make.

......................................................................................

*Jesus, thank You for being my example in putting others ahead of myself. Transform me from being selfish to being a servant as I seek You today, amen.*

# WEEK 39—FRIDAY
## The Mind of Christ

*Let this mind be in you which was also in Christ Jesus, who, being in the form of God, did not consider it robbery to be equal with God, but made Himself of no reputation, taking the form of a bondservant, and coming in the likeness of men.*

PHILIPPIANS 2:5–7

E very day, the news tells of conflict and war. For most of us it's out of sight and out of mind, and we don't let it dominate our thoughts. But we should be careful because conflict and war are closer than some realize. A war happens daily between our ears—the battle of the mind. The devil seeks access into our minds through his arsenal of fear, worry, lust, jealousy, and doubt. First John 4:4 reminds us, "He who is in you is greater than he who is in the world."

The indwelling Christ also accesses our mind. He fills us with faith, peace, joy, love, and courage. The battle of the mind must be fought and won daily through Christ's help.

Pray this verse back to Christ: "Let this mind be in [me] which was also in Christ Jesus." Confess any sin. Accept by faith that His Word is true and He answers your prayer. Do not live in fear and anxiety. You need not to announce to others you have the mind of Christ. Instead, let them see a Christ follower who walks in faith and victory.

........................................................................................................

*Christ, may Your mind be in me today. Dwell in me richly. Help me to think like You and to love like You. I want to be like You. I want others to see You in me, amen.*

Jeff Crook, Christ Place Church, Flowery Branch, GA

# Week 39—Weekend
## *God at Work*

*Therefore, my beloved, as you have always obeyed, not as in my presence only, but now much more in my absence, work out your own salvation with fear and trembling; for it is God who works in you both to will and to do for His good pleasure.*

Philippians 2:12–13

A road my family often travels always seems to be under construction. You've seen the familiar signs: Construction Area or Workers Present. Although road work signs are frustrating, they are an indication that progress is taking place. Our passage today reminds us, "for it is God who works in you both to will and to do."

God is always at work in our hearts. God works in trials and life changes. He is at work in the interruptions and the unexpected. God is always actively working in our lives for His good pleasure and for His purposes. When we respond in humility and obedience to God's work in our lives, something supernatural takes place. God's power energizes our wills to do what God wants for us. Progress takes place in our spiritual lives. We become stronger and more productive. Just as a newly opened road makes the journey smoother, God's glory radiates from lives that allow Him to work.

Don't allow feelings of frustration to enter your heart when construction is taking place in your life. Don't complain. Instead pause and worship your good Father who is at work. His work is never a waste; it is perfect and purposeful.

......................................................................................

*I know You love me, God. Your work in my life shows I am loved by You. Help me to cooperate with the work You are doing. Today, energize me to do Your will, amen.*

# Week 40—Monday

*Hold on Tight!*

---

*Holding fast the word of life, so that I may rejoice in the day of Christ that I have not run in vain or labored in vain. Yes, and if I am being poured out as a drink offering on the sacrifice and service of your faith, I am glad and rejoice with you all. For the same reason you also be glad and rejoice with me.*

Philippians 2:16–18

P aul spent much time, effort, and energy to ensure the Philippian believers grew in their relationship with Christ. He faced much toil and travail as he helped them advance in their spiritual journey. He likened his service among them as being "poured out as a drink offering." He shed his own blood, sweat, and tears to see these believers grow in their faith, and he wanted to make sure that he did not run or labor in vain. He challenged them to "hold fast" to "the word of life"—the gospel of Jesus Christ.

Paul knew that at the end of his life he would stand before Jesus. Because he was confident that the Philippian believers would remain faithful, Paul could rejoice and be glad, even as they faced persecution and suffering. Paul found joy in the fact that his spiritual children would remain strong in the faith.

The only way to stand confident before Christ on the Day of Judgment is to be certain that we hold "fast the word of life" and do not compromise the teachings of Scripture. It's impossible to be confident on the Day of Judgment if we've consistently lived in compromise.

---

*Father, help me to pour out my life so others will hear and believe the gospel, so they can stand with confidence on the Day of Judgment and rejoice in the presence of the Lord, amen.*

Dr. Jim Perdue, Second Baptist Church, Warner Robins, GA

# WEEK 40—TUESDAY

## *What Matters Most?*

*But what things were gain to me, these I have counted loss for Christ. Yet indeed I also count all things loss for the excellence of the knowledge of Christ Jesus my Lord, for whom I have suffered the loss of all things, and count them as rubbish, that I may gain Christ.*

PHILIPPIANS 3:7–8

I n two short verses, Paul sums up what his life is all about. A dramatic change in his perspective occurred when he met Christ. He says, "What things were gain to me, these I have counted loss for Christ." In other words, what had been important to him before didn't seem important any longer. He counted "all things loss for the excellence of the knowledge of Christ Jesus." Paul could think of nothing more important in life than knowing God. Compared to everything else, Paul considered the value of knowing Christ something of incomparable worth.

Paul suffered the loss of many things—his freedom, his health, his worldly possessions, and even his upbringing. But none of those things mattered when compared to Christ. This is a lesson that we all should learn. Knowing God is the most important thing in life.

As we look at our lives and what we value, can we say nothing compares to knowing God? Far too often we waste our lives on things that are ultimately unimportant, rather than investing our lives in what will last forever. Paul's greatest passion was to know Christ and to make Him known.

*Gracious Lord, help me to remember what matters most. Forgive me for placing value on earthly things instead of eternal things. Remind me each day of the surpassing value of knowing Christ, amen.*

# Week 40—Wednesday
*Knowledge or Wisdom*

---

*That I may know Him and the power of His resurrection, and the fellowship of His sufferings, being conformed to His death, if, by any means, I may attain to the resurrection from the dead.*

PHILIPPIANS 3:10–11

The Information Age has left us reeling with an overwhelming supply of knowledge. The amount of data available on the smart phone in your pocket or in your purse is unthinkable. Until 1900 human knowledge doubled approximately every century. By the end of World War II, knowledge doubled every 25 years. Today, on average, human knowledge is doubling every 13 months.

While knowledge and information seem ever to be increasing, wisdom seems to be in short supply. Maybe you have heard the joke by Miles Kington, "Knowledge is knowing that a tomato is a fruit. Wisdom is knowing not to put it in a fruit salad." Indeed, knowledge means that we know the truth. But wisdom means we know how to apply the truth.

Paul was determined to "know" Christ. In 1 Corinthians 2:2 he said, "For I determined not to know anything among you except Jesus Christ and Him crucified." Knowing Jesus is so much more than simply gathering information. It leads to transformation. When you determine to know Christ, you will gladly share in the "fellowship of His sufferings" and rejoice in the "power of His resurrection." Indeed, knowing Christ is the greatest wisdom you could ever attain.

---

*Lord, may my desire to know You far exceed my desire for any other information this world has to offer. Help me to know You in Your "sufferings" and in Your "power," amen.*

Dr. Jim Perdue, Second Baptist Church, Warner Robins, GA

# WEEK 40—THURSDAY
## *Press On!*

*Not that I have already attained, or am already perfected; but I press on, that I may lay hold of that for which Christ Jesus has also laid hold of me. Brethren, I do not count myself to have apprehended; but one thing I do, forgetting those things which are behind and reaching forward to those things which are ahead, I press toward the goal for the prize of the upward call of God in Christ Jesus.*

PHILIPPIANS 3:12–14

You probably know people who would have a hard time saying what Paul admitted in Philippians 3:12: "Not that I have already attained, or am already perfected." Unlike some people who pretend to be perfect, Paul recognized that he had not yet arrived. So what did he do about that?

Since he refused to feign perfection, Paul knew the next logical step was to "press on" to those things to which Christ had called him. He said, "Forgetting those things which are behind and reaching forward to those things which are ahead." He put his past in his rearview mirror and stared squarely out the windshield, looking ahead to the call of Christ.

Paul pressed on! He didn't let his past—neither successes nor failures— trip him up on his way to the finish line. Paul kept his eyes on the prize, and he remembered what mattered most. How often do we allow our past to cloud our vision of the future? What are some successes or failures we need to remove from our vision so we can "press on" in faith to claim what Christ promised?

*Faithful God, help me to "press on" in faith as I seek to follow Your will and bring You glory. I pray that I will faithfully reach for the prize You have set before me, amen.*

# Week 40—Friday
## *Learn from the Past, Look to the Future*

*Therefore let us, as many as are mature, have this mind; and if in anything you think otherwise, God will reveal even this to you. Nevertheless, to the degree that we have already attained, let us walk by the same rule, let us be of the same mind.*

PHILIPPIANS 3:15–16

P aul was laser-focused on running his race to the glory of God. But he didn't want to run alone. He understood that the Christian life was meant to be lived in the context of community. He challenged others to "walk by the same rule" and to "be of the same mind." He wanted other Christians to join him in this race. He called others to forget the past and focus on the future.

Far too many people live in the past. Some can't get over the past because of a hurt or tragedy they experienced. The pain and heartache are just too much for them to bear. Others can't get over the past because of previous success or nostalgia. They think the promise of the future will never compare to the joy of the past. The Bible makes it clear—we should learn from our past, but we shouldn't live in it. We should live in the present and look to the future.

When Paul invited the Philippian believers to join him in his race, he asked them to "walk by the same rule, which is" the Word of God. The Bible provides our standard for walking in righteousness and living in unity with other believers. As we follow the Word, we unify with other believers in purpose and passion.

............................................................................................................

*Lord, help me to live my life and run my race based upon the standards and rules that You have set forth in Your Word, amen.*

Dr. Jim Perdue, Second Baptist Church, Warner Robins, GA

# WEEK 40—WEEKEND
## Citizens of Heaven

*For our citizenship is in heaven, from which we also eagerly wait for the Savior, the Lord Jesus Christ, who will transform our lowly body that it may be conformed to His glorious body, according to the working by which He is able even to subdue all things to Himself.*

PHILIPPIANS 3:20–21

Because we have trusted Christ for salvation, our citizenship in heaven has already been decided. Citizenship in a country comes with certain rights. In America some of these rights are enumerated in the Bill of Rights and the Constitution. Beyond that laws of the land clarify and catalog the rights of American citizens.

Sometimes we forget, however, that citizenship also comes with responsibilities. Focusing on the rights of citizenship without remembering our responsibilities is dangerous. As citizens we are required to pay taxes, we are expected to vote, and we may be called upon to serve our country in various capacities.

But let us never forget this world is not our home. We are citizens of heaven. We are ambassadors from another kingdom, representing a sovereign king while we live on foreign soil. We must remember the rights and responsibilities of our heavenly citizenship. And while on this earth, we must do the will of our King!

*Heavenly King, help me to remember that my first allegiance is to represent Your kingdom and Your will on this earth. May "Your will be done on earth as it is in heaven" (Matthew 6:10).*

# Week 41—Monday

*Peace Through Prayer*

*Rejoice in the Lord always. Again I will say, rejoice! Let your gentleness be known to all men. The Lord is at hand. Be anxious for nothing, but in everything by prayer and supplication, with thanksgiving, let your requests be made known to God; and the peace of God, which surpasses all understanding, will guard your hearts and minds through Christ Jesus.*

Philippians 4:4–7

I recently asked my congregation to identify the obstacle that most hinders their walks with Christ. They were to write them on index cards provided by the church, bring them to the front of the auditorium, and leave them there. On Monday morning I surveyed the cards. Worry was by far the most frequently listed barrier to a rewarding Christian life.

There is a peace that is beyond the reach of our minds but within the scope of our Christian experience. To receive this "surpassing peace" we must stop worrying about everything and begin praying instead. Relinquishing our worries to Christ in prayer guards our thoughts and emotions from the attacks of the evil one.

Peace is the last thing the enemy wants you to experience. Unable to overcome the sentry placed around your heart and mind, he will tempt you to worry once again about those things you have submitted to Christ in prayer already. Don't do it. Give your concerns to Christ in prayer and enjoy the peace of God.

........................................................................................

*Lord, guard my heart and mind with Your peace. I trust You are more than enough to deal with those things that cause me to worry and fear. I give them to You and ask for strength to leave them there, amen.*

Dr. Ken Duggan, Dallas Bay Church, Hixson, TN

# WEEK 41—TUESDAY
## Your Thought Life Matters

*Finally, brethren, whatever things are true, whatever things are noble, whatever things are just, whatever things are pure, whatever things are lovely, whatever things are of good report, if there is any virtue and if there is anything praiseworthy—meditate on these things. The things which you learned and received and heard and saw in me, these do, and the God of peace will be with you.*

PHILIPPIANS 4:8–9

P aul is about complete his letter to the Philippians. As he concludes his thoughts, he lists things that should occupy a healthy believer's mind. He began his letter with the assurance that God had begun a good work in their lives and would complete that work (Philippians 1:6). Now he reminds them that their thought lives should reflect the progress of their transformations.

Believers are works in progress. Our thoughts reveal to us how far we have come in our faith. Rather than allowing our minds to be swept into the polluted current of this present world and hinder our walks with Christ, we should actively meditate on things that cultivate the peace of God.

Be honest: How different is your thought life now from before you became a follower of Christ? Paul indicates by his final words to the church at Philippi that pure thoughts don't come naturally. An undisciplined mind will naturally gravitate toward unhealthy thoughts. You need to guard against allowing unhealthy images having access to your mind while you purposefully pursue things that will not hinder the work Christ is doing in you.

*Dear Lord, give me wisdom to avoid things that will hurt my walk with You. Grant me access to things that are worthy of a child of God. I desire Your peace to fill my heart and mind, amen.*

# Week 41—Wednesday
## A Diluted Gospel

*Since we heard of your faith in Christ Jesus and of your love for all the saints; because of the hope which is laid up for you in heaven, of which you heard before in the word of the truth of the gospel, which has come to you, as it has also in all the world, and is bringing forth fruit, as it is also among you since the day you heard and knew the grace of God in truth.*

Colossians 1:4–6

The letter to believers in the ancient city of Colossae was received during a time the validity of early Christian doctrine was being challenged by false teachings emerging in the early church. The result of such false teaching was to mix error with the truth of the gospel. Such dilution tempered the fervency of the work of God among believers to bring forth good fruit. An uncertain gospel mixed with error causes a church to become lukewarm and repulsive to Christ (Revelation 3:16).

Incredibly not much has changed since then. The truth of the gospel is still being diluted to make it more palatable. Any attempt to alter the truth drains it of the power to save and offer hope. Often alterations to the gospel attempt to remove the role of grace that Paul calls "the grace of God in truth." Such grace-filled truth will not only bring forth fruit in your life, but in "all the world."

You are an important factor in producing fruit as you live out the truth of the gospel. You must seek to share a gospel that hasn't been watered down or mixed with false doctrines.

.................................................................................

*Heavenly Father, shine through me into the darkness of this world so others might see the hope I have in You, amen.*

Dr. Ken Duggan, Dallas Bay Church, Hixson, TN

# WEEK 41—THURSDAY
## *An Accurate View of Christ*

*And He is before all things, and in Him all things consist. And He is the head of the body, the church, who is the beginning, the firstborn from the dead, that in all things He may have the preeminence.*

COLOSSIANS 1:17–18

I listened as someone described to me a heavenly visitation that a colleague had experienced. The person telling the story wanted my opinion on the matter. It seems that Christ had appeared to this individual as he shaved while preparing for work. The Savior and this man had a conversation that left him feeling loved and accepted.

What was my response? "The man did not meet Jesus," I said. "If he had, he would not have been able to stand, much less shave, and continue a conversation." The presence of the person described in this passage by the apostle Paul would initiate at least an attitude of worship, if not outright terror if experienced here on earth.

Paul declares that Jesus is eternal and that Christ is the power that holds all things together. Because He had the power to overcome death and the grave, Christ is the leader of the church. The head not only sits atop the body, but also determines the actions and the direction in which the body goes.

Christ is not the copilot of our lives. He demands preeminence. Anything or anyone that comes before Christ is out of place. An accurate view of Him will help keep our lives in order.

.................................................................................................

*Lord, help me to keep You first in my life above all others, amen.*

# WEEK 41—FRIDAY

*Christot in You*

*The mystery which has been hidden from ages and from generations, but now has been revealed to His saints. To them God willed to make known what are the riches of the glory of this mystery among the Gentiles: which is Christ in you, the hope of glory.*

COLOSSIANS 1:26–27

P reviously in his letter to the Colossians, Paul had emphasized the preeminence of Christ. Now he would write of His permanence. How the Messiah would be eternally present with believers had remained a mystery until Christ revealed it to His saints.

Now we have the awesome privilege of living with the presence of God in us through the Holy Spirit. Why would God gift His saints with the presence of His Spirit when He had not revealed this mystery to previous generations? Because God has given us the tremendous privilege of taking the good news of Christ to the whole world. Imagine what a daunting task that must have seemed to the early church. A few of them were to take the message to the whole world. Such a task would have been impossible if God had not given them the power of the Holy Spirit (Acts 1:8).

The Great Commission is no less difficult today. In a world that is increasingly hostile to the gospel, Christians must rely on His power in them to fulfill their mission. If you will surrender yourself to Him, "Christ in you, the hope of glory" will give you the confidence to share your faith with those He places in your life. This continuing indwelling of the Holy Spirit enables and empowers you to be His light in a world of darkness.

*Heavenly Father, thank You for Your presence within me. Help me use Your power for Your glory, amen.*

Dr. Ken Duggan, Dallas Bay Church, Hixson, TN

# WEEK 41—WEEKEND

## *Lacking Nothing*

*For in Him dwells all the fullness of the Godhead bodily; and you are complete in Him, who is the head of all principality and power.*

COLOSSIANS 2:9–10

These words by Paul follow closely on the heels of a warning to stay in the truth that they had received from him: "Beware lest anyone cheat you through philosophy and empty deceit" (Colossians 2:8) It is in our human natures to learn. This inquisitive nature has been given to us by our heavenly Father. With that desire to learn He has also given us the source of all truth and knowledge. When we are led astray by human philosophy or a prideful desire to be recognized as a source of truth, we get into trouble.

The apostle presented Christ, as all his readers needed to have a full revelation of God. Paul declared that Christ is the "fullness of the Godhead." They lacked nothing because they were "complete in Him." But the Colossians were being challenged by those who had alleged to have extra knowledge greater than they had received through his teaching.

The temptation to know more than others is always present with us. Our flesh loves to be recognized and even admired. However, no believer has more access to truth and the deep riches of God than another. Even gifted preachers don't have extra truth to share with their church members. Their gift of preaching only allows them to share truth in such a way as to benefit those who will listen.

Rather than spending your time pursuing some new revelation, try pursuing God. You are complete in Him, lacking nothing.

......................................................................................................................

*Lord, open my eyes to all the riches I have in You. Amen.*

# Week 42—Monday
## An Eternal Mindset

*If then you were raised with Christ, seek those things which are above, where Christ is, sitting at the right hand of God. Set your mind on things above, not on things on the earth. For you died, and your life is hidden with Christ in God.*

Colossians 3:1–3

We live in a fast-paced culture filled with a variety of worldviews. It can be very easy to be influenced by the masses to the point we are no longer influenced by our Master. The apostle Paul instructs the church at Colossae to be focused completely on things of eternal value rather than of a temporary nature.

As Christians we have been redeemed by the blood of the Lamb and indwelt with the Holy Spirit. We have an eternal relationship with our heavenly Father through the sacrifice of His dear Son. We can see the world from heaven's point of view. We are not limited to our own intellect. We have tapped into the resources of a place called glory. How can this be?

Paul said it is because we died. When we trust Christ as Savior and Lord, we no longer live for ourselves. We now live for the glory of Christ as men and women who have been changed by the power of the cross. We now live to minimize ourselves by maximizing our Savior.

Start this week off right: set your heart and mind on Christ, and you will be blessed by how He will touch your life.

........................................................................................................

*Lord, help me to focus my heart and mind completely on You today. Help me to trust You in all things as You receive glory from my life, amen.*

Brent Thompson, Heflin Baptist Church, Heflin, AL

# WEEK 42—TUESDAY

## *Transformed by Christ*

*Do not lie to one another, since you have put off the old man with his deeds, and have put on the new man who is renewed in knowledge according to the image of Him who created him, where there is neither Greek nor Jew, circumcised nor uncircumcised, barbarian, Scythian, slave nor free, but Christ is all and in all.*

COLOSSIANS 3:9–11

In this passage the apostle Paul admonishes believers to recognize the transformation that has taken place within them. He reminds them the old man has been put off and the new man has been put on. As followers of Christ we no longer live to please ourselves. We now live to honor our Savior. The new man is a transformed man with a renewed mind who has been created to bring glory to God by walking in truth. We are no longer bound by the shackles of our sins. We can now live in complete victory and abundant joy. We no longer have to be guided by the latest trends and fads. We can now live with confidence in our relationship with Christ. We have been changed by His power and for His purpose.

One of the greatest attributes of our heavenly Father is that He shows no partiality to those whom He transforms. The blood of Christ crosses all man-made boundaries. Regardless of the racial, national, physical, or social barriers, the blood of Jesus covers the sins of all who come to Him by faith. We can rest in His faithfulness to provide love and care for those He has transformed.

*Lord, remind me today of all that You have done to change me from who I used to be. Thank You for transforming me, amen.*

# Week 42—Wednesday

*Living with the Peace of God*

*But above all these things put on love, which is the bond of perfection. And let the peace of God rule in your hearts, to which also you were called in one body; and be thankful.*

COLOSSIANS 3:14–15

W hen we try to think of words to describe the way most people live today, we probably think of words like *chaos* and *turmoil* rather than words such as *peace* and *love*. We live in a world where we spend a lot of time on things of minimal eternal value. Yesterday we talked about putting off the old man and putting on the new man. Today we discuss putting on love.

Many books and songs have been written on the subject of love, yet the ultimate authority on this subject is our Lord. He presented the greatest demonstration of love the world has ever known by giving His Son to die for the sins of all mankind. The apostle Paul experienced this love when his life was transformed during an encounter with Jesus. The key to loving others faithfully is by loving God supremely. When we enter into a personal relationship with Christ, we have a new purpose and perspective toward everything in our lives. He gives us true peace, which brings direction to our lives.

Jesus gave this same comfort to His disciples in John 14:27: "Peace I leave with you, My peace I give to you; not as the world gives do I give to you. Let not your heart be troubled, neither let it be afraid." Let's live today guided by the peace He brings.

....................................................................................................

*Lord, I trust You today to rule my life. You are my captain and I submit to Your authority, amen.*

Brent Thompson, Heflin Baptist Church, Heflin, AL

# WEEK 42—THURSDAY

## Consumed with Christ

*Let the word of Christ dwell in you richly in all wisdom, teaching and admonishing one another in psalms and hymns and spiritual songs, singing with grace in your hearts to the Lord. And whatever you do in word or deed, do all in the name of the Lord Jesus, giving thanks to God the Father through Him.*

COLOSSIANS 3:16–17

Some people are consumed with their work while others are consumed with their hobbies. Some people are consumed with making money while others are consumed with overwhelming debt. The apostle Paul reminds us that everything we do in our lives should be done in the name of Christ and for His glory. The key to being consumed with Christ is letting His Word dwell in us. When we are faithful to read and study His Word, it will affect every area of our lives. His Word will direct our thoughts and our decisions in a very positive way. His Word will teach us to live in total dependence upon Him as we are guided through life by the Holy Spirit.

When it dwells in us, the Word will flow from our lives and affect those in our circle of influence. We will be able to teach and encourage others from the overflow of God's Word from our lives.

Friend, make a wise decision today to be consumed with Christ. Let His love and Word flow from your life and be a blessing to those around you.

....................................................................................................

*Lord, help me to focus completely on You today. May I be consumed with You today and every day. In Jesus' name, amen.*

# WEEK 42—FRIDAY
*Welcoming the Word*

*For this reason we also thank God without ceasing, because when you received the word of God which you heard from us, you welcomed it not as the word of men, but as it is in truth, the word of God, which also effectively works in you who believe. For you, brethren, became imitators of the churches of God which are in Judea in Christ Jesus. For you also suffered the same things from your own countrymen, just as they did from the Judeans.*

1 THESSALONIANS 2:13–14

The church at Thessalonica was a body of believers that was very faithful and fruitful. In many ways this church serves as a great model for the body of Christ today. The believers were effective in proclaiming the Word of God faithfully to their region and beyond. This church was one that brought joy to the heart of the apostle Paul. His love for them is clear.

What was their secret? It's really no secret at all. They received the Word as a message from God. They understood and welcomed God's truth being spoken into their lives.

Today we have many critics of God's Word who constantly want to challenge its inspiration and authority. The Word of God has been under attack since the garden of Eden, yet it has withstood the test every time. God's Word is true, and it effectively works in the lives of all who receive it.

The Word will give you the ability to persevere even when you face suffering for the sake of the gospel. Friend, welcome the Word and allow the Word to direct your steps today.

.................................................................................................

*Lord, I welcome Your Word as truth. Give me strength to persevere faithfully, Amen.*

Brent Thompson, Heflin Baptist Church, Heflin, AL

# Week 42—Weekend
## Wisdom for the Weekend

*Indeed you do so toward all the brethren who are in all Macedonia. But we urge you, brethren, that you increase more and more; that you also aspire to lead a quiet life, to mind your own business, and to work with your own hands, as we commanded you, that you may walk properly toward those who are outside, and that you may lack nothing.*

1 THESSALONIANS 4:10–12

Good news! It's the weekend! After a week filled with testing and trials, hopefully you will relax and enjoy the next couple of days. When reading the Scriptures, I look for key words to better understand the meaning of each passage. In today's text key words help us gain some wisdom from God's Word.

The apostle Paul gives helpful instructions to the church at Thessalonica. Paul urges them to increase by reaching forward to what was ahead of them. He challenges them to live quietly. He certainly does not mean for them to live dull and boring lives, but to daily shine the light of Christ. He admonishes them to mind their own business and not engage in the sin of gossip and tearing down other people. His final word of instruction is for them to work with their own hands. He does not want them to live off the labors of others, but to give their best effort in everything they do.

The ultimate reason for Paul's challenging words is to inspire believers to walk properly and be faithful witnesses to those who do not have a relationship with the Lord.

Remember these admonitions from Paul as you worship this weekend.

*Lord, I bless Your holy name and I seek to walk daily in Your grace, amen.*

# WEEK 43—MONDAY
*Practical Pointers from Prophecy*

*Therefore comfort each other and edify one another, just as you also are doing. And we urge you, brethren, to recognize those who labor among you, and are over you in the Lord and admonish you, and to esteem them very highly in love for their work's sake. Be at peace among yourselves.*

1 THESSALONIANS 5:11–13

P aul turns his focus to practical Christian living and sets out to tell us how we should live considering prophetic truth. He begins with a gentle word about the church's leadership.

A consideration of the Lord's return should cause believers to acknowledge spiritual leaders. These leaders should be recognized as shepherds, who not only work "among" us, but are also "over" us. This attitude requires active involvement in a local church and submission to the leaders God has placed there.

Believers should also appreciate spiritual leaders. As the world grows darker and ministry becomes more challenging, leaders need encouragement. One way to "esteem them very highly" is by simple faithfulness. No words, notes, or pats on the back will ever fully compensate for old-fashioned faithfulness to the Lord's work.

Finally, Christians should assist spiritual leaders. Remember all of this is considering the return of Jesus. How should you respond to this glorious truth? Help leaders in their work. And do so peaceably. Teach a class. Give a gift. Fulfill your service. Find a ministry.

*Jesus, help me today to live and serve considering Your imminent return. Thank You for the spiritual leaders You have given me. Help me support their work with respect, honor, and faithfulness, amen.*

Mike Stone, Emmanuel Baptist Church, Blackshear, GA

# WEEK 43—TUESDAY
## *The Center of God's Will*

*Rejoice always, pray without ceasing, in everything give thanks; for this is the will of God in Christ Jesus for you.*

1 THESSALONIANS 5:16–18

M ost pastors say that the number-one question they hear deals with finding the will of God. It may be a single adult praying for a spouse or a high school senior praying about a career. It may be a senior adult praying about long-term care for his or her spouse or a young couple praying about buying their first home. But believers of all ages often find the will of God to be seemingly elusive.

In times like these the words of an old preacher are very helpful: "When you don't know what to say, say what you know to say. And when you don't know what to do, do what you know to do." The apostle Paul would have said "Amen" to this. In three short, power-packed verses, Paul reminds us that three things are always the will of God: praise, prayer, and gratitude.

Never will a time arise when it is out of the will of God to lift praise, voice a prayer, or express gratitude. Praise Him for who He is. Pray to Him in humility and present the requests of the day. Thank Him for what He has already done. This is God's will for each of His children today!

......................................................................................................

*Lord, I don't know what this season of my life holds. But whatever crossroads I face, I choose to live a life of praise, prayer, and gratitude. I will rejoice in all You are today. I will bring my needs to You in prayer. And I will glorify You for Your many deeds of faithfulness to me in the past, amen.*

# WEEK 43—WEDNESDAY
## Head, Heart, and Hands

*As I urged you when I went into Macedonia—remain in Ephesus that you may charge some that they teach no other doctrine . . . Now the purpose of the commandment is love from a pure heart, from a good conscience, and from sincere faith.*

1 TIMOTHY 1:3, 5

When Paul left Timothy in charge of the Ephesian church, he gave specific instructions to the young pastor. In one of the sternest passages of the Bible dealing with false teachers, the apostle reveals both the importance and the aim of sound doctrine.

Paul did not advocate sound doctrine merely for the sake of intellect and knowledge. Rather he knew the accurate teaching of God's Word would lead to right behavior and heartfelt worship of Jesus.

Spirit-led Bible study should never stay in the head. The purpose of learning sound doctrine is that we would know God more completely, love God more supremely, and obey God more faithfully. True doctrine is loved with the heart and lived with the hands!

Jesus often rebuked the scribes and Pharisees for what might be called "lifeless study." Even though they studied the Scriptures looking for eternal life, the One to whom those Scriptures pointed stood in their very midst, and they did not recognize Him. May God protect His people from orthodoxy that fills the mind with facts without warming the heart with truth.

. . . . . . . . . . . . . . . . . . . . . . . . . . . . . . . . . . . . . . . . . . . . . . . . . . . . . . . . . . . . . . . . . . . . .

*Father, may my pursuit of Your perfect Word always be a pursuit of Your perfect Son. And may the knowledge of Your truth cause me to love Jesus more passionately and follow Him more closely, amen.*

Mike Stone, Emmanuel Baptist Church, Blackshear, GA

# WEEK 43—THURSDAY
## *Thank God for the Bridge*

*Who desires all men to be saved and to come to the knowledge of the truth. For there is one God and one Mediator between God and men, the Man Christ Jesus, who gave Himself a ransom for all, to be testified in due time.*

1 TIMOTHY 2:4–6

The story is told of two men standing beside a road holding a sign that read, "Turn around before it's too late!" One driver went by in a truck, assumed they were gospel preachers, and yelled profanities at them. In a moment the men heard screeching brakes and a loud splash. One turned to the other and asked, "Do you think we should change the sign just to say that the old bridge is out?"

Paul's image of Jesus as the Mediator is a reminder that our sin has separated us from God. We need someone who can "bridge the gap" and reconcile us to God. There is no other bridge, no other go-between, no other mediator except Jesus Christ.

A safe bridge must be able to rest firmly on both sides of the divide. When it comes to the chasm that exists between God and men, only one person can grab hold of the bank of humanity and the bank of deity and bridge the gap between them. That person is the God-Man, Jesus Christ.

As we share the gospel of Jesus, we simply testify of this truth: There is eternal danger ahead, and all other bridges are out except for Jesus.

........................................................................................

*Father, Your Word says You desire all men to be saved. Use me today to speak Your truth and share Your gospel with someone who needs to know that Your Son, Jesus, can reconcile a sinner to You, amen.*

# WEEK 43—FRIDAY

*Who's Your Timothy?*

*You therefore, my son, be strong in the grace that is in Christ Jesus. And the things that you have heard from me among many witnesses, commit these to faithful men who will be able to teach others also. You therefore must endure hardship as a good soldier of Jesus Christ.*

2 TIMOTHY 2:1–3

As Paul wrote his final letter, he knew death was near. While his farewell was technically in chapter four, this entire letter to Timothy is rightly viewed as "parting words." Paul, ever the teacher, seemed concerned that the work of the gospel continued after his own death. He instinctively knew that the work of Jesus was, in human terms, always one generation away from extinction.

Paul's inspired plan was not merely to raise up a new generation (singular) of leadership. He wanted to see Timothy raise up multiple generations of Christ followers. The plan laid out in this text envisions four levels of Christian mentorship: Paul, Timothy, faithful men, and others.

God's plan is still that His children sit at the feet of mature disciples to learn, and then stand before less mature believers to teach. This learning and teaching is not necessarily in a formal classroom setting. Rather it is a God-ordained system that is to exist in the everyday life of a Jesus follower.

Even the great apostle Paul needed a Barnabas in his life. Paul in turn invested in Timothy. As a result Timothy was to pour his life into others. God's plan has not changed.

........................................................................................

*Lord, guide me into relationships in which I can both learn and teach the wonderful truths of Your Word, amen.*

Mike Stone, Emmanuel Baptist Church, Blackshear, GA

# WEEK 43—WEEKEND

*Running the Christian Race*

*And also if anyone competes in athletics, he is not crowned unless he competes according to the rules. The hardworking farmer must be first to partake of the crops. Consider what I say, and may the Lord give you understanding in all things.*

2 TIMOTHY 2:5–7

Having compared Timothy's ministry to being a teacher and a soldier (2 Timothy 2:2–4), Paul now compares it to being an athlete. The Greek games were ancient athletic contests that were popular. There were basic requirements to win a crown, and each of them has a point of application for a Christ follower.

The first requirement involved being a natural-born Greek. In the case of the Christian life, we would call it rebirth. Our first birth was into the sin nature. To be eligible for the crown of righteousness, a person must be born again.

The birth requirement was not all that was necessary "according to the rules." A Greek athlete had to run the race, which required preparation and training. To be successful athletes as believers, Christians must embrace the disciplines of prayer, Bible study, witnessing, and more.

Finally, the Greek athlete had to compete within the established guidelines. He could not step out of bounds or break the rules. A good athlete is marked not only by what he does but what he doesn't do. Similarly, if we are to run the Christian race, we must embrace godliness and shun the practices of disobedience and sin.

*Father, I thank You for the rebirth that put me on Your divine team. Help me to run this day with discipline and devotion for Your honor and glory, amen.*

# Week 44—Monday
*Approved Workers*

*Be diligent to present yourself approved to God, a worker who does not need to be ashamed, rightly dividing the word of truth. But shun profane and idle babblings, for they will increase to more ungodliness.*

2 Timothy 2:15–16

I f we are going to be used of God to reach others, we must be "approved" workers who are not ashamed because we correctly handle "the word of truth." The phrase "approved workers" speaks of craftsmen who are gifted and dedicated to doing excellent work.

Let me illustrate. A friend asked me to recommend a good mechanic because his car was having problems. I didn't hesitate—I was glad to mention a mechanic. The shop owner is a friend of mine, and I have gotten to know him well over the years. I do not use his shop because of our friendship, rather I keep going back because of the high quality of service. As far as I am concerned, my friend is an "approved worker" who does not need to be ashamed because he correctly handles the cars that come into his shop.

Likewise, those who serve the Lord must take care in the way they handle the Word of God. In verse fifteen, the phrase reads "rightly dividing." This speaks of making a straight path. We must not use the Word of God to support a pet theory or our own ideas, but we must follow the true teaching of the Word of God, making it the straight pattern for life. This involves knowing the Word and being able to explain it accurately to others.

*Father, thank You for Your Word that makes my pathway straight. As one who desires to be used by You, help me to take great care in how I handle the Word of truth, amen.*

Dr. Steven L. Kyle, Hiland Park Baptist Church, Panama City, FL

# Week 44—Tuesday
## Don't Let Them Get Under Your Skin!

*And a servant of the Lord must not quarrel but be gentle to all, able to teach, patient,*
*in humility correcting those who are in opposition, if God perhaps will grant them*
*repentance, so that they may know the truth.*

2 Timothy 2:24–25

Most of us know people who seem to have the "gift" of getting under our skin. Paul's advice is simple but not always easy to follow: Don't let them do it! We shouldn't let people get us riled up so we lose our cool and say things we shouldn't say.

We are not permitted to yell back at those who yell at us. We are not to curse at those who curse at us. We are not to intimidate those who try to intimidate us. In short, we are not to match the tactics of those who may oppose us and ridicule our faith. We must keep our cool at all cost.

One reason for this is very practical: we can't argue a person into the kingdom of God. We can't insult them into becoming a Christian. We can't intimidate them into accepting Christ as Savior. It is quite possible though to argue them away from the kingdom. Therefore, we must be gentle even when pushed to the limit. We must be patient toward those who oppose us, and we must with meekness tell them the truth. If we lose our temper, we may win the verbal battle, but we will surely lose the war for the soul.

*Heavenly Father, thank You for loving me unconditionally. Please help me to love others that way too. I ask the Holy Spirit to create in me a heart of compassion and forgiveness toward others. May my answers to opposition always be gentle in spirit, amen.*

# WEEK 44—WEDNESDAY

## *"Thus Saith the Lord!"*

*I charge you therefore before God and the Lord Jesus Christ, who will judge the living and the dead at His appearing and His kingdom: Preach the word! Be ready in season and out of season. Convince, rebuke, exhort, with all longsuffering and teaching. For the time will come when they will not endure sound doctrine, but according to their own desires, because they have itching ears, they will heap up for themselves teachers.*

2 TIMOTHY 4:1–3

To preach means to stand as a herald on the street corner. When a king wanted to send an important announcement to his subjects, he sent heralds who scattered across the kingdom, declaring the king's message. They went to every corner, every city gate, and every public marketplace, announcing the king's message. The herald had one responsibility—he was to announce only what the king told him to announce. He was not free to add or subtract or to summarize the king's message. He was not permitted to add his own opinions.

In this sense, to preach means to declare the truth of God authoritatively. That's why Luther and Calvin said that when the preacher truly preaches the Word of God, what the preacher says is what God says. That's right—as long as the preacher truly is preaching God's Word and not his own opinions.

We are to "preach the word"—not preach our ideas or preach our theories or preach our analysis of current events or preach the latest hot gossip. And we are not to preach *a* word, but *the* Word, the Word of the living God. We are to stand and declare to an unbelieving world, "Thus saith the Lord!"

..............................................................................

*Lord, please help me to proclaim Your Word boldly to a world that desperately needs inerrant truth, amen.*

Dr. Steven L. Kyle, Hiland Park Baptist Church, Panama City, FL

# WEEK 44—THURSDAY

*An Honest Day's Work*

*Exhort bondservants to be obedient to their own masters, to be well pleasing in all things, not answering back, not pilfering, but showing all good fidelity, that they may adorn the doctrine of God our Savior in all things.*

TITUS 2:9–10

I n the early church were many slaves. We don't have slaves in our American culture today, but we do have employees. Paul's words here apply to the modern workplace. Christian workers should faithfully submit to their bosses without grumbling or complaining.

Many a worker who professes Christ as Lord has griped about his boss to others on the job. Instead he should honor his boss as one to whom God has given authority and give an "honest day's work for an honest day's wage." Companies lose millions of dollars a year from employees who steal from them, everything from pencils and paper clips to bogus sick days. "I've earned it!" is no excuse. Neither is "Well, they owe it to me!"

Paul gives a great reason why Christian employees should be trustworthy or display "all good fidelity." He says, "That they may adorn the doctrine of God our Savior in all things." When we serve faithfully and respond differently from those employees who do not know Christ, we make the message of Jesus Christ more attractive to unbelievers. When we do a good job, we glorify the One who gave His life for us.

........................................................................

*Living God, thank You for being so faithful to provide daily for my needs. I ask You to guide me as I seek to honor You in all that my hands touch. I pray I will always be reminded that as a Christ follower I should approach all my work as though I am doing it for You, amen.*

# Week 44—Friday
## Praise God! I'm Not What I Once Was!

*For we ourselves were also once foolish, disobedient, deceived, serving various lusts and pleasures, living in malice and envy, hateful and hating one another. But when the kindness and the love of God our Savior toward man appeared, not by works of righteousness which we have done, but according to His mercy He saved us, through the washing of regeneration and renewing of the Holy Spirit.*

TITUS 3:3–5

John Newton was once a slave ship captain who was gloriously saved and penned the great hymn "Amazing Grace." He once wrote, "I am not what I ought to be, I am not what I want to be, I am not what I hope to be in another world; but still I am not what I once used to be, and by the grace of God I am what I am." This quote is a perfect summation of Titus 3.

Titus gives us a picture of how we were before we came to know Christ. We were once totally opposed to God. No work we have done has delivered us from our previous sinful selves, "but according to His mercy He saved us."

Becoming a Christian doesn't mean that you will turn over a new leaf; otherwise, you will find yourself writing the same things on the other side of the leaf. God extends His rich mercy to you. Through His mercy He washes and regenerates you through the power of the Holy Spirit. You are a new person in Jesus Christ.

......................................................................................................

*Father, thank You for Your salvation through Jesus. I praise You today for continuing the good work in me that You started when I came to saving faith. I pray I will be a glorious example of Your work of grace, amen.*

Dr. Steven L. Kyle, Hiland Park Baptist Church, Panama City, FL

# WEEK 44—WEEKEND
## *Streams of Grace*

*Whom He poured out on us abundantly through Jesus Christ our Savior, that having been justified by His grace we should become heirs according to the hope of eternal life.*

TITUS 3:6–7

I like the word *pour*. The word doesn't make me think of one who measurably trickles a liquid, but instead a picture of one lavishly cascading a stream of abundance.

In Titus 3, Paul reminds us God "poured out" His grace on us through Jesus. This flood of grace brought about our salvation in Christ. What is the goal of salvation? Why did God save us? Look at the end of verse seven: that "we should become heirs according to the hope of eternal life." Instead of living in the fear of death, the fear of hell, the fear of eternal punishment, and under the power of sin, we might be heirs of eternal life and live in the hope of heaven. In other words, He rescues us to change our eternal destinies and to fill our hearts with hope instead of dread.

God saved us, as Paul says in Romans 8:17, to make us "heirs of God and joint heirs with Christ." To give to us, as Peter says in 1 Peter 1:4, "an inheritance incorruptible and undefiled and that does not fade away, reserved in heaven for [us]." He saved us from the consequence of sin and the place of eternal death. We find hope in this knowledge of salvation.

......................................................................................................

*Lord, thank You for loving me the way You do and not the way I deserve. Thank You for Your grace that not only saves me, but makes me an heir with Christ and gives me hope for heaven, amen.*

# WEEK 45—MONDAY
## Not Ashamed

*For it was fitting for Him, for whom are all things and by whom are all things, in bringing many sons to glory, to make the captain of their salvation perfect through sufferings. For both He who sanctifies and those who are being sanctified are all of one, for which reason He is not ashamed to call them brethren.*

HEBREWS 2:10–11

I f we are followers of Jesus Christ, we have probably heard the scriptural admonition to be unashamed of the gospel of Jesus Christ (Romans 1:16). As Christ followers we should certainly be willing to proclaim boldly the truth and the hope of the good news. These verses in Hebrews, however, remind us of another scriptural truth: God is not ashamed of us.

Let that sink in. The God of the universe, the Creator of all that is, the One for whom and by whom all things exist, cares so much about you that He was not ashamed to become like you.

At the heart of the gospel is this central truth: God loves you so much that He became like you so you might become His. As this week begins take a moment to reflect on the love of the "captain of [your] salvation." God will never love you more than He has already loved you in Jesus, and as hard as it is to believe, God could never love you less than He does today.

God is not ashamed to call you His. Can you call Him yours?

......................................................................................................

*Heavenly Father, thank You for allowing me to begin another week of life. As I reflect on Your unashamed love for me, I commit to live unashamedly for You. In Jesus' name, amen.*

Paul Purvis, First Baptist Church of Temple Terrace, Temple Terrace, FL

# WEEK 45—TUESDAY
## *The Anchor Holds*

*This hope we have as an anchor of the soul, both sure and steadfast, and which enters the Presence behind the veil, where the forerunner has entered for us, even Jesus, having become High Priest forever according to the order of Melchizedek.*

HEBREWS 6:19–20

I n this world you will have trouble. That's not a prophecy—that's a promise. The words of Jesus in John 16:33 remind us that things will get difficult in this world on this side of heaven, but Jesus reminds us that our hope is in Him and not in this world.

The writer of Hebrews speaks of that hope as "an anchor of the soul, both sure and steadfast." Has Jesus become the anchor of your soul?

We are tempted to put our trust in so many unreliable anchors. Sometimes relationships become our anchors. At other times resources become an anchor, and all too often we rely on our own strength to hold us steady during life's troubling storms. But all those anchors fail.

Take time to renew your trust in the one true anchor for your soul. Meditate on God's Word, and find your sure and steadfast rest in Jesus today.

.........................................................................................................

*Thank you, Jesus, the captain of my salvation, for being an anchor for my soul this day and every day, amen.*

# WEEK 45—WEDNESDAY
## He Is Able

*But He, because He continues forever, has an unchangeable priesthood. Therefore He is also able to save to the uttermost those who come to God through Him, since He always lives to make intercession for them.*

HEBREWS 7:24–25

Scripture constantly reminds us that nothing is impossible with God (Matthew 19:26; Luke 1:37; Philippians 4:13). Nevertheless, most of us find ourselves doubting, or at the very least, failing to depend upon His sufficiency. This passage reminds us that since God can do that which only He can do, "save to the uttermost," He is certainly able to meet our every need for His glory.

Take time today to preach the truth of the gospel to yourself. If God can "save to the uttermost," He is able to handle anything in your life. The power of the gospel means that God can transform your relationships, your finances, your emotional health, and every other thing in your life.

What are you facing today that can only be overcome by Jesus through the power of the gospel? As you think about your needs, any overwhelming circumstances, the difficult situations you face, rest in this truth: "He is able!"

*God, I know that You are able. I trust You to handle that which I can't handle today. In Jesus' name, amen.*

Paul Purvis, First Baptist Church of Temple Terrace, Temple Terrace, FL

# WEEK 45—THURSDAY

*Power in the Blood*

*How much more shall the blood of Christ, who through the eternal Spirit offered Himself without spot to God, cleanse your conscience from dead works to serve the living God? And for this reason He is the Mediator of the new covenant, by means of death, for the redemption of the transgressions under the first covenant, that those who are called may receive the promise of the eternal inheritance.*

HEBREWS 9:14–15

Have you ever had a stain that was hard to get out? Have you ever been so dirty that you had difficulty getting clean?

The Bible teaches sin stains the inner beings of our humanity. We are not sinners simply because of what we do; rather we are sinners because of who we are. Our very nature is marked with sin. Even our conscience needs to be cleansed; and on our own, we will never experience the cleansing we desire nor the cleansing we need.

But we try. We try religion. We try rituals. We even try to make things right on our own.

And we fail.

When we reach this point of failure and desperation, we can understand the power of the blood of Christ. The blood of Jesus gives us a deep cleansing. The Spirit of God goes below the surface, beneath the outer person, into our very conscience where our guilt resides, and He cleanses us.

......................................................................................................

*Jesus, thank You for shedding Your blood for the redemption of my sin, amen.*

# WEEK 45—FRIDAY

## A Divine Appointment

*And as it is appointed for men to die once, but after this the judgment, so Christ was offered once to bear the sins of many. To those who eagerly wait for Him He will appear a second time, apart from sin, for salvation.*

HEBREWS 9:27–28

On February 21, 2018, international media reported the death of Dr. Billy Graham. After nearly one hundred years of life on earth, the famed evangelist entered his eternal reward. Upon his death, many people quoted Graham's well-known adaptation of Dwight L. Moody's words:

"Someday you will read or hear that Billy Graham is dead. Don't you believe a word of it. I shall be more alive than I am now. I will just have changed my address. I will have gone into the presence of God." [8]

Dr. Graham understood the biblical principle taught in Hebrews 9:27: death is an appointment every man or woman must keep, but death is not the end. After death we will give an account for this life, and we will spend eternity somewhere.

God's Word teaches that Jesus the Christ died "to bear the sins of many," so we could spend eternity with Him in heaven. However, to be ready on that day, we must ensure that we have trusted Christ.

........................................................................................

*Jesus, I understand that You paid the price for my sins. I trust You this day to prepare me for that day, amen.*

Paul Purvis, First Baptist Church of Temple Terrace, Temple Terrace, FL

# WEEK 45—WEEKEND
## *You Can Trust Him*

*Let us hold fast the confession of our hope without wavering, for He who promised is faithful. And let us consider one another in order to stir up love and good works, not forsaking the assembling of ourselves together, as is the manner of some, but exhorting one another, and so much the more as you see the Day approaching.*

HEBREWS 10:23–25

A s you end this week, think about these words: "He who promised is faithful." Nothing you have faced, nothing you are facing, and nothing you will face is too great for His faithfulness, because great is His faithfulness.

Don't ever forget that simple truth. He is faithful. In your pain—He is faithful. In your fears—He is faithful. In your trials—He is faithful. In your sorrow—He is faithful. In your uncertainty—He is faithful. In a world of unfaithfulness—He is faithful.

So trust Him. Hold fast to the truth of His faithfulness, the confession of your hope, and do not waver. You will have those days when the waves of doubt sweep over you, and you begin to question His faithfulness. You may even encounter seasons in which you wonder about His presence. That's why Christians need one another. That's why believers must come together. Set aside time this weekend to gather with other Christ followers and encourage one another in His faithfulness. You won't regret it, and He will be faithful.

..........................................................................................................

*Dear heavenly Father, "Great is Thy faithfulness! Great is Thy faithfulness! Morning by morning new mercies I see. All I have needed Thy hand hath provided. Great is Thy faithfulness, Lord, unto me!" Amen.*

# Week 46—Monday
*Don't Quit!*

*Therefore do not cast away your confidence, which has great reward. For you have need of endurance, so that after you have done the will of God, you may receive the promise.*

HEBREWS 10:35–36

My wife's favorite movie is *The Count of Monte Cristo*. In an unforgettable scene, Edmond Dantès sits alone in his prison cell at the infamous Château d'If, when suddenly he sees an old priest, Abbé Faria, come bursting through the floor. Faria spent years digging an escape tunnel, but made an unfortunate miscalculation that placed him in the middle of Dantès' cell instead of outside the prison compound as he had hoped. Instead of abandoning his escape plan and getting discouraged, Faria solicits Dantès' help, and together they mastermind an impressive prison break. Faria and Dantès provide an inspiring example of what it looks like to remain confident despite very real adversity.

Does life have you on the ropes? Do you ever feel imprisoned by fear, despair, loneliness, or unmet expectations? The author of Hebrews encourages you to remain confident in the face of the fiery trials. Of course, quitting often feels easier. But quitting isn't for Christians because Christ persevered all the way to the cross. Be encouraged today, for victory is on the other side of your trial. Persevere in the power of Christ your Savior. He knows exactly where you are. Your reward is in His hands!

........................................................................................

*Dear Father, enable me to persevere. Help me to remember You when I am tempted to quit. I trust You to finish the work You have begun. In Jesus' name, amen.*

Rev. Jeremy Morton, Cartersville First Baptist Church, Cartersville, GA

## *Time to Grow Up*

*By faith Moses, when he became of age, refused to be called the son of Pharaoh's daughter, choosing rather to suffer affliction with the people of God than to enjoy the passing pleasures of sin, esteeming the reproach of Christ greater riches than the treasures in Egypt; for he looked to the reward.*

HEBREWS 11:24–26

Today's passage mentions "Moses, when he became of age." Like most people prior to adulthood, Moses had little opportunity to decide things for himself. It was Moses' parents who protected him in infancy from the wicked Pharaoh's genocide against babies (Exodus 1–2). It was his mother's idea to hide Moses in a basket coated with pitch and courageously set him afloat on the Nile River while his sister, Miriam, kept watch. It was Pharaoh's daughter who adopted Moses and raised him in the palace with all the access to Pharaoh's luxury. But when Moses became of age, he had to decide for himself who he was, what he believed, and how he would live.

That day inevitably comes for all of us. Joshua said, "Choose for yourselves this day whom you will serve" (Joshua 24:15). Moses had the correct vision for his life. He knew deep in his heart that his worst day of suffering as a child of God was far better than his best day outside the will of God.

Where are you today? Are you willing to walk away from what the world defines as success? By faith, Moses saw that obedience to God is the real substance of success.

.........................................................................................................

*Heavenly Father, give me eyes to see Your calling for my life. Help me to treasure You with all my heart. I ask this in the name of Jesus, amen.*

# Week 46—Wednesday

*Run with Endurance*

*Therefore we also, since we are surrounded by so great a cloud of witnesses, let us lay aside every weight, and the sin which so easily ensnares us, and let us run with endurance the race that is set before us, looking unto Jesus.*

Hebrews 12:1

The sun was setting and only a few thousand people remained in the stadium at the 1968 Olympics in Mexico City as John Stephen Akhwari of Tanzania limped across the finish line of the marathon—more than an hour behind the winner. He had cramped up and been badly injured during the race. When asked why he didn't just drop out of the long-distance run, Akhwari said, "My country did not send me five thousand miles to start the race. They sent me to finish the race." [9]

The list of faith heroes in Hebrews 11 serves as motivation for today's believer to run the race for Christ and finish well. How can we run effectively? By eliminating everything that slows us down or distracts us. Just as a long-distance runner removes all unnecessary weight, believers must look to Christ and trust Him to eliminate the things that hold them back from fulfilling God's calling.

Today what needs to be discarded from your life? A cynical attitude? A bad habit? A toxic relationship? You need the Holy Spirit to help you keep your eyes on Christ, run hard, and finish well.

........................................................................................

*Dear God, I cannot run today's race without Your strength. I lean on You, Holy Spirit, to guide my every step. Amen.*

Rev. Jeremy Morton, Cartersville First Baptist Church, Cartersville, GA

# Week 46—Thursday
## Pain Serves a Purpose

*If you endure chastening, God deals with you as with sons; for what son is there whom a father does not chasten? . . . Now no chastening seems to be joyful for the present, but painful; nevertheless, afterward it yields the peaceable fruit of righteousness to those who have been trained by it.*

HEBREWS 12:7, 11

When parents take their child to visit the doctor, the typical questions on the child's mind go something like this, "Is this going to hurt? Do I have to get a shot?" No one looks forward to pain and suffering. We usually take drastic measures to avoid pain at all costs.

However, today's passage reminds us that the process of pain or discipline can be beneficial. Just as no reasonable parent would allow the doctor to inflict unnecessary pain on his or her child, our heavenly Father watches over our lives with tender compassion. This does not mean life is always easy or painless. To the contrary, the painful seasons most often cause our faith to grow.

Can a parent expect good behavior without disciplining the child? Can an athlete expect to remain fit without exercise? Can a vine continue to produce fruit without pruning? Of course not! Nor can we become healthy, mature followers of Christ without our heavenly Father's tender rebukes.

God allows pain and discipline in our lives because He loves us, and He knows what we must endure to keep growing into Christlikeness.

*Heavenly Father, please grant me a teachable spirit. I want to receive Your discipline with a humble heart, so I might continue to grow. In Jesus' name, amen.*

# WEEK 46—FRIDAY

*Christ Is Our Contentment*

*Let your conduct be without covetousness; be content with such things as you have. For He Himself has said, "I will never leave you nor forsake you." So we may boldly say: "The LORD is my helper; I will not fear. What can man do to me?"*

HEBREWS 13:5–6

As a comedian, Jim Carrey is one of the most successful actors in American film. He is a recipient of numerous honors. Carrey has earned millions of dollars for his work in comedy and film. Which makes it even more sobering to consider Carrey's recent comment on being rich and famous, "I think everybody should get rich and famous and do everything they ever dreamed of so they can see that it's not the answer." [10]

Though known for his humor, Carrey's statement about money and success is insightful. We struggle with covetousness—desiring possessions that do not belong to us—since Adam and Eve lusted after the one tree God forbade in Eden.

We are obsessed with money, success, large homes, fast cars, and luxury clothes. Followers of Christ must ask, "What do I most desire for my life?" The truth is, through Christ, we have all we could ever need and more. Christ can do exceedingly, abundantly more than we could ever imagine (Ephesians 3:20). Christ is our sufficiency, and He is the secret to contentment.

*Dear God, in a world known for materialism and greed, please help me to live generously, simply, and with contentment. Set me free of covetousness. For Christ's sake, amen.*

Rev. Jeremy Morton, Cartersville First Baptist Church, Cartersville, GA

# Week 46—Weekend
## *Rejoice in God's Plan*

*My brethren, count it all joy when you fall into various trials, knowing that the testing of your faith produces patience. But let patience have its perfect work, that you may be perfect and complete, lacking nothing.*

JAMES 1:2–4

Joni Eareckson Tada is a bright light for Christ. At age seventeen, Joni was severely injured in a diving accident that resulted with her becoming a quadriplegic in a wheelchair. As tragic as Joni's accident was, it was the beginning of a deep work of grace in her life. Through her injury and God's obvious hand of power upon her, Joni has turned her captivating ability as a Christian speaker into a platform to accelerate ministry in the disability community and also to do missionary work all over the world.

Think of the daily struggles for those with physical disabilities. What some might consider ordinary, mundane tasks present many challenges to individuals such as Joni. But Joni has chosen to count it all joy! Obviously, being joyous when pain afflicts us isn't natural, but it is supernatural when we step back and trust God. We don't rejoice over pain. But we rejoice that our sovereign God in heaven can use every circumstance in life for a divine purpose that glorifies His name and strengthens our character (Romans 8:28).

Are you going through a storm? Instead of cursing the storm, ask God to reveal what He intends to teach you. Ask God to make you a joyous, shining testimony. God doesn't waste your pain. He uses it!

.............................................................................

*Heavenly Father, help me to rejoice in You in every situation. Conform my character to Christ by the power of the Holy Spirit. Use me, Lord! Amen.*

# WEEK 47—MONDAY

*Accessible Answers*

*If any of you lacks wisdom, let him ask of God, who gives to all liberally and without reproach, and it will be given to him. But let him ask in faith, with no doubting, for he who doubts is like a wave of the sea driven and tossed by the wind. For let not that man suppose that he will receive anything from the Lord.*

JAMES 1:5–7

The whole counsel of God says wisdom is both essential and accessible. While this passage emphasizes how we access wisdom, it does so with an underlying assertion that drives the quest. Before we unpack keys to unlock wisdom's treasures, we must first esteem it as valuable, for no man asks for a thing until he is convinced he needs it.

But just because something is essential doesn't mean it is easy to access. After all, one of the most deflating things in life is to long for something we never obtain.

In this passage we find wisdom is attainable. We shout for joy. Our text emphasizes two postures required for finding heavenly insight: humility and faith. Humility is a prerequisite, for we must believe we need God's wisdom and be willing to admit we are not self-sufficient. Admitting our need and our inability to solve problems alone is humbling. Once we hit our knees we must grab hold of faith, trusting that the One from whom we ask can indeed answer.

...................................................................................................

*Father God, I know You are the One who is maker of heaven and earth, and You can grant me the insight I need. Please provide me the wisdom for life's challenging questions, making the answers accessible, amen.*

Micah McElveen, Vapor Ministries, VaporMinistries.org

# WEEK 47—TUESDAY
## *Well Off*

*Let the lowly brother glory in his exaltation, but the rich in his humiliation, because as a flower of the field he will pass away. For no sooner has the sun risen with a burning heat than it withers the grass; its flower falls, and its beautiful appearance perishes. So the rich man also will fade away in his pursuits.*

JAMES 1:9–11

James reminds us of a pragmatic truth: a materially poor brother is less tempted to find his security in money because he doesn't have any money in the first place. His position causes him to look for assistance outside himself. The humility needed to acknowledge one's need for help and to seek it from God comes more naturally to him.

On the other hand, the rich person is tempted to lean on his savings and trust in his earning potential instead of truly resting in God's provision. Money for the rich is often elevated to a place of worship, used outside of God's intended purposes, and held over the heads of those in need. While mammon can prop a man up for a season, it cannot satisfy or save a soul.

One day soon that false god, whose reliable persona lures so many, will wither like winter rye in the summer heat, and all who idolize it will wilt. Many once proud and wealthy will kneel in the ashes of their god, filled with acute humiliation. Next to them the poor, who looked to Jesus, will stand exalting in the hope of glory.

.............................................................................................

*Wake me up, Lord. Help me trust You more and steward your resources in line with Your desires. Help me love, serve, and learn from the poor. Grant me heaven's perspective on how to live truly well off, amen.*

# WEEK 47—WEDNESDAY

*Home, Not Heaven*

*Blessed is the man who endures temptation; for when he has been approved, he will receive the crown of life which the Lord has promised to those who love Him. Let no one say when he is tempted, "I am tempted by God"; for God cannot be tempted by evil, nor does He Himself tempt anyone.*

JAMES 1:12–13

T he primary temptation James instructs us to "endure" is the one he talked about in the verses immediately preceding—the temptation to allow material goods to take an improper place in our lives. Not only do we tend to worship money, use funds for selfish ends, and hoard resources intended for God's work, but we are tempted to blame the money rather than our use of it. The disease infecting our first parents, blame-shift sickness, is a virus now universally contracted.

James responds to those who blame God for their giving into temptations with three important truths: God is impervious to evil and does not tempt anyone with sin. Temptation comes from our lust to have our way over God's. God grants endurance and reward to those who turn from evil to Him.

The fight against evil requires a commitment to truth and reliance on grace, and it comes with a reward for the steadfast. In Christ alone lies the truth and grace needed for salvation and the endurance leading to eternal rewards.

........................................................................................

*Lord, help me to see myself in the light of truth, confess where I fail, and endure in the grace found through Christ's gospel, amen.*

Micah McElveen, Vapor Ministries, VaporMinistries.org

# Week 47—Thursday
## *All-Good*

*Do not be deceived, my beloved brethren. Every good gift and every perfect gift is from above, and comes down from the Father of lights, with whom there is no variation or shadow of turning. Of His own will He brought us forth by the word of truth, that we might be a kind of firstfruits of His creatures.*

JAMES 1:16–18

Having previously reminded us that God tempts no man with evil, James exhorts us to guard our minds against lies. The liar would not only have us believe falsehoods about God but would also keep us from knowing good truths about our heavenly Father. In that vein, James reminds us that God is not just void of evil—our matchless Lord is entirely perfect. Furthermore, God is not only all-good, but all good comes from God. Think on that. Every good thing that exists originated in God.

Our text reminds us the majestic heavenly lights that grant energy and sustain life on our planet come from God. He goes on to note that the One who spoke the heavens into existence granted us the very Word of God. Having made Himself knowable through the Word, He then makes the connection that all who believe in Him are afforded a new birth and a special place among His creation. Indeed, we who were far off are adopted as children of God by the goodness of heaven. Now that is good news!

........................................................................................

*Father God, thank You that unlike human attempts at goodness, Your faithfulness and goodness are unwavering. Thank You that You are unchanging and the shadow that Your good form casts never varies, no matter the light of day. You indeed are all-good, amen.*

# WEEK 47—FRIDAY
## Faith with Feet

*What does it profit, my brethren, if someone says he has faith but does not have works? Can faith save him? If a brother or sister is naked and destitute of daily food, and one of you says to them, "Depart in peace, be warmed and filled," but you do not give them the things which are needed for the body, what does it profit? Thus also faith by itself, if it does not have works, is dead.*

JAMES 2:14–17

This passage implies two age-old issues. The first involves right thinking versus right doing. Some emphasize right doctrine, where it appears God would have our minds without our backs. Others emphasize right doing, where it would seem Jesus would have our hands without our heads.

The truth is we cannot work our way to a right standing with God. But to think God intended His people only to come to right conclusions is dead wrong and produces "dead faith." Head knowledge apart from action produces pride and leaves us bloated. James tells a chronically heady audience that they will miss Christ's way if they have faith statements on their walls that aren't lived out.

The second issue, while subtler, challenges the notion that we are to choose between caring for a person physically or spiritually. James reminds us that Christ asks Christians to care for both the body and soul, just as Christ does for us.

........................................................................................................

*Heavenly Father, as I walk through life, help me to remember both to meet needs and feed souls. Remind me that in the realm of King Jesus I build His kingdom by practicing faith with feet, amen.*

Micah McElveen, Vapor Ministries, VaporMinistries.org

# WEEK 47—WEEKEND
## *Happily Wed*

*Adulterers and adulteresses! Do you not know that friendship with the world is enmity with God? Whoever therefore wants to be a friend of the world makes himself an enemy of God. Or do you think that the Scripture says in vain, "The Spirit who dwells in us yearns jealously"?*

JAMES 4:4–5

We all have ambitions that flow from our hopes and desires. The first few verses in James 4 remind us that dissension in Christ's family chiefly flows from ungodly ambitions being pursued in ungodly ways. Like a hot knife through butter, verse four cuts to the chase. It effectively tells Christians: You are with me or you are against me. "Choose this day whom you will serve" (Joshua 24:15) . . . and if it is me, then love me exclusively and follow me wholeheartedly.

James uses language from the bedroom, reminding us that we sleep around on God when we choose the world over Him. He explains cheating creates division in the family and sows discord between us and God. He pulls from other verses, highlighting that God, like a good husband, has a zealous and jealous love for His bride. He reminds us that anyone who violates the intimacy meant between exclusive lovers becomes the enemy of the betrayed.

......................................................................................

*Father, help me to quit vacillating and embrace the hope of heaven, the desires of the lover of my soul. Help me to align myself with the ambitions of my bridegroom, Jesus Christ. Transform my will to Yours, my maker, Savior, and Lord, that we would walk in our union, happily wed, amen.*

# Week 48—Monday
*Draw Near to God*

*Submit to God. Resist the devil and he will flee from you. Draw near to God and He will draw near to you. Cleanse your hands, you sinners; and purify your hearts, you double-minded.*

JAMES 4:7–8

I n this passage James calls Christians to action. James starts off by saying we are to say yes to God's will. In humble submission we are to come under the authority of the One who is completely sovereign. We are to bend to God's will. This passage connects closely to the one before. James reminds his readers that submission to God is a cure for worldliness.

We are to take our stand against the evil one. In other words, we are to "resist" Satan. When we do, he will "flee" as a defeated foe. When believers draw near to God, they have the promise that God will draw near to them. Through the indwelling power and presence of the Holy Spirit, God is actively present in our lives.

James adds an injunction: "Cleanse your hands, you sinners; and purify your hearts, you double-minded." God does not work through dirty hands and hearts that are polluted from the world. We are not to cling to our own selfish desires and at the same time have a desire to please God—that's being double-minded.

However, when we follow each one of these imperatives, we can draw near to God, being assured He will draw near to us.

........................................................................................

*Dear Jesus, help me to say yes to Your will, and by Your power and presence, take a stand against the evil one. Thank You that when I confess my sins, I have the promise of Your forgiveness, amen.*

Dr. Christopher M. Webb, Ten Mile Center Baptist Church, Lumberton, NC

*Confess your trespasses to one another, and pray for one another, that you may be healed. The effective, fervent prayer of a righteous man avails much.*

JAMES 5:16

The main subject James addresses in this verse is prayer. The concept of prayer is demonstrated when a child of God makes a petition to an all-knowing, all-loving, and all-wise God. James informs his readers that Christians are to confess their sins to one another; Christians also are to pray for one another. Without confession of sins, prayer, and forgiveness, there will be no healing.

James provides an example in the next verse (5:17) by using the prophet Elijah. The prophet prayed that it would not rain and God heard his request (1 Kings 17:1). In using the prophet as an example, James explains how the prayer of the righteous has power. One should note that prayer points to God as the active agent: prayer is impactful because of God's response to it.

That's the reason Christ followers should abide by what James teaches in this verse. When we confess our sins to one another and pray for one another, God responds to our prayers. He hears the prayers of His children.

With a clear conscience and with boldness, let us always continue to pray.

...................................................................................................

*Father, thank You for the privilege and power of prayer, amen.*

# WEEK 48—WEDNESDAY

*Restore the Erring One*

*Brethren, if anyone among you wanders from the truth, and someone turns him back, let him know that he who turns a sinner from the error of his way will save a soul from death and cover a multitude of sins.*

JAMES 5:19–20

All believers have the potential to stumble and stray away from the truth. We must take heed to maintain a Christian character and conduct. Truth has to do with truthfulness in Christian conduct, not the correctness of Christian belief. The focus is more moral than intellectual.[11] Christians must have the understanding that all believers are accountable to one another. When someone errs from the truth, it is the responsibility of the Christian community out of love to come alongside the errant one and help restore him or her back into a faithful and fruitful fellowship with God.

Paul makes note: "Brethren, if a man is overtaken in any trespass, you who are spiritual restore such a one in a spirit of gentleness, considering yourself lest you also be tempted" (Galatians 6:1). James assures his readers of two truths: whosoever causes a sinner to listen to God again will rescue this sinner from death, and God will forgive the many sins of the one who has erred.

*Lord Jesus, empower me with Your Holy Spirit to help restore those who have erred from the truth. Thank You for the forgiveness You extend to those who will repent and turn back to You, amen.*

Dr. Christopher M. Webb, Ten Mile Center Baptist Church, Lumberton, NC

# WEEK 48—THURSDAY
## *We Have Hope*

*Blessed be the God and Father of our Lord Jesus Christ, who according to His abundant mercy has begotten us again to a living hope through the resurrection of Jesus Christ from the dead, to an inheritance incorruptible and undefiled and that does not fade away, reserved in heaven for you.*

1 PETER 1:3–4

God is a promise keeper. It is sad, but people often will say one thing and do another. Not God! Whatever He has said, He will do.

There are times we do not understand why we experience suffering, pain, and trials. But as born-again believers in Christ, we remember, rely, and rest in the hope we have in God. As Peter reminds his readers, the hope we place in God is "through the resurrection of Jesus Christ from the dead." Because Jesus lives, we are confident that regardless of what we experience, we have hope. The hope we have is not wishful thinking. We stand and live in the power, presence, and peace of the hope we have in God.

Peter experienced firsthand that God keeps His promises. Jesus said that He would be crucified, buried, and raised on the third day. This came true when Peter saw the resurrected Christ. He also heard Jesus say He would build His church, and in the book of Acts, Peter experienced the birth and expansion of the church. What Jesus said, He did.

Jesus is the same yesterday, today, and forever. This gives us hope!

........................................................................................................................

*Father, thank You for the hope I have in You. Because of Jesus, I live in the present and look toward the future, knowing what I have in Jesus will not fade away, amen.*

# Week 48—Friday

*A Precious Faith*

*That the genuineness of your faith, being much more precious than gold that perishes, though it is tested by fire, may be found to praise, honor, and glory at the revelation of Jesus Christ, whom having not seen you love. Though now you do not see Him, yet believing, you rejoice with joy inexpressible and full of glory.*

1 Peter 1:7–8

While Christianity is full of trials, tests, and temptations, as believers in Christ Jesus we are overwhelmed with great joy. As Christians, our faith will be tested. During our times of distress, like fire refines gold from its impurities, so will the trials do to our faith. When gold is melted in fire, the impurities float to the top and can be removed. When the refining fire is over, the gold is even more valuable.

So it is with our faith in God. The proof or "genuineness" of our faith is demonstrated when we experience the hard knocks of life and come out on the other side victorious. As Spurgeon once said, "Expect trial, also, because trial is the very element of faith. . . . Faith without trial is like an uncut diamond, the brilliance of which has never been seen. . . . What a fish would be without water, or a bird without air, that would be faith without trial."[12] If you have faith, you may surely expect that your faith will be tested.

...........................................................................................................

*Dear Father, I praise You for times of distress. Even though at times it is hard, I still rejoice in the precious faith You have extended to me. This faith refines me to become to Your very image, amen.*

Dr. Christopher M. Webb, Ten Mile Center Baptist Church, Lumberton, NC

# WEEK 48—WEEKEND
## *Ready for Battle*

*Therefore gird up the loins of your mind, be sober, and rest your hope fully upon the grace that is to be brought to you at the revelation of Jesus Christ; as obedient children, not conforming yourselves to the former lusts, as in your ignorance.*

1 PETER 1:13–14

As fully devoted Christ followers, we are called to action. We are called to stand firm, focused, and faithful in the truth of God's Word. When we have been touched by the truth, as Peter uses this metaphor to explain, we are called to right thinking that leads to godly actions and attitudes. We are called to live with self-control and to be alert morally. We are to have a fixed hope as we look forward with great expectation to our glorious future we have in Christ.

How are we able to live in such a way? Peter says God's grace, the unmerited favor of God, enables, empowers, and equips us for battle. In other words, His grace leads us to victorious living. Peter reminds his readers that because we have been touched by the truth, we are to live obedient lives. Now that we have been touched by the truth, we no longer live as we did before being saved.

Therefore, let us live in such a way that we are ready for action.

........................................................................................

*Father, thank You for Your saving and sustaining grace that empowers me to be ready for action. Thank You for the truth that is found in my knowing and growing in Your Son, the Lord Jesus Christ. For it is in His name I pray, amen.*

# WEEK 49—MONDAY
## *The Lost Doctrine of the Church*

*As He who called you is holy, you also be holy in all your conduct, because it is written, "Be holy, for I am holy."*

1 PETER 1:15–16

I t has been said, "Holiness is the lost doctrine of the church." Many professing believers put holiness on the bottom of the list of Christian virtues. This mindset leads to the loss of their gospel witness because of the lack of holiness.

Peter tells us that God is holy. Because God is holy, we as His children should be holy. Hebrews 12:14 teaches us that without holiness, no man will see God. How are sinners made holy? By repentance and faith in the Lord Jesus Christ. Only through the power of the Holy Spirit who indwells every believer can we be holy.

This type of life comes from the sanctifying power of God's Holy Spirit. Most little boys don't like to take baths, something that must be done daily to keep the "dirt crust" from growing. Bathing may not be fun, but it is necessary in order to live without becoming odious. Each of us must submit to God daily in absolute surrender, confessing and repenting of sin, or we will become odious and our lives will not be holy!

Come to God today and take a spiritual bath. You will be better for it, and you will influence others by your witness of the cleansing power of the blood of Jesus Christ!

..........................................................................................................

*Father, create in me a clean heart and fill me with your Holy Spirit. Enable me by Your Holy Spirit to live a holy life. In Jesus' name, amen.*

Dr. Dan Lanier, Northcrest Baptist Church, Meridian, MS

*Headed to Jesus*

*Beloved, I beg you as sojourners and pilgrims, abstain from fleshly lusts which war against the soul, having your conduct honorable among the Gentiles, that when they speak against you as evildoers, they may, by your good works which they observe, glorify God in the day of visitation.*

1 PETER 2:11–12

P eter says that the Christian life is a continual journey, not an experience. As Christians, we are to be moving forward continually. Our goal is not a place but a person: Jesus.

The Greek words that Peter uses for sojourners and pilgrims connote "a foreigner alongside." We are in this world but not of this world. We are just passing through this one. The issue for us today is this: Are we making a difference on this journey?

We are at war with the flesh, constantly battling the old man. Our lifestyles are to present a clear witness of the gospel of Jesus Christ to those whom we meet on this journey. Our works, the things that we say and do on this journey, should bring glory to God every day.

Get up, get moving, go forward! What are you going to do today that will bring glory to God?

........................................................................................

*Father, thank You for a new day on the journey that You have entrusted to me. Help me to be a good witness, to move forward in my faith and walk with You. Enable me by Your Holy Spirit to make a difference in someone's life today. In Jesus' name, amen.*

# WEEK 49—WEDNESDAY
## Polished and Shined

*For what credit is it if, when you are beaten for your faults, you take it patiently? But when you do good and suffer, if you take it patiently, this is commendable before God. For to this you were called, because Christ also suffered for us, leaving us an example, that you should follow His steps.*

1 PETER 2:20–21

A diamond is one of the hardest minerals on earth. A natural diamond forms under high temperatures and extreme pressure. To be used commercially, a diamond must be mined, cut, and then polished. It takes time, labor, and detail to get the finished product. After the process is completed, the resulting diamond radiates beauty.

This is also true for the Christian. God uses the heat and pressures of life to make us profitable for His kingdom. What sometimes hurts us may bring about the greatest healing. What we are going through today may be God's removing from our lives imperfections that don't bring glory to Jesus Christ. He polishes our lives to reflect the beauty of Christ. This process occurs as we daily submit to Him. Our reactions to the struggles of life speak volumes to those who do not know Christ. People are watching to see how we react, what we do, and what we say during the valleys.

Be submissive to the working of God today. He is polishing and shining you to look like Jesus!

..................................................................................................

*Father, help me to live surrendered to Your will today, amen.*

Dr. Dan Lanier, Northcrest Baptist Church, Meridian, MS

# WEEK 49—THURSDAY
## *Nothing but the Blood!*

*"Who committed no sin, nor was deceit found in His mouth"; who, when He was reviled, did not revile in return; when He suffered, He did not threaten, but committed Himself to Him who judges righteously; who Himself bore our sins in His own body on the tree, that we, having died to sins, might live for righteousness—by whose stripes you were healed.*

1 PETER 2:22–24

I love the old hymn "Nothing but the Blood." The hymn writer, Robert Lowry, had correct theology. Throughout the Old Testament mankind is presented with the need for a perfect sacrifice for sin. All the sacrifices made by the Jews under the old covenant were not sufficient. Sin still separated man from God. For man to have a relationship with God, the sin debt had to be paid. A sinless sacrifice was needed to pay for man's sin.

John 1:29 says Jesus is "the Lamb of God who takes away the sin of the world." Man's sin problem could only be taken care of by God Himself. Jesus Christ, fully God yet fully man, died as the sinless Lamb of God, the supreme sacrifice on the cross of Calvary, to pay for our sins. When we place our faith in Jesus, He washes away our sins forever! He makes us righteous and gives us the power to be victorious over sin.

.......................................................................................................

*Father, thank You for forgiving all my sins. Thank You for the cleansing power of the blood of Jesus Christ. Please help me today to walk in Your forgiveness and power, amen.*

# WEEK 49—FRIDAY
## A Reason for Hope

*And who is he who will harm you if you become followers of what is good? But even if you should suffer for righteousness' sake, you are blessed. "And do not be afraid of their threats, nor be troubled." But sanctify the Lord God in your hearts, and always be ready to give a defense to everyone who asks you a reason for the hope that is in you, with meekness and fear.*

1 PETER 3:13–15

An unknown author said, "Man can live forty days without food, four days without water, and eight minutes without air, but only for one second without hope." What is hope? Mr. Webster says in his dictionary that hope is a desire accompanied by expectation or the belief in fulfillment.

Peter wrote to those who suffered great persecution for their faith in Jesus Christ. He encouraged these believers to remain faithful, to never give up, for their hope was secure in Christ. The witness of their lives would cause others to ask, "What is the reason for your hope?" Real hope is not in a religion or a ritual, but in the person of Jesus Christ! We are to live the kind of lives that witness to a lost world our hope is steadfast and sure.

Are others asking questions about the peace and hope you have during this wicked world? People are looking for hope. As a Christian you can give them hope by introducing them to Jesus Christ!

*Father, thank You for the hope that You have given to me through Jesus Christ. Help me to make this hope known to those around me, amen.*

Dr. Dan Lanier, Northcrest Baptist Church, Meridian, MS

# WEEK 49—WEEKEND
### *Alive in Christ*

*For Christ also suffered once for sins, the just for the unjust, that He might bring us to God, being put to death in the flesh but made alive by the Spirit.*

1 PETER 3:18

The greatest miracle that ever happens is for a lost sinner to be raised from spiritual death. The Bible teaches us that we are dead in trespasses and sins. We are sinners by birth, by nature, and by practice. Not enough goodness in all of humanity can save one lost soul.

In today's verse Peter tells believers that Jesus Christ suffered, bled, and died for the sins of man. Jesus Christ paid the debt that man could never pay. He took our sin, our suffering, and our shame in order that we might have His righteousness, His holiness, and His life.

Jesus died for the sins of man, but He did not stay dead. He arose! His tomb is empty! Through His resurrection, Jesus overcame man's greatest enemies: death, hell, and the grave. Jesus Christ is not the best way to heaven or just one of the ways to heaven: Jesus Christ is the only way to heaven. When we place our faith in Jesus Christ as our Lord and Savior, God gives us resurrection life. One day just as Jesus was raised from the dead, we too will be raised from the dead.

Does the world know you are alive in Christ?

........................................................................................................

*Father, thank You that I have been made alive in Christ. Amen.*

# Week 50—Monday

*Buckle Up!*

*Therefore, since Christ suffered for us in the flesh, arm yourselves also with the same mind, for he who has suffered in the flesh has ceased from sin, that he no longer should live the rest of his time in the flesh for the lusts of men, but for the will of God.*

1 Peter 4:1–2

In this passage Peter encouraged believers not to be distracted by worldly pursuits and passions, but to live wholeheartedly for the Lord. He charges them to "arm [themselves]" with the mind of Christ. This is a charge for believers to make their minds ready, to "buckle up," and prepare for any turbulence they may face. He did not want them to be caught off guard or surprised when faced with opposition, but always to endure.

Jesus, our example, came not "to be served, but to serve, and to give His life a ransom for many" (Mark 10:45). Jesus "has loved us and given Himself for us" (Ephesians 5:2). As grateful beneficiaries of His suffering and death, should we not be willing to live for Him—no matter what?

Jesus spoke directly to His followers about the suffering and tribulation they would face. Jesus' warnings were not intended to discourage or dissuade anyone from obediently living according to God's will. Rather His warnings were to prepare them. In addition, Jesus clearly promised His disciples both victory and His presence. He declared in John 16:33, "Be of good cheer, I have overcome the world." He also promised in Matthew 28:20, "I am with you always, even to the end of the age." In light of those promises we have nothing to fear.

.....................................................................................................................

*Lord, give me faith always to live on a mission and according to Your will, amen.*

Mark Lashey, LifeHouse Church, Middletown, DE

# WEEK 50—TUESDAY

*Fervent Love*

---

*And above all things have fervent love for one another, for "love will cover a multitude of sins." Be hospitable to one another without grumbling. As each one has received a gift, minister it to one another, as good stewards of the manifold grace of God.*

1 PETER 4:8–10

F ervent love is faithful love. It's not the kind of love we may have for pizza or kittens or the color blue. Rather it is a deep and abiding love that flows from the Father. It is the kind of love that we as His children are to be marked by.

The importance of loving one another in this way cannot be underestimated, as evidenced by Peter's exhortation to prioritize its application "above all things."

Needless to say, it's easier said than done. When we put people in the mix, we put problems in the mix. Nevertheless, this kind of love trumps many problems and is empowered to "cover a multitude of sins."

If God can equip us with the ability to love our enemies (Matthew 5:44), surely He can give us the ability to "have fervent love for one another."

Fervent love is love that requires faith. It is love that is from God and never fails. It is love that is willing to sacrifice and go the extra mile.

This love by its very nature demands expression and cannot be contained. Each one of us is to demonstrate fervent love by employing his or her God-given gifts.

*Lord, please give me more love and opportunities to use the gifts You have given me to minister to my brothers and sisters in Christ, amen.*

# Week 50—Wednesday

*Treasured Trial*

*Beloved, do not think it strange concerning the fiery trial which is to try you, as though some strange thing happened to you; but rejoice to the extent that you partake of Christ's sufferings, that when His glory is revealed, you may also be glad with exceeding joy. If you are reproached for the name of Christ, blessed are you, for the Spirit of glory and of God rests upon you. On their part He is blasphemed, but on your part He is glorified.*

1 PETER 4:12–14

Never doubt God's love and concern for you. Never think God has forgotten you or is unaware of your "fiery trial." As Paul wrote: "But God demonstrates His own love toward us, in that while we were still sinners, Christ died for us" (Romans 5:8).

In 2 Corinthians 12, Paul testified of a "thorn," that despite his desperate prayers, the Lord did not remove. Rather God gave Paul the ability to see a purpose in it. In addition, the Lord gave Paul sufficient grace to overshadow the thorn in such a powerful way that Paul could rejoice in it, knowing that because of the thorn he was able to experience the grace and power of Christ in a way he would not have been able to otherwise.

The truth is when trials test our faith, we have the opportunity to grow and mature in Christ. Like Paul and his thorn, we too can experience God and trust Him for sufficient grace and power while experiencing trials. We can endure in such a way that we consider trials to be treasures.

..........................................................................................................................

*Lord, I trust You for sufficient grace and power to endure any trial and to see it as a treasure, amen.*

Mark Lashey, LifeHouse Church, Middletown, DE

# WEEK 50—THURSDAY
## *All Things*

*As His divine power has given to us all things that pertain to life and godliness, through the knowledge of Him who called us by glory and virtue, by which have been given to us exceedingly great and precious promises, that through these you may be partakers of the divine nature, having escaped the corruption that is in the world through lust.*

2 PETER 1:3–4

Our God is faithful. He has uniquely created and called each of us to specific works and ordained purposes (Ephesians 2:8–10).

We can easily feel inadequate or incapable of accomplishing the opportunities the Lord places before us. (We should.) In addition, the "life and godliness" He calls us to can seem beyond our reach. (They are.)

However, we can be encouraged by Paul's words in Philippians 2:13, where he told believers that God is at work in them, and that God gives them both the desires and the power to do what pleases Him. In other words, not only does God give them hearts to do what He calls them to accomplish, God also gives them the ability, the power, to do it. (He always does!)

God does not save us, instruct us, and then just leave us to it. He "has given to us all things that pertain to life and godliness" (2 Peter 1:3).

We must not forget what Jesus told His disciples in John 15:5: "Without Me you can do nothing." We also know that "without faith it is impossible to please Him" (Hebrews 11:6). Therefore, by design, we are to walk in constant dependence while trusting in His enduring faithfulness.

........................................................................................................

*Lord, I praise You for Your enduring faithfulness and all Your precious promises. Thank You for giving me everything I need that pertains to "life and godliness," amen.*

# WEEK 50—FRIDAY

## Not Weighed, Obeyed

*Knowing this first, that no prophecy of Scripture is of any private interpretation,*
*for prophecy never came by the will of man, but holy men of God spoke as they were*
*moved by the Holy Spirit.*

2 PETER 1:20–21

We must never take for granted the precious Scripture to which we have access. We must receive it for what it is: God's Word. His Word is the map that equips us to navigate treacherous seas, and the weapon to help us victoriously endure the battles we face. His Word sustains and nourishes our hungry souls as we journey through the wilderness.

God's Word is more than suggestions or options to be weighed. His commands are to be obeyed for our good. Scripture equips us "for every good work" (2 Timothy 3:17). The Word of God provides a platform for us to remain standing upon while weathering any storm life brings our way (Matthew 7:24–27). The Word of God is the protection we need to ensure that we remain steadfast and pure (Psalm 119:9–11).

Even though the Word of God sometimes "cuts" (Hebrews 4:12) and can be a hard pill to swallow at times, it is truth. The Word of God is life (John 6:63).

......................................................................................

*Lord, please give me a greater appetite and appreciation for Your holy Word,*
*amen.*

Mark Lashey, LifeHouse Church, Middletown, DE

# Week 50—Weekend

*Not Late*

*But, beloved, do not forget this one thing, that with the Lord one day is as a thousand years, and a thousand years as one day. The Lord is not slack concerning His promise, as some count slackness, but is longsuffering toward us, not willing that any should perish but that all should come to repentance.*

2 Peter 3:8–9

As we wait upon the Lord for His return to witness the picture painted for us in 1 Thessalonians 4:16–17 when Jesus will dramatically descend from heaven and we will rise to meet Him, we must realize that His seeming delay is intentionally gracious. Although we wait, we must understand that He is not late. He did not forget to set His alarm clock or forget about us altogether. He is not stuck in traffic or detained against His will. He is not dragging His feet or slacking to make good on His promise. He is always faithful! Although He will make a grand and glorious entrance, that is not a deciding factor on when He will come.

Paul tells us in 2 Corinthians 6:2 that today "is the day of salvation." The implication, in light of that proclamation, is that tomorrow may never come. As such men have the gracious opportunity to repent of their sins and call upon Jesus' name for salvation today. When the Lord returns, that opportunity will have passed, and men who have not done so will perish. Therefore, as the Lord tarries we should not neglect the opportunity we have by the grace of God to continue working with Him as He brings about salvation (2 Corinthians 6:1).

..................................................................................................

*Lord, give me faith to trust Your perfect plan and to work with You today as You continue to seek and save the lost, amen.*

# WEEK 51—MONDAY
## Steadfast Truth

*You therefore, beloved, since you know this beforehand, beware lest you also fall from your own steadfastness, being led away with the error of the wicked; but grow in the grace and knowledge of our Lord and Savior Jesus Christ. To Him be the glory both now and forever. Amen.*

2 PETER 3:17–18

T oday we see that false teachers even speak evil of the authorities that seek to enforce God's law in this world. They always make it about themselves and what they can do. A Christ follower should always point to Jesus, the ultimate authority.

Paul also dealt with false teachers in Colossae. The Word tells us in Colossians 1:18: "And He is the head of the body, the church, who is the beginning, the firstborn from the dead, that in all things He may have the preeminence."

We are complete in Christ. Why would we seek anything or anyone else?

True Christians cannot fall from salvation and be lost, but they can fall from their own "steadfastness." The truth is born-again believers cannot be defeated by Satan, but the enemy will distract us, and we will defeat ourselves.

Be steadfast in the Lord. As Paul also wrote: "Therefore, my beloved brethren, be steadfast, immovable, always abounding in the work of the Lord, knowing that your labor is not in vain in the Lord" (1 Corinthians 15:58).

........................................................................................

*Lord, may I stay steadfast, looking to You as You reveal truth to me. I pray that I put my trust fully in You and not place confidence in man or in myself. Lead me as I yield to Your Spirit. May I always be on guard. In the mighty name of King Jesus, amen.*

Chad Burdette, Macedonia Baptist Church, Ranburne, AL

# WEEK 51—TUESDAY

## *This Truth Touched Me*

*If we say that we have no sin, we deceive ourselves, and the truth is not in us. If we confess our sins, He is faithful and just to forgive us our sins and to cleanse us from all unrighteousness.*

1 JOHN 1:8–9

John was an evangelist, and he opened his discourse with a testimony asserting personal experiences with Jesus Christ, the Son of God (1 John 1:1–3). I must share my testimony with you, as I have vowed to my King never to stop telling it.

I was raised in a Christian home. After being introduced to prescription pain pills through two surgeries, I subsequently began using them for pleasure rather than pain. Eventually physicians and emergency rooms dismissed me due to drug-seeking behavior. I began buying drugs on the streets. It was like a bear trap: the harder I tried to pull away, the tighter it would squeeze. I was in a downward spiral. Regrettably I went to jail seven times due to my addiction. In one month I received five speeding tickets and two DUIs. After a drug overdose while behind the wheel, I was airlifted to the university hospital. Realizing I had a problem greater than myself, I sought rehabilitation.

I was reminded of the One who is greater than all strongholds. I got on my knees and prayed, "Lord Jesus, help me!" I then found a Gideon Bible in the nightstand by my bed. I had gone from a drug overdose to a good dose of the Holy Ghost and haven't been the same since!

........................................................................................................................

*Lord, help me, in the mighty name of King Jesus! Amen.*

# Week 51—Wednesday
*Walking in Truth*

*I write to you, little children, because your sins are forgiven you for His name's sake. I write to you, fathers, because you have known Him who is from the beginning. I write to you, young men, because you have overcome the wicked one. I write to you, little children, because you have known the Father. I have written to you, fathers, because you have known Him who is from the beginning. I have written to you, young men, because you are strong, and the word of God abides in you, and you have overcome the wicked one.*

1 John 2:12–14

John began this chapter by giving the basis of assurance: our obedience, which means "walking" in the way Christ walked (1 John 2:1–6). John followed the statements on obedience by defining the context of obedience as love, which encompassed the commandments of both the Old Testament and the new way of Jesus. Accordingly, the one who loves others belongs to the light, whereas the one who hates others belongs to the blinding darkness (1 John 2:7–11). John then used a series of couplets to reason that believers' sins had been forgiven in Christ and that they were victorious over the evil one, as seen in our text for today.

We are overcomers because Christ overcame. We are in Christ, and He is in us. Our identity is in Christ. It's not about imitation, but rather incarnation. Christ lives His life through us. If we are in control, He isn't in control.

Give your life to Him. You can overcome.

........................................................................................

*Father, thank You that because You overcame, I can overcome. As I yield to Your Spirit, empower me to walk in the truth. In the mighty name of King Jesus, amen.*

Chad Burdette, Macedonia Baptist Church, Ranburne, AL

# WEEK 51—THURSDAY
## *Abiding Truth*

*Do not love the world or the things in the world. If anyone loves the world, the love of the Father is not in him. For all that is in the world—the lust of the flesh, the lust of the eyes, and the pride of life—is not of the Father but is of the world. And the world is passing away, and the lust of it; but he who does the will of God abides forever.*

1 JOHN 2:15–17

W e learned from yesterday's devotion that we are victorious overcomers in Christ. In today's text John wants to make sure we understand what being an overcomer means, so he warns about the wrong kind of love, namely desiring the things of the world that have no eternal value. The temporal, the world, is passing away. On the other hand, eternal things abide forever.

When we do anything, it will either make God smile or Satan smile; they won't smile at the same thing.

I remember a story of a missionary who went to an Indian reservation. The missionary led one particular person to the Lord. When the missionary returned to the same reservation a year later, he ran into his brother in Christ and asked him, "How are things going?"

The man replied, "Well, it's as if I have a good dog and a bad dog inside of me, and they're fighting all the time."

"Which one is winning?"

"Whichever one I feed."

*Father God, keep me ever mindful that Your will is the best for me—not my own will or the ways of the world. Empower me, strengthen me, and lead me in Your perfect will. Thank You, Lord, that Your will abides forever. In the mighty name of King Jesus, amen.*

# WEEK 51—FRIDAY
*Surrendering to Truth*

*And you know that He was manifested to take away our sins, and in Him there is no sin. Whoever abides in Him does not sin. Whoever sins has neither seen Him nor known Him. Little children, let no one deceive you. He who practices righteousness is righteous, just as He is righteous.*

1 JOHN 3:5–7

T he same John who penned the gospel according to John also wrote the Johannine letters.

In 1 John, he employed many major themes from the gospel of John, such as the importance of life and death, truth and lying, light and darkness, remaining in a proper relationship, being born of God, and, of course, the significance of love.

First John, as any Bible student will acknowledge, is rather easy to read. Such an assertion does not mean that the document is easy to interpret.

How does all of this apply to us in everyday life? Well, in Christ's first coming in the flesh, He came to take away sin and destroy the works of the devil. So to continue in a pattern of sin is clearly a violation of God's intended way for humanity. John's words are not a focus on works of self-righteousness but what it means to be clothed in the righteousness of Christ. Christianity is Christ-in-me-ity. Surrendering daily to Him should be one's focus. To be born of God means that one lives an authentic, worship-filled life of love in Christ.

........................................................................................

*Father, You are righteous. I submit myself to You today. In the mighty name of King Jesus, amen.*

Chad Burdette, Macedonia Baptist Church, Ranburne, AL

# Week 51—Weekend

*Assuring Truth*

*My little children, let us not love in word or in tongue, but in deed and in truth. And by this we know that we are of the truth, and shall assure our hearts before Him. For if our heart condemns us, God is greater than our heart, and knows all things.*

1 John 3:18–20

True Christian love means loving in deed and in truth. Warren W. Wiersbe said in his book *Be Real*, "The opposite of 'in deed' is 'in word,' and the opposite of 'in truth' is 'in tongue.'" [13]

People struggling with doubt, or the lack of assurance. One of the awesome blessings of today's verse is the assurance we receive in our hearts when we practice obedience "in deed and in truth."

The enemy wants us to doubt our salvation, which in turn makes it highly improbable that we will share Christ with a lost and dying world. Our assurance is a must because the Great Commission is an obligation, not an option. Blessed assurance causes us to be intentional in evangelism with our personal testimony, just as John gave his testimony in the opening of this epistle.

A condemning heart or an accusing conscience robs a believer of peace. Christians must not live with guilt of the sins of the past. When you take it upon yourself to condemn others, you deny them the same grace you may need before the day is over.

...................................................................................................

*Father God, Your Word reveals that whoever walks in love has a heart open to You. Lead me to show love to others. In the mighty name of King Jesus I pray, amen.*

# WEEK 52—MONDAY

*God in the Flesh*

---

*Beloved, do not believe every spirit, but test the spirits, whether they are of God; because many false prophets have gone out into the world. By this you know the Spirit of God: Every spirit that confesses that Jesus Christ has come in the flesh is of God.*

1 JOHN 4:1–2

One of the greatest needs in every believer's life is spiritual discernment. The apostle John places unsurmountable importance on the doctrine of the person of Christ. Who is Jesus?

Every generation has false teachers who proclaim teachings that are contrary to the Word of God. One of the primary false teachings that John encountered in His day was Gnosticism. This taught that Christ did not actually have a body of flesh; rather He just seemed to have one. To them the flesh was evil and God was good; therefore, God would never have placed Himself in flesh. Yet the apostle affirms the reality of the incarnation.

The Spirit of God guides us into the truth of God (John 16:13). The same Spirit of God came to not speak of Himself but to glorify Jesus (John 16:14). To confess that Jesus came in the flesh is to agree with another part of the Godhead.

The teaching that "Jesus Christ has come in the flesh" is a belief in the God of the Old Testament, who in the person of His Son, became incarnate in human flesh without its sin. He died on the cross to satisfy the just demands of the law and raised Himself from the dead. As a result He is the living Savior of the sinner who places his faith in Him and what He did on the cross.

...........................................................................................................

*Lord, thank You that even though You are Spirit, You clothed Yourself in flesh for me. Bless Your holy name, amen.*

Dr. Johnny Hunt, First Baptist Church Woodstock, Woodstock, GA

# WEEK 52—TUESDAY
## *The Love of God*

*Whoever confesses that Jesus is the Son of God, God abides in him, and he in God.*
*And we have known and believed the love that God has for us. God is love, and he who*
*abides in love abides in God, and God in him.*

1 JOHN 4:15–16

This passage makes much of God's love. It is a love that we as individuals can experience, and as we grow in His love, we begin to be expressions of His love and extensions of His love to others.

The Bible often speaks of how, at salvation, God Himself is imparted to us and He puts His love in our hearts. Thus, the love of God: Originated with the Father, was manifested with the Son, is perfected in His Family. A good way to say it is: The greatest revelation of God's love is Jesus Christ in the flesh. The second greatest revelation of God's love is Jesus Christ manifesting His love through His family.

Our love for others displays that God is real. When we love one another, we put God on display. The unseen God reveals Himself through the visible love of believers.

The fact that God abides in us speaks of a relationship, and His presence allows us to behave according to His behavior. As we love God and others, the Holy Spirit confirms our relationship with Him by the fruit He produces in us and the power He provides.

......................................................................................................

*Lord Jesus, Your love is overwhelming and encouraging. Love others through me*
*as I love You, amen.*

# WEEK 52—WEDNESDAY
*Eternal Life*

*And this is the testimony: that God has given us eternal life, and this life is in His Son. He who has the Son has life; he who does not have the Son of God does not have life. These things I have written to you who believe in the name of the Son of God, that you may know that you have eternal life, and that you may continue to believe in the name of the Son of God.*

1 JOHN 5:11–13

I am so grateful for God's salvation, given to me so rich and free. Not only has He given me salvation, He confirms it with His Spirit. As Romans 8:16 says: "The Spirit Himself bears witness with our spirit that we are children of God."

As if this were not enough, He gives us the testimony of His Word. John wrote, "This is the testimony: that God has given us eternal life." The words speak of the gift of His Son as a historic fact. They remind us of the reality of the grace aspect: His salvation is undeserved and unearned.

Today's passage serves as one of the most powerful biblical passages on the confidence of the believer's salvation, which is all predicated on the work of God. How encouraging to know that salvation is true in our lives and God has given proof of His presence within us. As a result, if we have the Son of God in our lives, then we know we have eternal life.

........................................................................................

*Lord, You are gracious, good, and glorious. Your salvation is unbelievable, yet I believe, amen.*

Dr. Johnny Hunt, First Baptist Church Woodstock, Woodstock, GA

# WEEK 52—THURSDAY
*Confidence in Him*

*Now this is the confidence that we have in Him, that if we ask anything according to*
*His will, He hears us. And if we know that He hears us, whatever we ask, we know that*
*we have the petitions that we have asked of Him.*

1 JOHN 5:14–15

The Lord gives confidence, which translates into freedom of speech. We can come to Christ freely and tell Him our needs. This confidence speaks of a boldness before the Lord. This confidence that gives boldness is seen several times in 1 John. In 1 John 2:28, we can have confidence before Him and not be ashamed at His coming. In 1 John 3:21, we are told that we can have confidence toward God. And in 1 John 4:17, we are told that we can have confidence on the Day of Judgment.

Note this confidence is "in Him!" This speaks of an intimate relationship, and it means we are engaged in prayer with God. This intimacy allows us to know what to ask for and allows us to ask "according to His will." We find ourselves in unity with Him when there is not unconfessed sin in our lives, which is a serious obstacle to answered prayers. We must make sure nothing is between us and any other brother or sister; if there is, we must settle it.

Martin Luther said, "Prayer is not overcoming God's reluctance. It is laying hold of His willingness." [14] Robert Law said, "Prayer is a mighty instrument, not for getting man's will done in heaven, but for getting God's will done on earth." [15] These three things can help us in our prayer lives: 1. Desiring God's will; 2. Discerning God's will; 3. Doing God's will. Obedience is the key.

...............................................................................

*Lord, I desire for me what You desire in me. In Jesus' name, amen.*

# WEEK 52—FRIDAY
*We Are of God*

*We know that we are of God, and the whole world lies under the sway of the wicked one. And we know that the Son of God has come and has given us an understanding, that we may know Him who is true; and we are in Him who is true, in His Son Jesus Christ. This is the true God and eternal life.*

1 JOHN 5:19–20

What a statement: "We know that we are of God." This implies a rebirth and a proceeding forth as well as a change of status. All of this is true because of who He is. The principle of 2 Corinthians 5:17 is so true: "Therefore, if anyone is in Christ, he is a new creation; old things have passed away; behold, all things have become new."

Note the contrast between "we are of God" and "the whole world lies under the sway of the wicked one." The Lord changes us and gives us a new nature and a new disposition, but at the same time Satan has an influence on the whole world. The bottom line is Satan can do nothing for us that is of any spiritual significance.

Where Satan can do nothing, our dear Lord Jesus brings assurance to the lives of those who trust in Him. "We know that the Son of God has come" speaks of an experiential knowledge that brings assurance with it. He has arrived, and we have the privilege of becoming acquainted with Him.

John makes it all too clear that we worship Jesus because He is God alone. Jesus is the true expression and revelation of God.

......................................................................................

*Lord, thank You for showing me who You are, amen.*

Dr. Johnny Hunt, First Baptist Church Woodstock, Woodstock, GA

# Week 52—Weekend

## Our Devoted Christ

*"Behold, I stand at the door and knock. If anyone hears My voice and opens the door, I will come in to him and dine with him, and he with Me. To him who overcomes I will grant to sit with Me on My throne, as I also overcame and sat down with My Father on His throne."*

REVELATION 3:20–21

I f I were to choose a title or theme for this passage, it would be "Our Devoted Christ." It is here that we see our risen Lord patiently standing at the door of the church or at the door of our lives. He is knocking, which is a picture of His persistence. He knocks through His Word, His Holy Spirit, His people, His providence, our circumstances, and other things He allows into our lives.

What a great truth that we can hear His voice. As Romans 10:17 asserts: "So then faith comes by hearing, and hearing by the word of God."

I will be forever grateful for the day His voice was so loud and clear in my life, calling me to a relationship with Him. As I opened the door of my life, He came in just as He promised. The fellowship He offers has been the greatest pleasure and joy I have ever known.

Verse twenty-one is such a great promise of Christ's reign in our lives. I believe Paul had this same idea in mind when he gave us 2 Timothy 2:11–13: "This is a faithful saying: For if we died with Him, we shall also live with Him. If we endure, we shall also reign with Him. If we deny Him, He also will deny us. If we are faithless, He remains faithful; He cannot deny Himself."

............................................................................................................

*Lord, You are a promise keeper, and I praise You for what You've done in my life, amen.*

# Contributors

# NOTES

**WEEK 10**

1. A retelling. Ray Johnson, *The Hope Quotient: Measure It. Raise It. You'll Never Be the Same* (Nashville: W Publishing, 2014), 55.

**WEEK 23**

2. Bryan A. Follis, *Truth with Love: The Apologetics of Francis Schaeffer* (Wheaton: Crossway Books, 2006), 131.

**WEEK 24**

3. C. S. Lewis, Letters to Malcolm, Chiefly on Prayer (New York: HarperCollins, 1964), 125.

**WEEK 29**

4. Charles R. Swindoll, *Insights on Romans* (Carol Stream, IL: Tyndale House Publishers, 2015), 296.

**WEEK 30**

5. C. S. Lewis, *Mere Christianity* (New York: HarperCollins, 1952), 179.

**WEEK 34**

6. Scott Conger, "What Does Your MBA say About You?" *LinkedIn.com*, May 20, 2016, https://www.linkedin.com/pulse/what-does-your-mba-say-you-scott-conger.

**WEEK 38**

7. E. M. Bounds, *The Complete Works of E. M. Bounds* (Grand Rapids: Baker Books, 1990), 299.

**WEEK 45**

8. Kayla Root, "'Someday You Will Hear Billy Graham Is Dead. Don't Believe a Word of It'": His 7 Best Quotes about Heaven, February 25, 2018, http://www1.cbn.com/cbnnews/us/2018/february/someday-you-will-hear-billy-graham-is-dead-dont-believe-a-word-of-it-his-7-best-quotes-about-heaven.

**WEEK 46**

9.  "Tanzania's Most Inspriational Athlete," May 11, 2016, https://www.olympic.org /athlete365/news/tanzanias-most-inspirational-athlete/.

10. Justin Gammill, "Inside the Beautiful Mind of Jim Carrey," *iheartintelligence.com*, http://iheartintelligence.com/2016/02/11/beautiful-mind-jim-carrey/.

**WEEK 48**

11. I-Jin Loh and Howard Hatton, *A Handbook on the Letter from James*, UBS Handbook Series (New York: United Bible Societies, 1997), 197.

12. Charles H. Spurgeon, "2055. The Trial of Your Faith," Sermon, The Metropolitan Tabernacle, Newington, 2 December 1888. *Answers in Genesis*, accessed 26 March 2018. https://answersingenesis.org/education/spurgeon-sermons/2055-trial-of-your-faith/

**WEEK 51**

13. Warren Wiersbe, *Be Real*. (Colorado Springs, CO: David C. Cook, 1972), 129.

**WEEK 52**

14. Ron Rhodes, *1001 Unforgettable Quotes about God, Faith, and the Bible* (Eugene, OR: Harvest House Publishers, 2011), 168.

15. Warren W. Wiersbe, *The Wiersbe Bible Commentary: New Testament* (Colorado Springs: David C. Cook, 2007), 1004.

# SCRIPTURE INDEX

## PROVERBS

## ECCLESIASTES

## ISAIAH

## JEREMIAH

## LAMENTATIONS

## LUKE

## JOHN

## ACTS

## ROMANS

# 1 CORINTHIANS

# 2 CORINTHIANS

# GALATIANS